The Maronites

CISTERCIAN STUDIES SERIES: NUMBER TWO HUNDRED FORTY-THREE

The Maronites
The Origins of an Antiochene Church
A Historical and Geographical Study
of the Fifth to Seventh Centuries

Abbot Paul Naaman

Translated by
The Department of Interpretation
and Translation (DIT),
Holy Spirit University
Kaslik, Lebanon
2009

α

Cistercian Publications
www.cistercianpublications.org

LITURGICAL PRESS
Collegeville, Minnesota
www.litpress.org

Maps adapted from G. Tchalenko, *Villages antiques de la syrie du Nord* (1953), T. II Pl. XXIII, Pl. XXIV, Pl. XXV. Used with permission.

A Cistercian Publications title published by Liturgical Press

Cistercian Publications
Editorial Offices
Abbey of Gethsemani
3642 Monks Road
Trappist, Kentucky 40051
www.cistercianpublications.org

Library of Congress Cataloging-in-Publication Data

Naaman, Paul, 1932–
    The Maronites : the origins of an Antiochene church : a historical and
    geographical study of the fifth to seventh centuries / Paul Naaman ;
    translated by the Department of Interpretation and Translation (DIT), Holy
    Spirit University, Kaslik, Lebanon.
        p. cm. — (Cistercian studies series ; no. 243)
    Includes bibliographical references and index.
    ISBN 978-0-87907-243-8 (pbk.) — ISBN 978-0-87907-794-5 (e-book)
    1. Maronites—History.   2. Catholic Church. Maronite Patriarchate of
    Antioch (Syria)—History.   3. Catholic Church—Maronite rite—Middle
    East—History.   4. Middle East—Church history.   I. Title.   II. Title:
    Origins of an Antiochene church.

BX182.N33 2011
281'.509021—dc22

                                                                    2010048732

To my nephews and nieces

To Professor Norman ASMAR

*So that they may realize from which mountain
rock they were carved, and from which
fountainhead springs their spiritual wealth*

Contents

Foreword

Some attribute early Christianity's worldwide growth to the peace of Constantine in AD 313 and his support of the Church. This assumption, however, does not consider the heroic missionary movement of the early Christians, even in the midst of stiff opposition and martyrdom. In fact, Christianity reached all parts of the Mediterranean basin, as well as India and perhaps China before it became the "state religion" of the Roman Empire.

Another movement, equally heroic, which flourished *after* the peace of Constantine and had a stabilizing effect on culture and Church order, was monasticism, the story of countless men and women who gave up everything for the sake of Christ and the Gospel.

Egypt had Saint Anthony, and Europe, Saint Benedict. Anthony's way was solitary, that is, hermits for God alone, Benedict's way communal—"a school for the Lord's service." Both pioneers spearheaded spiritual movements which are still vibrant today and have left a lasting mark on Church and society.

The story of Maron, a fifth-century hermit-priest, and the community gathered around him, later called Maronites, is part of this fascinating story of monastic and missionary movements in the Church. In the context of Syrian monasticism, which has always been a combination of both solitary and communal life, the Maronite story is one of a community of Christians who navigated through rough seas of political divisions and ecclesiastical controversies.

Today, the Maronite Church is one of twenty-one Eastern Catholic Churches in communion with the Pope of Rome. Her patriarch resides in Lebanon and forty-three bishops and approximately ten million faithful make up her presence throughout the world.

Abbot Paul Naaman, a Maronite scholar and former superior general of the Order of Lebanese Maronite Monks, wisely places the study of the origins of the Maronite Church squarely in the midst of the history of the Church. This book offers plausible insights into her formation and early development, grounding the Maronite Church in her Catholic, Antiochian, Syriac, and monastic roots.

Abbot Naaman maintains that Theodoret, the bishop of Cyr, himself a monk for seven years and the author of *Religious History* written in 444, along with the support of the Byzantine emperor, Marcian, founded a monastery from among numerous monks and hermits in order to support the definitions of the Council of Chalcedon (451). The monastery was named after the hermit-priest Maron, who was well known in that region for his sanctity.

According to Naaman, citing Theodoret's *Religious History*, there were two monastic realities in northern Syria: one was *coenobitic*, that is, monastic communities in the region of Apamaea. The other was *eremitical*, that is, hermits living in the region of Cyr. Ironically, Saint Maron, a hermit, lived in the region of Cyr; however, after his death, the monastery of Saint Maron was founded in the region of Apamaea. Naaman offers the following explanation.

During the christological controversies of the fifth century, there was a severe lack of discipline among monks and hermits, according to Theodoret. The monastery of Saint Maron, and soon, other Maronite monasteries in the region, provided stability and support to the efforts of Theodoret to arrest the spread of Monophysitism (Christ had only one nature, i.e., a fusion of human and divine) and promote orthodox faith. Naaman notes that this balanced faith and careful discernment served Maronites well in their beginnings, throughout history, and up to the present day.

Naaman, basing his argument on primary and contemporary sources, also recounts the zeal of the monks of Saint Maron in the spread of the Gospel and the effort to defend the Council of Chalcedon, and notes that the head of the monastery of Saint Maron was ordained a bishop in order to assure apostolic succession for the nascent Maronite monastic movement in the midst of threatening influences from other monasteries in the area.

Naaman's insightful history, which needs balance from another perspective, namely, the Eastern Orthodox point of view, nonetheless sheds light on the early Maronite monastic and missionary movement. It has been said that the rudder of a ship is small and goes almost unnoticed, yet it would be impossible to direct a ship without it. The case of the beginnings of the Maronite Church in the post-Chalcedonian Middle East is similar.

We are grateful that Abbot Naaman has taken the time and effort to navigate the uncharted waters of the origins of the Maronite Church by means of various manuscripts, and to attempt to discover this tiny rudder of her beginnings. His many years of dedication and commitment to this research have shown that even in the midst of the christological controversies, the history of the Maronite Church can still shed light for Catholics and Orthodox alike.

Although this book is rather complex and rests on certain assumptions, it is, nevertheless, well worth the effort to read. Abbot Naaman himself admits that his hypothesis is in need of completion through further research, and he hopes to inspire the student of history to look deeper.

According to the respected French theologian and orientalist Jean Gribomont, this book is definitively groundbreaking: "For the essential point, namely the date and the circumstances of the foundation of the Monastery (of Saint Maron) around which the Maronite nation forms itself, the shadows and controversy are definitely left behind."[1]

This is a treasured work for anyone interested in acquiring a historical perspective of the origins of an Antiochene Church, ecumenical in nature, Chalcedonian in faith, Catholic by communion, ancient yet ever new, which even today combines a missionary and monastic dynamism.

At the close of this Jubilee Year of Saint Maron, marking sixteen hundred years since his death, we are grateful to so many who have supported the publication of this scholarly volume. May the prayer of Saint Maron be with us all.

✛ Bishop Gregory J. Mansour
   Bishop of the Eparchy of Saint Maron of Brooklyn
   March 2, 2011, Feast of Saint John Maron

---

[1] *Revue d'Histoire ecclésiastique* 1972, no. 1.

Acknowledgments

I wish to thank everyone who made the publication of this book possible. First and foremost, Bishop Gregory Mansour, bishop of the Eparchy of Saint Maron in Brooklyn.

Special thanks are due to Roula Ghoushend for her initial translation and Dr. Mario Kozah who finalized the book with the comments of Rev. Joseph Azize and the help of a team at the DIT, Holy Spirit University of Kaslik in Lebanon.

Thanks also to Dr. John Bequette of the University of Saint Francis for his diligent assistance.

Finally, I wish to express my deepest gratitude to Hans Christoffersen of Liturgical Press and Fr. Mark Scott of Cistercian Publications whose loving patience and understanding allowed for this volume to be available at the conclusion of the 1600th anniversary year of Saint Maron.

Abbot Paul Naaman, LMO

Introduction

As the title *The Maronites: The Origins of an Antiochene Church. A Historical and Geographical Study of the Fifth to Seventh Centuries* suggests, this book is only a prolegomenon to the lengthy research which we intend to carry out later. This essay aims to clarify some points concerning the history of the Maronite Church which are still obscure.

The historian who views the Eastern world is immediately confronted by a phenomenon which is difficult to explain: the Arab conquest of the seventh century coincides with the decline of the preexisting Syro-Aramaic culture. This culture seems to sink into a progressive mummification. During this same period, the center of attention is diverted away from Antioch and Alexandria and henceforth focused on Byzantium and Rome, centers of Hellenic and Latin culture respectively.

Today, this Eastern world enjoys relative peace in comparison to previous ages. Time has succeeded in compensating, at least in part, for the harm particularly caused by Ottoman rule. Thus, the current situation renders the historian's work a little easier. Research on both the historical and archaeological levels has now become possible and imperative. Such work is indispensable to clarify the origins of the Eastern Churches in general and of the Maronite Church in particular. Let us hasten to say that in relatively recent times, this investigation has found its pioneers, but perhaps they have not all operated according to a stringently objective and systematic methodology. This methodological inadequacy is due less to the incompetence of the historians than to the highly regrettable traditional compartmentalization of the literary disciplines. This division sets up the Hellenists, on one hand, and the Easterners, on the other hand, to believe that they can solve the problems of Eastern history within the limited framework of their respective specialties. However, there is an inevitable overlap between such closely related fields, and coordination is therefore indispensable. Whether they be Hellenists or Easterners, it is no longer permissible for historians to operate in isolation from each other or, even worse, to depreciate each other's work.

The problems raised by the history of the Maronites have tempted two categories of historians. Those of the first category, non-Maronites, have often dealt with the questions in a purely marginal and superficial way. They have worked on apocryphal texts, incomplete or taken out of their context, and so have been unable to reach valid conclusions. Those of the second category, Maronites or pro-Maronites, being exasperated by attacks more or less justified, have inevitably been driven by apologetic motives. Thus they have neglected the problem of the origins to venture into the debate over Monothelitism: a debate which has no solution, as it involves a subject of extreme complexity which even today has not been clarified in a satisfactory manner. That theological problem still awaits its Joseph Lebon.[1]

Our inquiry is, therefore, situated in a context of intrigue, and is woven in a web of ambiguities and passionately interesting difficulties. Situated at the dawn of the history of the Maronites, its center of interest is the monastery of Maron, in Syria Secunda, near Apamaea, cradle of the movement we shall refer to by the term "Maronitude." Our objective is to try to situate this monastery in its *Sitz im Leben*, in its geographical, historical, political, theological, and monastic context. We think, following the "Gestalt" method, that the whole constitutes a new structure which is different from, and more than, the sum of the elements of which it is composed. Further, while affording a panoramic view of events, the restored whole affirms a proposition of primary importance, namely, the salient role played by the monastic community of Beit Maron in the Chalcedonian and neo-Chalcedonian christological crises. We shall see a clear and close connection between the founding of the

---

[1] Cf. bibliography.

monastery of Saint Maron, the disciplinary decrees of Chalcedon, and the preponderant influence exerted by the civil authority (in the person of the emperor Marcian) and the religious authorities (the bishops Domnus and Theodoret). Moreover, the attachment of the Maronites to the Chalcedonian and neo-Chalcedonian theology is the main explanation for the preeminence of this monastery among a flourishing monastic confederation in Syria Secunda. Finally, the founding of this monastery would be difficult to explain if we did not take into consideration the geographical and topographical data of this part of Syria. By taking into account the great ease of communication by road that existed between the different regions of Syria, we hope to give our work precision, for this factor has perhaps been overlooked by other investigators.

The method used here is simple: it consists of gathering the scattered fragments of the most ancient documents that refer to Maron and the monastery built in his honor. These documents cover the period which begins in the year 444, when the *Religious History* of Theodoret was written, until 957, the date of the death of the Arab historian al-Mas⁽ūdī:, who honored this monastery with a description, the only one left to us. We were able to gather and date these precious documents, which form the subject of this present study. We studied them separately at first and then compared them with each other in the light of general history of the Church, whose development was almost exclusively in the Eastern regions. One of these documents, unfortunately comparatively recent, summarizes in a few words the elements which constitute the framework of our thesis. This document is the testimony of the Arab historian Abū l-Fidā, governor of Ḥamah, the region in which the monastery once stood. Abū l-Fidā states precisely in his *Universal Chronicle* that "during the second year of his reign (452), Emperor Marcian built the monastery of Maron in Ḥoms." To this relatively late testimony, we have dedicated the first chapter of our work, in order to verify its authority.

In the second chapter, we have tried to present a clear idea about the two monastic centers of northern Syria: Cyr, a region much favored by Maron and his disciples, monks who lived in the open air; and Apamaea, where Theodoret of Cyr lived as a monk before being raised to the bishopric of Cyr. Our nearly exclusive source is the *Religious History* written by Theodoret. It is fundamental for our knowledge of Syrian monasticism from the beginning of the fourth century to the first half of the fifth century.

In the third chapter, while emphasizing the close relations between Theodoret and the two religious communities of Cyr and Apamaea, we have tried to discover the spiritual, ideological, and human bonds which brought together these two communities. The similarity of views in almost all fields, and particularly in religious politics during the christological crisis, then becomes apparent. One could not hope to provide conclusive proof in such a field of history, where documents and studies are so few; but to establish our thesis it is sufficient for us to point to the convergence of the evidence. Negatively, any thesis which cannot weave the evidence into a harmonious pattern is undermined. Positively, a convergence of all data and lines of enquiry fortifies us in our thesis.

Abbot Paul Naaman

Kaslik, 2009

Chapter One

The Evidence of Abū l-Fidā as to the Founding of the Monastery of Maron

The only document that mentions a specific date for the founding of the monastery of Maron is that of the Arab historian Abū l-Fidā (1273–1331), who states in his *Universal History* that during "the second year of his reign, the emperor Marcian (451–57) built the monastery of Maron in Ḥoms."[1] Arthur Vööbus in his *History of Asceticism in the Syrian Orient* refers to this belated testimony without, however, giving an opinion about its historical value: "The only source who claims to know more, is Abū l-Fidā. According to his information, the emperor Marcian built the monastery of Maron in the second year of his reign, i.e. AD 452. Nothing is known about the value of his information."[2]

We suggest making a complete critical study of this testimony, covering source criticism, internal criticism, and analysis of its accuracy.

---

[1] Abū l-Fidā, *Abrégé de l'histoire du genre humain*, vol. 1 (Beirut: Dar Al-Kitāb Allubnānī, 1960), 81. Another Arab historian, ʿOmar Ibn al-Wardī (1349), mentions the establishment of the monastery by Emperor Marcian, but the history of Ibn al-Ward is only a supplement to the *Universal History* of Abū l-Fidā, as Ibn al-Wardī admits himself.

[2] Arthur Vööbus, *History of Asceticism in the Syrian Orient*, vol. 2, *Early Monasticism in Mesopotamia and Syria*, C.S.C.O., 197, subs. vol. 17 (Louvain: Peeters, 1960), 252.

External Criticism

The Text

The text has been established through the diligence of the German scholar Henry Fleischer, from two manuscripts in the Royal Library of Paris, numbers 101 and 615. Personal consultation of these manuscripts establishes the fidelity of this great scholar to the original text, and we may therefore adopt his text and his translation as follows:

" ثم ملك بعده (ثاودوسيوس) مرقيانوس " من القانون". ملك سبع سنين، ولسنة

خلت من ملكه بنى دير مارون الذي بحمص. و في ايامه لعن نسطوريوس و نفي و

كان موت مرقيانوس في منتصف سنة ٧٦٢ "

"Ei successit Marcianus, qui," secundum Al-Kānūn,[3] "7 annos regnavit. Primo regni anno exacto, Emisae exstruxit Coenobium Maronis. Eodem regnante Nestorius divis devotus in exiliumque actus est. Marciano, anno 762 dimidio vita defuncto."[4]

Source Criticism

Once we possess a "reliable" text, we are in a position to analyze the source. Who was its author? What were the circumstances of its composition?

---

[3] *Al-Kānūn al Masʿūdī fī l'hay'a wa-l-nūjūm* by Abū l-Rayḥān Muḥammad Al-Bīrūnī; a treatise on mathematical geography written after the death of Sultan Maḥmūd and dedicated to his son and heir Masʿūd (421–32). Thus the title *Al-Kanūn al Masʿūdī*. Abū l-Fidā often quotes him, calling him "Master." The treatise is still in manuscript form, extant in Oxford, in the British Museum, London, and in Berlin, vide: (a) *Catalogue of the Oriental Manuscripts of the Oxford Library* (Bodleianae Bibliothecae) by Alexander Nicoli, vol. 2, 370 (Oxford, 1835), 360–63; (b) Supplement to the Catalogue of the Arabic manuscripts in the British Museum, 1894, n. 756, 513–19; (c) *Die Handschriften—Verzeichnisse der koeniglichen bibliothek zu Berlin der Arabischen Handschriften von W. Ahlward*, n. 5667 (Berlin, 1893), 150–55.

[4] *Abul Fedae Historia anteislamica, Arabice, E duobus codicibus bibliothecae regiae parisiensis, 101 and 615*, edidit Fleischer Henricus Orthobius, versione latina, notis et indicibus auxit (Lipsiae, 1831),113.

All authors, ancient and modern, agree that the book known as *The Universal History* is the principal work of Abū l-Fidā. Moreover, one has only to read the second part of this history, written in the form of memoirs, to be left without any doubt whatsoever about the author's identity. From this same part of *The Universal History*, we learn that Abū l-Fidā was born in Damascus in the year 672/1273[5] of a noble Arab family, that of Takī-al-Dīn ʿUmar, the son of Šahanšah, the elder brother of Saladin, who granted Takī-al-Dīn ʿUmar the government of Ḥamāh.[6]

Abū l-Fidā received a religious and literary education. He was given the Qurʾan and some didactic treatises to learn by heart. He devoted himself to an in-depth study of the principles of Islam, the Arabic language, jurisprudence, and history and letters. At the same time, he took part in certain wars in which his family and his suzerain were involved.

In the year 709/1310 the Mamlūk sultan al-Malik al-Nasir promised to grant Abū l-Fidā the principality of Ḥamāh under the same conditions as those enjoyed by his ancestors. Abū l-Fidā followed him to Cairo but at first he received only the title of lieutenant of the sultan.[7]

In 710/1312 he went again to Cairo. He now received the title which had belonged to his ancestors: "At last, the Sultan conferred upon me the title of Prince of Ḥamāh, Maʿrrā and Bârin."[8]

The Sultan sent his army against the city of Melitene, situated in northern Syria, in 715/1315. "Together with the troops of my principality," said Abū l-Fidā, "I joined the expedition. We went in turn through Aleppo, ʿAyn-Tab, Raban . . . . While crossing Nahr-al-Azrak (the Blue River), which flows into the Euphrates, I noticed a bridge of Roman construction built with large stones, its width surpassing all that I have seen of this type. Leaving Ḥiṣn-Manṣour

---

[5] The first date is that of the Hegira, the second that of the Christian era.

[6] Around 574/1178, Saladin joined Syria to his other conquests and established there a certain number of principalities, which he distributed among members of his family and also among the bravest of his emirs. Cf. Abū l-Fidā, *Abrégé* (n. 1), 5:82.

[7] Ibid., 7:69.

[8] Ibid., 7:72.

on our right, we reached the range that lies beyond the Taurus. There we had to cross such a narrow gorge that the army took two days and two nights to pass through it. After, we went to Zebetra, a small town falling into ruins. We reached the gates of Melitene on Sunday 22 Muḥarram" (27 April 1315).[9]

Thus, even in the midst of wars and continual movements of troops, Abū l-Fidā pursued his research and his scientific work, taking pains to observe and study the geography of this part of northern Syria.

It was at this time that he wrote his *Short Guide to Universal History*. He died at the age of fifty-eight on 23 Muḥarram 732/27, October 1331, in Ḥamāh. He wrote several books, among which we note two: *A Treatise on Geography*, a remarkable work translated from Arabic into French by J. T. Reinaud in 1848;[10] and the *History*. The author himself titled it *A Short Guide to the History of Human Kind* (المختصر في اخبارالبشر). Starting with the creation of the world, it ends slightly before the author's death. The period preceding Muḥammad, which includes the pertinent testimony, is covered very briefly. The *History* is divided into an introduction (فاتحة) that mentions his sources, a preface which expounds his method, and then five chapters of text.

The testimony we are studying is found in the third part, which deals with the caesars and the Roman emperors. In Fleischer's edition this part is found between pages 104–14.

This *History* is a compilation, summarizing the main histories published previously. It is difficult, in spite of the accurate indication of the sources, to determine what belongs exclusively to the author. However, as we shall see, Abū l-Fidā did not blindly copy from his sources. He was sufficiently intelligent, critical, and impartial to avoid falsehood, error, and exaggerated narratives.

[9] Ibid., 7:88.

[10] *Encyclopédie de l'Islam*, new edition, 1:122; "Takwīn al-buldān," a book of descriptive geography with a supplement containing data of physics and mathematics in the form of tables. It was edited *in toto* by J. T. Reinaud and Mac Guekin de Slane (Paris, 1840), and translated by Reinaud (Paris, 1848) and Stanislas Guyard (Paris, 1883). The first volume of the translation consists of a classic exposition titled *General Introduction to the Geography of the Orientals*.

This led Reinaud to comment: "There is good reason to consider the chronicle of Abū l-Fidā as the most important historical monument of the Arabs that has been published in its entirety in Europe up till now. The success that it has obtained is founded not only on the long succession of centuries that it covers . . . . Besides, the author has a merit that is rare among the writers of his nation. That is, instead of seeking marvelous or strange accounts, particularly those concerning Muḥammad and the Islamic religion, he sticks to historical facts and to what presents a positive interest. . . . His family had always been distinguished by its taste for literature and had collected a number of objects that were most precious for an intelligent, active and naturally curious mind."[11]

Few writers of his time enjoyed such an advantageous position for obtaining information and writing about the history and the geography of this part of Syria which he governed. His rank, culture, relationships, and voyages brought to his attention everything considered noteworthy. In addition, he had access to a rich library in Ḥamāh.

He devoted himself to the most diverse occupations in Ḥamāh and in the towns where he stayed. He took pleasure in gathering educated men around him regardless of the kind of studies to which they dedicated themselves. Religion, jurisprudence, poetry, history, geography, astronomy, and medicine, all were of interest to him. In any assembly he was outstanding for the extent of his knowledge.

Critical Classification of the Sources

Abū l-Fidā used two types of sources: general sources concerning the whole book and particular or special sources appropriate to each particular chapter.

In his introduction or Fātiḥah, Abū l-Fidā successively enumerated fourteen books that he used as general sources in his *History*. Several other books were used for writing the individual chapters. Of all these, we shall mention only two: (1) *Al-Kāmil fi-l*

---

[11] Abū l-Fidā, *Géographie*, 37–38.

tārīḫ by Ibn al-Aṯīr, used as a primary source and as a model for the *History*;[12] and (2) *Al-Kānūn al Masʿūdī* by Abū l-Rayḥān Muḥammad al-Bīrūnī, cited as the author's specific source in drawing up the chronology of the emperor Marcian (451–57). Under the reign of that emperor, the monastery of Maron was established.[13] But, as we have seen, these two sources do not mention the founding under Marcian of the monastery dedicated to Maron. Therefore, they cannot be the source of the testimony in question.

By ascertaining his sources, we may be able to infer whether the author was a direct witness. If so, his testimony is then a primary source. If not, there are two possibilities: either an unknown original source(s) alone was used; or an unknown source(s) was used and supplemented by the author's own testimony. If it is impossible to ascertain his sources, then the author's opinion must be acknowledged, but treated with reserve, and it must enjoy less authority. In our case, the author is certainly not a direct witness, because between the founding of the monastery in the fifth century,[14] and the birth of Abū l-Fidā, there is an interval of approximately nine centuries. However, his source has been lost, so we must either provisionally accept the testimony, or test its accuracy using indirect means and methods. Critical study is not excluded, but historians must concentrate their attention on the text itself, which might supply us with some indications about its sources. These sources, arranged and interpreted in relation to the events of the period, might furnish us with sufficient understanding to make an evaluation of their reliability possible.

[12] *Al-Kāmil fi-l tārīḫ* or the *History of Ibn al-Aṯīr* in 12 volumes (Leiden: Brill, 1867). He begins with the creation of the world and ends with the year 628/1230. It should be noted that Ibn al-Aṯīr, like at-Tabarī (839–923), describes the appearance of Maron, to whom is attributed the existence of the Maronites, as occurring during the reign of the emperor Maurice (582–602). This is an error already recognized as such by historians who cannot be suspected of sympathy for the cause of the Maronites. See Pierre Dib, *Histoire de l'Eglise Maronite* (Beirut: La Sagesse, 1962), 45–46; P. S. Vailhe, *Echos d'Orient* 4 (1906): 261–66, "L'Eglise Maronite du Ve au IXe siècles."

[13] Cf. footnote 3.

[14] See Dib, *Histoire*, 8–9.

Internal Criticism

The Context

Before we study the text itself, it will be helpful to analyze the context in which it was written. This is to be found in the chapter that deals with Roman history; more precisely, it is in a small note devoted to Emperor Marcian (451–57). The chapter begins with the legend of the founding of Rome by Romulus and Remus and ends with the accession of Heraclius (610), during whose reign the Hegira took place in 622.

Abū l-Fidā wanted above all to arrange a chronology of the emperors. However, his chronology is not entirely free from errors, despite the many references and the author's diligence. The events illustrating the reign of each emperor are succinctly and precisely selected. They are either general events like the birth of Jesus Christ under Augustus (31 BC–AD 14) or specific events concerning Syria, especially the region under Abū l-Fidā's authority, such as the construction of the walls of Ḥamāh (Epiphania) under Anastasius I (491–518).[15]

The Text

The language used by Abū l-Fidā is clear, sober, and precise. It is the style of a historian who records the facts as they strike his intelligent mind. We do not see any linguistic difficulties in the text. The author refers to the construction, and not to any enlargement,[16] under the emperor Marcian of a monastery by the name of Maron in Ḥoms.

It is worth pointing out here that Abū l-Fidā is the first, and to our knowledge the only one, among Arab historians to attribute the origin of this monastery to the fifth century. All other historians, including those such as Ibn al-Aṯīr and al Masʿūdī,[17] who served

---

[15] Abū l-Fidā, *Hist. Anteislamica* (n. 4), 110.

[16] Dib, *Histoire*, 7.

[17] al-Masʿūdī (Abū al-Ḥasan ʿAlī-al), born in Baghdad, died in Cairo in 345/956, named al-Masʿūdī after an ancestor, Masʿūd, who lived in Mecca, and whose son accompanied the prophet to Medina. He wrote several books

as his most illustrious models and sources, dated its foundation
to the reign of the emperor Maurice (582–602). When writing of
Maurice, Abū l-Fidā ignores these writers. By doing so, he accepts
the Maronite tradition which identifies the illustrious anchorite
whom Theodoret mentions in his *Religious History* with the patron
of this monastery, which is considered to be the cradle of the
Maronite Antiochian Church. He agrees also with the numerous
ancient and authentic documents, which speak of the monastery
of Maron and mention it as having been founded long before the
reign of Maurice, as we shall see in the following pages.

The formula used to proclaim this is not an ordinary one.[18] The
sentence has the concise style generally found in writing inscriptions,
highlighting the recorded fact and also its date. It is written so as
to be memorized. We might even speculate whether Abū l-Fidā
did not find an inscription recording Marcian's foundation of the
monastery during one of his many voyages.

Abū l-Fidā uses this formulaic style eight times in his chapter
on the Roman emperors. He uses it four times to describe events
which are related to general history and four times when relating
events that are of concern only to Syria:

1. The ascension of Jesus Christ

2. The Egyptian revolt against Diocletian (284–305)

3. The founding of Constantinople by Constantine (312–37)

4. The discovery of the True Cross by Helena, Constantine's
   mother

5. An invasion of locusts causing famine in the East during
   the reign of Anastasius (491–518)

6. The fortification of Ḥamāh under Anastasius in 492

---

of which the most important are (1) *Meadows of Gold*, written between 332/943
and 336/947. It was published in English by M. Sprenger in 1841 as *El Masʿūdīs
Historical Encyclopedia, Entitled 'Meadows of Gold'* (London: Printed for the Oriental
Translation Fund of Great Britain and Ireland, 1841); (2) *The Book of Advice*. This is
a collection of observations on history, geography, and philosophical doctrines.
The last book he wrote bears the date of his death, 345/956.

[18] Abū l-Fidā, *Hist. Anteislamica*, cf. footnote 12.

7. The taking of Apamaea by Chosroes in 573, during the reign of Justin II (565–78)

8. The founding of the monastery of Maron in 452 under Marcian (451–57)[19]

The events other than the founding of the monastery are well-known historical facts of signal importance, deserving emphasis. In addition, we cannot fail to notice that Abū l-Fidā is more precise when determining the date of an event with a direct relation to his region: such events gain in precision what they lack in importance.

Now, in spite of having occurred in the region in which the author is directly interested, the founding of a monastery in general circumstances is not a historical event of great importance for a Muslim historian. Why, then, should the author have wished to give as much importance to this specific event as to the other great events? Is it simply that a precise date was available to him, either through local tradition, or through some epigraphic inscription commemorating the event, or both?

What is certain is that Abū l-Fidā *treats the event in a way indicating that he considers it important, and presents the facts in an authoritative manner.*

Criticism of Accuracy

Both external and internal criticism help in understanding the text, in appreciating its authenticity, and in revealing Abū l-Fidā's personality. Sometimes criticism stops here, but equally, it can often go further. Once the text has been classified and the original form established, the historian seeks the facts, passing from document to reality, from signifier to signified; for as Marshal de Moltke expressed it, "the field and the historical site are the only remaining reality of an event in the past."[20]

"We shall take no witness at his word," said Robert Marichal. "The historian would be wrong to classify the evidence of witnesses as admissible or inadmissible, as in a court of law, and to accept

[19] Ibid., 110–13.
[20] P. Peeters, "Hypathius et Vitalien," in *Mélanges H. Grégoires*, vol. 2 (Brussels, 1950), 32–33.

the 'admissible' evidence every time he sees no 'special reason' for doubting it. The historian cannot be satisfied with negative arguments. He cannot accept anything that is not 'scientifically proven.' How then can we attain 'scientific truth' in history? The secret lies entirely in knowing how to interrogate the text." [21]

This implies an interrogation to discover the sources, and to study circumstances of each assertion, to uncover grounds for doubt or trust, as may be. Thus, we shall draft two sets of questions concerning the testimony in question.

The first set relates to the founding of the monastery by Emperor Marcian, and the second to its location in Homs.

a) *Is it true that the emperor Marcian built monasteries? Is it true that he built the monastery of Saint Maron? If so, under what circumstances?*

Marcian was a native of Thrace, "of a humble family," according to Tillemont, "but one which for several generations had always followed the Orthodox faith."[22] He was renowned for his kindness and bravery, rising from the rank of ordinary soldier to general, and then to senator.

Upon the unexpected death of Theodosius on 28 July 450, Pulcheria, his sister, "an intelligent and energetic woman"[23] of remarkable ability, seized power and gave orders for the execution of Chrysaphius the eunuch, who was close to and protected Eutyches, and had been the "evil genius and all-powerful counsellor" of the late emperor.[24] Then, as she did not feel powerful enough to rule alone, she married the elderly senator Marcian, and caused the senate and the military to proclaim him emperor on 24 August 450.[25]

---

[21] Robert Marichal, "L'Histoire et ses méthodes," in *Encyclopédie de la Pléiade* (Paris, 1961), 1341.

[22] Louis Sebastien Le Nain de Tillemont, *Histoire des empereurs* (Paris, 1700–1738), 4:280–305.

[23] Pierre Thomas Camelot, *Éphèse et Chalcédoine*, in *Histoire des conciles*, vol. 2 (Paris, 1961), 115.

[24] P. Goubert, "Le rôle de Ste Pulchérie et de Chrysaphios," in *Das Konzil von Chalkedon*, vol. 1 (Echter-verlag Woerzburg, 1953), 203–21.

[25] Eugène Marin, *Les moines de Constantinople* (Paris, 1897), 7.

Following the examples of Constantine, Helena, and almost all the great personalities of the empire, Marcian, and particularly Pulcheria, the new empress, were moved sometimes by piety and sometimes by vanity to build religious foundations, and to erect and richly endow churches, hospitals, and especially monasteries. Marcian built, amongst many others, the religious houses of Saint Zoe and of Saint Irene, and those of Myroceratum.[26]

The empress Pulcheria acquired some renown in this respect. "It would take us too long," says Sozomenes, "to describe how many churches were built by this pious princess . . . how many monasteries were built by her to which she left rents and revenues for the support of the people who withdrew to them."[27] We must conclude that Marcian and Pulcheria diligently engaged in building monasteries and churches.

But in our particular case, there were more specific motives which may have prompted Marcian and Pulcheria to found the monastery of Saint Maron: the new regime had inherited a critical religious situation. The patriarch of Alexandria continued the policy of his predecessors in favoring the enemies of Flavian, the former patriarch of Constantinople.[28] The palace revolution which brought Marcian to power brought about a change in ecclesiastical policy. The disgrace of Chrysaphius meant the defeat of the party of Dioscoros and Eutyches, and the victory of Flavian, and Theodoret of Cyr. Eutyches was exiled from his monastery and confined somewhere near Constantinople. Meanwhile, Flavian's body was brought back to Constantinople, the exiled Catholic bishops were recalled, and a council was convoked and opened on 8 October 451.

More light is shed on the founding of the monastery of Maron in the proceedings of the sixth session, held in the presence of the emperor himself, during which the Chalcedonian creed was solemnly proclaimed. During a solemn session, the emperor and Pulcheria were acclaimed as "the torch-bearers of the orthodox faith,

---

[26] Ibid., 7, 16.
[27] Sozomene, *Hist. Eccl.* PG 67:9:1:1596.
[28] Goubert, "Le rôle de Ste Pulchérie," 309.

Marcian, the new Constantine, and Pulcheria, the new Helena."[29]
The emperor gave thanks to Jesus Christ for the restoration of unity
and threatened severe punishment to private individuals, soldiers
and clergy alike who might raise other difficulties concerning the
faith,[30] and he proposed no less than three edicts concerning the
founding of monasteries, the civil affairs of the clergy and monks,
and the transfer of clergy from one church to another. However, he
left the details for the council to decide, being matters that fell within
its domain rather than that of the imperial authority: "There exist,"
said Marcian, "some articles concerning discipline which we have
respectively reserved, considering it suitable that they be decided
canonically by the Council rather than imposed by our laws."[31]

Beronician, the secretary, read them out: "We consider worthy of
honor those who embrace sincerely the monastic life; however, as
there are some who find any excuse to cause trouble in the Church
and in the State, we have given orders that *no one should build a
monastery without the approval of the bishop of the region and the owner
of the land.* We once again remind the monks of the cities as well as
those of the countryside that they should *submit to their bishop* and
that their life is above all *a life of peace, fasting and prayer, having nothing
to do with the affairs of the State and of the Church"* (emphasis added).[32]

In fact, the council, in agreement with the emperor, decreed
canons IV, V, and VI as he had proposed. A reading of canon IV
reveals that the abuses it suppressed were the work of the civil
policy of the state as much as of any ecclesiastic discipline.

The counter-attack against the Eutychian monks of Bar Sauma
causes no surprise, since at Chalcedon the prevailing spirit was
one of reaction against the excesses committed at Ephesus in 449.[33]

[29] J. Mansi, *Sacrorum conciliorum omnium nova et amplissima collectio,* vol. 7
(Florence and Venice, 1759–98), 129ff.; Hardouin, *Acta conciliorum et epistolae
decretales ac constitutiones summorum pontificorum,* vol. 2 (Paris, 1715), 2:463ff.

[30] Mansi, *Sacrorum conciliorum,* 7:170ff.; Hardouin, *Acta conciliorum,* 490ff.

[31] Labbe, *Concilia,* 4:608.

[32] Héfélé-Leclercq, *Histoires des Conciles,* vol. 2 (Paris, 1907), 732–35 and 779ff.

[33] Henri Marrou, *Nouvelle Histoire de l'Eglise,* vol. 1 (Paris: Ed. du Seuil, 1963),
395: "The Council of Chalcedon was not an act of revenge for the brigandage
of 449, although the Monophysites later pretended it was an act of revenge for
the Council of Ephesus."

So it was that, after the closing of the Council of Chalcedon early in November of 451, Marcian, who had made a promise during the sixth session to prevent any further religious dispute, promulgated a law on 7 February 452 in which he expressed his joy at seeing disputes calmed by the authority and the decisions of the council.[34]

On 6 July 452, he promulgated a decree abrogating the law of Theodosius II against Flavian, Eusebius, and Theodoret.[35] Finally, on 28 July 452 he issued a very severe decree against the monks and other followers of Eutyches forbidding them from holding any meeting, building any monastery, or living together in monasteries. Further, their meeting places were confiscated. Eutychians who had previously been clergy of the orthodox faith, and the monks who had inhabited "the cavern of Eutyches," were banished from the territories of the Roman Empire.[36]

Also in 452, the monks of Palestine who were in revolt against the Council of Chalcedon and the patriarch Juvenal of Jerusalem wrote what was considered to be an insolent petition to Pulcheria and Marcian.[37]

It was during this same year, AD 452, notable for the agitation caused by the monks of the East, that according to the Arab historian Abū l-Fidā, the emperor Marcian founded the Chalcedonian monastery of Saint Maron in the region of Homs.

Although late, this testimony dovetails with all known facts and circumstances of the period, especially that Marcian was conscious of his dignity as orthodox emperor, and had been responsible for the success of the Council of Chalcedon, as Constantine had been for the success of the Council of Nicea in 325.

So by promulgating these edicts against the Eutychian monks, Marcian intended not to undermine the monastic life, but to reform and purge his empire of the enemies of the social and religious order which he and the empress supported. Marcian is known to have honored peaceful, prayerful monks, who stayed where they

---

[34] Héfélé-Leclercq, *Histoires*, 2:844.

[35] Mansi, *Sacrorum conciliorum*, 7:498; Hardouin, *Acta conciliorum*, 2:675ff.

[36] Mansi, *Sacrorum conciliorum*, 7:502; Hardouin, *Acta conciliorum*, 2:675ff.

[37] Baluze, *Concilium appendix* (Paris, 1683); see Le Nain De Tillemont, *Mémoires pour servir à l'histoire ecclésiastique des six premiers siècles* (Paris, 1693–1712), 15:180.

were put until their bishop allowed them leave, and caused no trouble to the state or the church. He desired to have these monks replace those whom he considered to be bad monks. We now come to our second question.

b) *Is it true that Marcian built this monastery in Ḥoms?*

Answering this question is more difficult, but it is most decisive. First, it is appropriate to recall here some geographical facts about the division of Syria first under the Romans and then under the Arabs following the conquest of Syria by the Muslim general Abū-Bakr in 632–36.

Syria, a Roman Province

We know that Syria was established as a province by Pompey in the year 64 BC[38] when he dethroned the last Seleucid king, Antiochus Asiaticus. But we are uncertain of the precise boundaries of this province. Indeed, while Pompey completely divested Antiochus Asiaticus of his possessions, and took possession of all Syria from the upper Euphrates and the Gulf of Issus to Egypt and the Arabian Desert, he considered it impossible to give Syria one united organization, either because of its diverse nationalities, or because of the political dissensions which had split the country during the last days of the Seleucid dynasty, or both. In 63 BC, following the storming of Jerusalem, Pompey organized the new province. Judea or *Syria Palestina* remained separated from Syria proper, which latter was divided much later on, probably under Severus in the year 194, into two provinces, namely, *Syria Magna* or *Syria Cœla* and *Syria Phoenicia*. Later, in the fourth century, these three provinces, *Syria Palestina*, *Syria Cœla*, and *Syria Phoenicia*, were transformed into seven provinces, as follows:

1. Syria Prima, with Antioch, Seleucia, Laodicea, Gabala, Poltos, Beræa and Chalcis

2. Syria Secunda, with Apamaea, Epiphania, Arethusa, Balanea, Seleucabelos and Raphanea

---

[38] Philip Hitti, *History of Syria* (London: McMillan, 1951), 249–50.

3. Euphratia, with Cyr (Cyrrhus), Hierapolis (Membej), Samosata, Zeugma, and Germanicia

4. Phoenicia, with Tyre, Ptolemais, Sidon, Berytus, Byblos, Bostroys, Tripoli, Arca, Arados and Panæas

5. Lebanese Phoenicia, with Ḥoms, Laodicea, Heliopolis (Baalbek), Abila, Damascus and Palmyra

6. Palestina Prima, with Caesarea, Diospholis (Lydda), Azotus (اشدود), Aclia Capitolina (Jerusalem) (اورشليم), Neapolis (نابلوس), Sebastes, Anthedon (نازله), Joppa (يافا), Gaza and Ascalon

7. Palestina Secunda, with Scythopolis (بيسان), Gadara, Antiochia ad Hippum, Tiberias and Gabac

(Khun states that Euphratia was established between 341 and 343, while Syria Cœle, Syria Phoenicia, and Palestine remained united until 381 at least. They were probably divided only under Arcadius from 395 till 399. Such is also the opinion of Mommsen.)

Syria under Islam

Syria and Palestine submitted to Islam following the battle of Yarmuk, fought in 636 by Abū-Bakr. Then, at the conference of Jabiyah, Syria was divided into four districts or military regions (Jund جند).[39] These were Damascus, Ḥoms, Jordan, and Palestine. The district of Jordan included Galilee and stretched out east toward the desert. Palestine included the southern region of the plain of Esdrelon (Marj-ibn ʿAmer), while Damascus stretched out northwards as far as Heliopolis.

Finally the district of Ḥoms included all northern Syria and in particular the cities of Apamaea, Epiphania, and Schaizar as far as Chalcis (Qinnisrin). It was only under the caliph Yazid (680), son of Moawiyya, that the new district of Qinnisrin was established by

---

[39] Jabiyah is one day's journey southwest from Damascus, and the settlement of the Ghassanid Emirs of Japhnah. When the Arabs conquered Damascus, they made it a military and administrative base. There they shared among themselves the spoils of victory after Yarmuk, and discussed the problems of the conquest. Thus we have "Jabiyah Day" and the "Speeches of Jabiyah."

separating Chalcis from Ḥoms and by adding Antakhyāh, Manbij, and Al-Jazirāh (Mesopotamia). Then under the caliph ʿAbd-el-Malik in 685 Al-Jazirāh was separated from Qinnisrin and made into another independent district.

It is clear that Ḥoms under the Romans was the metropolis of Lebanese Phoenicia. Its activity was thus essentially oriented toward the south, toward Heliopolis, Damascus, and Palmyra. However, under Islam, it became the provincial capital of a very large district or military region. Ḥoms became the Islamic military base for the northward march of conquest, in the direction of Ḥamāh, Apamaea, Chalcis. Hence, as the conquest progressed, new districts began to be established in the north. Even before Islam, as Henri Lammens points out, Ḥoms had begun to extend northwards after the repeated incursions of the Persians and the Lakhmid Arabs had destroyed Apamaea.[40]

c) *Is there in fact a monastery under the name of Maron in Ḥoms?*

Of all the surviving ancient documents that mention a monastery of Saint Maron, none names such a monastery in Ḥoms. On the contrary, all agree in locating a monastery of Saint Maron in the region of Apamaea and therefore in Syria Secunda and not in Syria Prima.[41] Only two documents, probably dating from the period of the conquest of Syria by the Muslims, mention the city of Ḥoms when speaking about the monks or the monastery of Maron. One is taken from the Chronicle of Denys of Tell-Mahré and the other from the Syriac manuscript number 234 in the National Library of Paris.

In the first document, which relates the visit of Emperor Heraclius to Syria and its consequences, the Jacobite patriarch of Antioch says, "This persecution has lasted long and many monks adhered to the Synod (Chalcedon). The monks of Beit-Maron, at

---

[40] Henri Lammens, *Le Liban* (Beirut: Imprimerie Catholique, 1906), 83ff. Extract from *Al-Machriq*; Georges Tchalenko, *Villages antiques de la Syrie du Nord*, vol. 1 (Paris, 1953), 426–27 and note 1.

[41] Coll. Avellana, Pars 2 (Vindobonae, 1898), 565–71, letter 139, 572–84; letter 140; Mansi, 8:882, 911, 930, 939, 945, 995, etc. ACO Coll. *Sabbaitica*, ed. Eduard Schwartz, vol. 3 (Berolini: de Gruyter, 1940), 60–62 and 106–10.

Mabboug (Hierapolis), Ḥoms, and the regions of the South showed their malice."[42]

The text does not allow us to conclude that there existed a monastery by the name of Saint Maron in Ḥoms, otherwise we would be obliged to conclude likewise that there existed several monasteries under that name, in Mabboug, in Ḥoms, and in the regions of the south. The author refers rather to the "monks of Beit-Maron" who were in Mabboug, Ḥoms, and so on, an expression which allows us to infer either that there existed a *monastic grouping,* or a *monastic confederation, that came under the authority of the monastery of Saint Maron near Apamaea,* or simply that there existed a monastic grouping confessing the same doctrine as that of the monks of this monastery of Saint Maron. This latter possibility is suggested in some sixth-century documents, namely, the two petitions written by the monks of Syria Secunda in which they attacked Severus of Antioch (512–18) and Peter of Apamaea. These petitions were submitted to Pope Hormisdas in 517 and to the synod of the province of Apamaea in 518. The other documents include the Acts of the Council of Constantinople held in 536 in the presence of the Catholic patriarch Menas.[43]

The second document relates the story of a "blessed one who dwelt in a tree in Ir'enin, a small village dependant on the metropolis of Apamaea." The manuscript mentions neither the date of the work nor the name of the author, but F. Nau, who translated

---

[42] Michel le Syrien, *Chronique de Michel le Syrien, patriarche Jacobite d'Antioche* (1166–1199), édition et traduction par J.-B. Chabot, Syriac text (Paris, 1899–1924), 4:410; translation, 2:412.

[43] The Acts of this council were edited for the first time by Severin Binius in 1618, according to a manuscript of the library of Heidelberg, which is very incomplete and even contains errors. In that same year, Fronton-le-Duc wrote a better version of the text, to which Labbe made a few amendments. This last version is considered generally as a reference; Caesar Baronius, *Annales ecclesiastici, ad ann.* 536, nn. 71–93, T. 9, 500–45, *Caesaris S.R.E. Card. Baronii, Od. Raynaldi et Jac. Laderchii, denuo excuse et ad nostra usque tempora perducti ab Augustino Theiner* (Barri-Ducis: Ludovicus Guerin, 1867); Labbe, *Concilia,* 5:1–276; Hardouin, *Coll. Concil.,* 2:1185; Mansi, supplement 1:416, *conc. ampliss.* vol. 8: 870; Héfélé-Leclercq, *Histoires,* 2.2:1142ff.; ACO *Sabbaitica,* ed. Schwartz, 3:131–34, 136, nn. 68ff.

and edited this account, thinks that it was probably written by one of the monks of the monastery of Saint Maron near Apamaea.[44] This text demonstrates the importance of Homs and the monastery of Maron near Apamaea. Summarized, it says that a "man of God" dwelt in a large cypress tree in Ir'enin, a village in the vicinity of the metropolis Apamaea. One night, the secluded one secretly came down from the tree and went toward Jerusalem. On his way, he came to a desert, which he crossed with difficulty, and reached "the region of the barbarians." In that region, he met a native of Homs who asked him where he was from. The man of God answered him: "*I am from Homs*, because," continues the author of the account, "*Apamaea is a dependency of Homs*" (emphasis added).

This episode has a double interest: first, it must have been written either at the time of the Islamic conquest or a short time before, following the Persian incursions, when the metropolis Apamaea began to lose some of its authority to Homs. Second, it provides an example of a custom of identifying the capital Homs with other cities dependent on it. According to H. Lammens, there is nothing surprising about the fact that a great number of authors used Homs in the calculation of distances and talked about Hamāh and Apamaea as two cities in its vicinity, for Homs was one of the largest central cities of Syria and the two cities Hamāh and Apamaea were governed by it.[45]

Abū l-Fidā's expression "monastery of Maron in Homs" need not be interpreted to mean "in the city of Homs." It could equally mean "the monastery of Maron in the region of Homs," or "in the region dependent on Homs." As we shall see, the monastery of Maron was a few kilometers away from Apamaea and was not dependent on any village or city. It could then be easily affiliated to Apamaea or to Homs, to the metropolis or the capital. Abū l-Fidā, writing when Apamaea was in ruins, could speak of the monastery of Maron near Apamaea as well as the monastery of Maron in the region of Homs.

Abū l-Fidā himself, the governor of Hamāh, writes in his *Universal History*: "Schaizar (Larissa) and Hamāh were very small

---

[44] François Nau, *Opuscules Maronites*, in *Revue de l'Orient Chrétien* (1899), 4:337ff.; cf. also Zotenburg, *Catalogue*, ms. n. 234.

[45] Lammens, *Le Liban*, 2:83.

at the time of the Arab conquest and were part of the region of Ḥoms, which was the capital." Then he continues: "Ḥamāh and Schaizar, according to the commentators, are two villages of the region of Ḥoms."[46] We know that the distance between Schaizar and Apamaea was about twenty kilometers while the distance separating Apamaea from Ḥoms was eighty-eight kilometers.[47] The monastery of Maron according to al-Masʿūdī and other historians was situated on the east side of Ḥamāh and Schaizar.[48]

General Conclusion

We clearly see following this detailed critical study that there is no genuine reason for doubting the testimony of Abū l-Fidā. On the contrary, everything is in its favor: Abū l-Fidā had opportunities for gathering information, based upon his rank, culture, his travels, and his many contacts. Further, there is a complete harmony between the asserted fact and the circumstances prevailing around AD 452.

Thus we can safely answer questions (b) and (c) in the affirmative, and accept as a fact that there was indeed a monastery of Maron near Apamaea, which could be described as being in (the province of) Ḥoms, and which was built on the orders of Emperor Marcian in 452, that is to say following the Council of Chalcedon, when on 28 July 452, the emperor had issued a stringent law against the monks and the followers of Eutyches.[49] This monastery would later become the headquarters of the Chalcedonians in the sixth and seventh centuries.

[46] Aboulfida, *Annales muslemici*, edition Reisk and Adler, 1:224–25.

[47] René Mouterde and Antoine Poidebard, *Les limes de Chalcis* (Paris, 1945), 26.

[48] Al-Masʿūdī, *Kitāb at-tanbih wal-ishraf*, edition De Goeje (Leyde, 1894), 153–54; see also the translation of Carra de Vaux, *Imprimerie nationale* (Paris, 1897), 211–12, *Appendice*, 202–3; Arabic text ed. Dar at-Turāth (Beirut, 1968), 131–32; see also Tchalenko, *Villages antiques* (n. 41), 2:23, *Région archéologique du Massif Calcaire*; cf. A. Daou, *Histoire des Maronites* (in Arabic), ed. Dār an-Nahār (Beirut, 1970), 145ff.

[49] Mansi, *Sacrorum conciliorum*, 7:502; Hardouin, *Acta conciliorum*, 2:675. See also Schiwietz, *Das morgenlandische Moenchtum*, vol. 3 (Wien, 1938), 242–43, n. 3; Dib, *Histoire* (n. 12), 7.

Chapter Two

Maron and Marcian

North Syrian Monasticism in the Fourth and Fifth Centuries

We can, then, accept Abū l-Fidā's statement that after the Council of Chalcedon in 452, the emperor Marcian built the monastery of Maron "in Ḥoms" (Emessa).[1] But which Maron was he referring to? In Syria, many had borne this name.

Maronite tradition identifies this Maron as the most famous one, the anchorite of Theodoret's *Religious History*. His Beatitude the Syrian Orthodox Patriarch Ignatius Jacob III, in his article *Severus and the Monks of the Monastery of Maron*, attempted to list the different bearers of that name.[2] Since the custom of giving a person's name to a monastery is generally a testimony to the veneration in which the memory and the virtues of some holy monk are held, and Marcian was an upholder of doctrinal orthodoxy, the Maron in question must have enjoyed a significant, not to say respectable, reputation in the monastic milieu of northern Syria, and have died before 452.

Of those known to us, only the Maron of the *Religious History* satisfies all of these conditions. All the others ever put forward are posterior. The other Marons are the following:

---

[1] See chap. 1, n. 1.
[2] *The Patriarchal Magazine*, 2 (1963), n. 12, 70–82.

1. Maron, correspondent of Severus of Antioch (512–18)[3]

2. Maron, correspondent of Jacob of Serugh (+521)[4]

3. Maron, lector of Anazarbes[5]

4. Maron, the hermit of the Amid district[6]

5. Maron, orthodox superior of the monastery of the Easterners in the Roha mountain, exiled by Justinian (518–22)[7]

6. Maron, superior of the monastery of the Tree in Daraia, "he who signed the orthodox letter around the year 570"[8]

7. Finally, Maron of the *Religious History* (+410)[9]

But how are we to explain the presence of a monastery in or around Apamaea or Homs, dedicated to a monk who had been a hermit and who had spent all his life in Cyr, when the distance between the two regions is about 150 kilometers? Was there any relationship between these regions, or their religious communities? The present chapter, which has as its principal source Theodoret's *Religious History*, will be divided into three parts: (1) an essay on the ecclesiastical history and geography of northern Syria, theatre of the exploits of the heroes of the *Religious History*, particularly Cyr and Apamaea; (2) Marcian and his disciples, or the cenobitic life in Apamaea in the fourth and fifth centuries; and (3) Maron and his disciples or the eremitic life in Cyr in the fourth and fifth centuries.

In the beginning of the second part, we will briefly study Theodoret's *Religious History*, which is the only source that talks about Maron, Marcian, and their disciples.

---

[3] E. W. Brooks, ed., *Patrologia Orientalis*, vol. 12 (1919) and vol. 14 (1920) (Turnhout, Belgium: Brepols), 1:196ff.

[4] Olinder, *Jacobi Saruq, Epist* (Lund, 1939).

[5] Ernst Honigmann, *Évêques et évêchés monophysites* (Louvain: L. Durbecq, 1951), 64, n. 4.

[6] *Vie des pères et ermites orientaux*, 1:56.

[7] Zacharias Rhetor, *Hist. Eccl.*, ed. E. W. Brooks, in CSCO 83–84 (Paris and Louvain, 1919–21), 2:81.

[8] Doc. Monoph., ed. I. B. Chabot, in CSCO, n. 17 (103) (Paris, 1908), 220.

[9] *H.R.* in *P.G.* 82:16, col. 1418–19.

Northern Syria

General Surroundings[10]

The region that served as an apparently natural setting for the anchorites spoken of in the *Religious History* is now one of the main archaeological regions of Syria. It is located to the north and at the same time extends toward Asia Minor, the Mediterranean and the steppes to the east. It is surrounded by the great ancient cities of Cyr to the north, Apamaea to the south, Antioch to the west, and Chalcis and Aleppo to the east. The major part of this region is made up of a secondary range of mountains around which stretch out large and fertile interior plains. To this whole region, almost abandoned until recently, the archaeologist G. Tchalenko gave the name of "the Limestone Massif of Belus."[11]

This limestone massif is surrounded on the north and northwest by the folds of Kurd-Dāğ, and all along the west by the meridian faults in which flow the Orontes and the Afrin rivers. In the south it ends near Apamaea at the bend of the Orontes, and finally to the east it merges progressively into the interior plateau, where it is distinguished by the nature of its soil (see Map II). This massif, which is about 150 kilometers long north-south and twenty to forty kilometers wide west-east, formed the cradle of those who were later to be called *the monks of Beit-Maron*, or simply *the Maronites*. It includes four groups of mountains: immediately to the north of that region and to the east of Cyr, the Parsa Dāğ; to the northeast, a little lower, Gebel Halaqa, which continues to the north to form Gebel

---

[10] See the excellent G. Tchalenko, *Villages*, 1:1–91; J. Mattern, *Villes Mortes*, in *Mélanges de l'Université de Saint Joseph* (Beirut, 1933), 17:10ff.; René Dussaud, *Topographie historique de la Syrie antique et médiévale* (Paris: P. Geuthner, 1997); J. Lassus, *Inventaire archéologique de la region au Nord-Est de Hama, Documents d'études orientales de l'Institut français de Damas*, 4, 2 vols. (Damascus, 1935); Melchior de Vogue, *Syrie centrale, Architecture civile et religieuse, du Ier au VIIe siècles*, 2 vols. (Paris: J. Baudry, 1865–77); AAES, *Publications of an American Archaeological Expedition to Syria* in 1899–1900 (New York, 1903–30); and PAES, *Publications of the Princeton University Archaeological Expeditions to Syria* in 1904–5 and 1909 (Leiden, 1907–49).

[11] Tchalenko, *Villages*, 1:55–56, n. 1.

Seiḫ Barakat of Gebel Semᶜan; in the middle, a group composed of three parallel ranges; finally in the south, Gebel Zawiye or Gebel Riha. Of these four groups, the first and the fourth are of interest to us because the Parsa Dāǧ seems to be, according to P. Canivet, the place of Saint Maron's retreat and it is surely in the neighborhood of Gebel Zawiye that the monastery of Maron was established, as we shall observe.

The Parsa Dāǧ dominates from above the range that overlooks the Afrin. Like Sheikh Barakat, it is a high place, often attractive to monks.[12] It has three distinct and very close summits. The southernmost summit dominates the village of Maᶜarin, and seems to have been a significant religious site, consecrated to Artemis Parsaia.[13] It also presents the two following elements: (1) a *wali* named "Parsa Khatoum" located on the southern extremity of the summit; and (2) a temple sixty meters away to the north of the wali, on a higher part of the mountain. The ruins indicate a rectangular edifice, oriented north-south, twelve meters long and four meters wide. "If a temple really existed here," concludes Pierre Canivet, "we would then be in the presence of an ancient temple in the location of Cyr. In fact, we have to bear in mind that the Parsa Dāǧ was a part of Cyr, like Azaz. . . . The religious continuity from the pagan temple to the Wali would be assured. In the event of a cult substitution, a pagan cult would have been followed by a Christian one, that of Maron, which with Islam would itself have undergone transformation."[14]

Gebel Zawye or Riha is the most extended, elevated, and level part of what Tchalenko called the limestone massif of Belus. Its core is formed of two massifs separated by a large valley which is occupied by the large and ancient agglomeration of El-Bara. Gebel Zawiye rises to a sheer, uninterrupted wall above the Rūg and the plain of Gāb, where the Orontes forms swamps. The ruins of

---

[12] Pierre Canivet, *Mission en Syrie du Nord* (August–September, 1965): unpublished, which the author kindly provided to me, from which I have drawn information about Parsa Dāǧ.

[13] D. Sourdel, *Ruḥin, lieu de pélerinage musulman de la Syrie du Nord au XIIIème siècle*, in *Syria* (1953), 30:88–107, quoted by Canivet, *Mission en Syrie*, 14.

[14] Tchalenko, *Villages*, vol. 4, APP. 2:13; quoted by Canivet, *Mission en Syrie*, 15.

24 The Maronites

Apamaea are found at the southern foot of Gebel Zawiye, above Gāb. The general altitude of the massif is four hundred to five hundred meters. The crests reach an altitude of six hundred meters, while only a few summits exceed a height of eight hundred meters.[15]

Population: Origin and Language

This northern region between the Mediterranean and the Euphrates represents the most Hellenized part of Syria. It is adjacent to those cities which were the center of Hellenistic civilization, namely, Antioch, Seleucia, Apamaea, and Laodicea. It occupies the center of Seleucia and is also the first region to have been organized by the Romans after the coming of Pompey. On the other hand, it maintained great indigenous traditions. These traditions made it highly accessible to currents of civilization coming from the East, from Osroene, starting from the fifth century.

Its population was of Aramaean origin, as was its language. But following several consecutive occupations and the influence of economic and commercial factors, the big cities, particularly Antioch, became cosmopolitan, with Greeks, Romans, Armenians, Arabs, Persians, and Jews. However, it is certain that the overwhelming majority of the population, except perhaps in Antioch, was Syrian Aramaean.

As for language and literature, the problem is complex. Hellenism penetrated into Syria with the Seleucids, and enjoyed great success in the time of the Romans,[16] "but," according to Peeters,

> it dominated only one region, and even that very incompletely. The cities where it ruled were like islets of an archipelago, close together in some places but very much scattered in others. Its supremacy was reduced in fact to a kind of aristocratic precedence. Even in Antioch, the most Hellenized city in Roman Syria, people spoke fluent Syriac. . . . In how many other cities of Roman Syria did the old Aramaean stock not persist under

[15] Tchalenko, *Villages*, 2:73; J. Mattern, *Villes mortes, dans Mélanges de l'Université Saint-Joseph* (Beirut, 1933), 10.

[16] Paul Peeters, *Le Tréfonds oriental de l'hagiographie byzantine, Subsidia Hagiographica*, 26 (Brussels, 1950), 15.

the official exterior imposed by the conquest? Greek remained the language used in the administration but the army and the judiciary spoke Latin. This dualism had deeply affected the prestige previously enjoyed by Hellenism. As long as Roman domination continued, the obvious superiority of its culture was not questioned; but to conclude from this that the Syrians of that time, because they were following its school, accepted to consider themselves an inferior race . . . is to take too big a step, one we measure quite well when present-day Orientals, having no interest in flattering us, reveal their true inner thought.[17]

Libanius, for example, so proud of his Hellenism, does not hesitate in several of his writings to call himself Syrian and Phoenician. Besides, his name implies as much and when the Syrians were turned against him, he considered himself a coward if he kept silent.[18] Theodoret of Cyr himself, after having blamed the Greeks who boasted about the privilege enjoyed by their culture, adds:

I do not say this to belittle the Greek language, which is mine, to a certain extent, or to be ungrateful for the culture that it has given me, but rather to silence those who boast about it, to make them cast their looks down and to teach them not to make fun of a language which has the glow of truth, and not to pride themselves for having delivered speeches written with consummate artistry but lacking in truth. I say so to make them admire the spokesmen of truth who have not learned to embellish and polish their speeches with a beautiful style but who show, in its bareness, the beauty of truth without the slightest need for foreign embellishments imported from outside.[19]

Noldeke raised some interesting considerations in answer to Mommsen, who in Book V of his Roman history somewhat disparaged

---

[17] Ibid., 16. Cf. also Peeters, "Encore le coq sacré d'Hiérapolis," in *Bulletin de la classe des lettres de l'Académie royale de Belgique, Vème série* (1943), 29:303–10.

[18] Canivet, *Histoire d'une entreprise apologétique au Vème siècle* (Paris, 1957), 25 and n. 5.

[19] Theodoret of Cyr, *Thérapeutique des maladies helléniques*, in *Sources Chrétiennes* 57 (Paris: Cerf, 2001), 1:250–51.

the civilization of the Aramaean provinces of the empire.[20] Noldeke
said,

> It is an exaggeration to affirm that the Syriac language was
> abolished in the civilized centers. In fact, long before, civilized
> people had spoken and written in Aramaic according to consis-
> tent rules at a time when the people of Rome and its surround-
> ing villages did not even know the alphabet. At the time of the
> Persian kings, Syriac was adopted as an official language in
> Egypt and in Asia Minor, that is, outside its native country. Even
> during the time of the first Roman caesars, Aramaic was the of-
> ficial language not only of Palmyra but also of the Nabataean
> kingdom as far as the Arabian Peninsula and the Ḥijaz, that is
> to say here again outside its natural home. This was not simply
> the after-effect of a temporary victory, for the ruins of Palmyra
> and of Nabat clearly show that this language developed and
> flourished even after the Persian kings.

Aramaic and Syriac literature produced some original works
whose value is beyond dispute, particularly since, with the
outstanding example of Saint Ephrem, it became widely known
through the translations of the church fathers. From that time this
literature, after becoming well-known thanks to Saint Ephrem,
began to influence the works of the church fathers.[21]

The Great Communication Routes[22]

The Roman Empire organized two principal road networks for
commercial communications between the Mediterranean and Asia,

[20] Noldeke, *ZDMG* (1885), 39:331–51, quoted by Lammens, *Le Liban*, 61.

[21] Canivet, *Mission en Syrie*, 24, n. 2; 27, n. 2; Peeters, *Tréfonds*, 17, says: "Of all
the literatures that have repaid Hellenism part of the services received, Syriac
literature comes unquestionably in the first place. And if we find in Syria a class
of bilingual intellectuals, something lacking in Egypt, we also find among them
those who contented themselves with writing in their own language, while
nevertheless having all the means of access to another superior culture. Even
many of their readers easily consoled themselves for not knowing Greek."

[22] On the great ancient routes exterior to the massif, see: Poidebard, *La Trace
de Rome dans le désert de Syrie* (Paris, 1934); Mouterde and Poidebard, *Les limes
de Chalcis*; Tchalenko, *Villages*, 1:84ff. See Map I.

and to form its line of defense: in the north, in Cappadocea, that of Sebastes; in the south, in upper Syria, that of Antioch. With this large Antiochian network, there were the very important Syrian networks of Apamaea and Chalcis, where several roads intersect. We will only mention the most important ones.

1. *The Apamaea-Chalcis-Hierapolis (Membej) route.* This had twice the traffic on the military route Antioch-Hierapolis, and directly linked the Orontes and the Euphrates. It was, according to Tchalenko, the great ancient lateral link—with respect to the massif already described. It still exists today. But Tchalenko adds: "Due to the form of the massif, it is the communications north-south which give it its cohesion and not those running east-west; the massif, where it is crossed by this road from Antioch to Chalcis, is only ten kilometers wide." Hence, the importance of the route *Cyr-Chalcis-Apamaea.*

2. *The Cyr-Chalcis-Apamaea route.* The Cyr-Apamaea route that crosses Chalcis was the central part of the great communications line parallel to the line of battle leading from Samosata to the coastal ports.[23] The archaeological unity of the massif, noted by Tchalenko, was perhaps a function of the easy contacts and frequent travel all along the *Cyr-Chalcis-Apamaea* axis.

3. *The Antioch-Apamaea-Heliopolis route* or the great *Route of the Orontes.* This was a Roman route oriented north-south. It followed the gully of the Orontes between Gebel Nosayri and Gebel Zawiye, and then went on through the Bekaa Valley, between the mountains of Lebanon and Anti-Lebanon. It put Antioch in direct communication with Apamaea and Homs, which was itself at the crossroads of the inland towns, namely, Damascus, Heliopolis, and Chalcis ad Libanum (Anjar).[24] *This road would be taken later by a group*

[23] Tchalenko, *Villages*, 85. The author has tried to uncover traces of this important route. The valleys of the Gāb and the Rūg between Gebel Zawiye and the ranges of the middle provide a passage from south to north. That passage extends from the Dana plain, passing by the foot of Cheiḫ Barakāt and going down to Deir Simᶜan in the valley of Afrin. It is the natural road from Apamaea to Cyr.

[24] Tchalenko, *Villages*, 431–37. Aurel Stein, "Surveys on the Roman frontier in Iraq and Trans-Jordan," in *Geographical Journal* (1940), 430ff.

of Syrians, the Maronites, going to settle in north Lebanon, following the economic decline of the limestone massif, and motivated by other political and religious reasons.

Cyr[25]

Cyr in History

Cyr is now best known as the episcopal seat of the "great theologian and controversialist of the fifth century, Theodoret."[26] The city was a Seleucid colony.[27] It seems it had been the principal urban center of all the region of northern Syria. In Roman times, the province of Cyr was a region on the frontier between the kingdom of the Arsacids and the territories of Commagenea and Cilicia, which were still independent. Location and other strategic factors saw Cyr designated as the center of the military command. Under Tiberius (AD 14–37), it became the camp of the Legio Fretensis until the war of Judea. Under Vespasian, in 73, when Cilicia was established as a province, Cyr lost its strategic importance; however, some troops were kept there to provide for its security.

In the fourth century, Cyr was part of the new province of Euphrates, of which Hierapolis was the metropolis. Theodoret tells us of the extent of its territory: "It is forty miles long and wide. But there are many great mountains, some utterly bare and others covered with non-fruit-bearing trees."[28] It included around

[25] On the history and the topography of Cyr and its region, in addition to the study of Franz Cumont, *Etudes Syriennes* (Paris: Picard, 1917), 221–45; and *Inscriptions*, ibid., 330–40 (nn. 38–41); see Dussaud, *Topographie*, 470–72; Lammens, *Le Liban*, 58–75; Chapot, *Frontière de l'Euphrate*, 340ff.; Droysen, *Histoire de l'hellénisme*, trans. Bouché-Leclercq (Paris: E. Leroux, 1885), 3:727.

[26] Cumont, *Etudes Syriennes*, 221.

[27] The Seleucid Dynasty was founded in Persia and Asia Minor by Seleucos I Nikator, a general under Alexander. It ruled from around 312 till 64 BC. Having conquered Syria in 200 BC, its territory was reduced to that of a province in the first century BC.

[28] Theodoret of Cyr, Ep 42; trans. Yvan Azéma, Théodoret de Cyr, *Correspondence*, 4 vols., *Sources Chrétiennes* 40, 98, 11, 429 (Paris: Cerf, 1955, 1964, 1965, 1998), 2:111. See also Epp 32, 139, 144–46.

eight hundred parishes.[29] From the *Religious History* we know the names of certain villages such as Omeros (1429-B), Tillima (1452-D), Targala (1453-D), Kitta (1457-D), and Parthen, or Parthes, which left its name to Parsa Dāğ, eight miles southeast of the town.[30]

At the time of Theodoret, Cyr was of very little importance. It was far from the main lines of communication and the bishop had to go to Antioch to send and to receive letters.[31] He also talked about the "desolation" of the small town, which "in one way or another concealed its ugliness by the building of sumptuous and diverse edifices."[32]

Although the valley of Afrin was fertile, the region was not rich, and the town, perched on a height, was without water. The financial situation of the town was critical; overburdened with taxes, its resources dried up due to the exodus of its notables and the emigration of its villagers, who left the fields untilled.[33]

The violence caused by the theological disputes also disturbed the population. When in 449 Theodoret, suspected of adhering to Nestorianism, had to abandon his episcopal seat to return to his monastery near Apamaea, many of his supporters left Cyr with him.[34] During his episcopate, Theodoret took pride in putting his ingenuity and even his "ecclesiastical revenues" toward carrying out the indispensable works of town planning, such as the building of porticos for the public, bridges and public baths, and the construction of an aqueduct to bring water, etc.[35] By the beginning

---

[29] Ep 113; Azéma, 3:63.

[30] For these names and others, see in particular: Dussaud, *Topographie*, 470–72; Cumont, Études *Syriennes*, 226ff.; E. Honigmann, *Historische Topographie von Nordsyrien im Altertum, ZDPV* (1923): 149 and (1924): 1 (Leipzig, 1923), in particular numbers 216, 470. See also *Analecta Bollondiana* 29 (1900): 307ff.

[31] Synodicon, 107 (letter from Theodoret to Himerus of Nicomedia), cf. R. Devresse, *Le Patriarcat d'Antioche* (Paris, 1945), 285.

[32] Ep 139; Azéma, 3:147.

[33] Epp 42–43; Azéma, 2:107–16.

[34] Epp 114–15; Azéma, 3:69.

[35] Ep 81; Azéma, 2:193. Epp 66, 67, 68; Azéma, 2:147–50. Epp 42–47; Azéma, 2:107–23. Ep 115; Azéma, 3:69. In his letters, Theodoret takes pleasure in invoking the name of James (Jacob), the disciple of Maron, for his great prestige and reputation for saintliness.

of Justinian's reign (527–65), Cyr was a small, totally neglected town until the emperor restored its lost power.[36] Under Islam, Cyr (Qoūrouš) became one of the seven towns of the Province of the Fortresses (جند العواصم) created by Harūn al-Rashīd at the end of the eighth century.

Cyr and Christianity

Christianity had been introduced early into Cyr, as in all of Syria. The church of Cyr, certainly established before the Council of Nicea, to which it sent its bishop Siricius, claimed to have its beginnings with Simon the Zealot and to preserve the remains of Saints Cosmos and Damien. Toward the end of the fourth century and the beginning of the fifth, slightly before the time of Theodoret, the town became a center of fervent religious devotion. In the surrounding mountains, the anchorites were venerated for their asceticism. We know, thanks to the *Religious History*, a great number of these paragons of eremitic virtue.[37]

Upon his arrival, Theodoret found an already fervent Christian presence with numerous parishes and monasteries. But there were also many heretics: Marcionites, Arians, and Macedonians. "I had the joy," he wrote in 445 to the consul Nomus, "of bringing back to the right path eight villages infested by the heresies of Marcion . . . I brought to the light of the knowledge of God another village full of Eunomians and another one full of Arians and thank God not a single wisp of heresy has remained among us. I have not accomplished this task without facing danger, but by often shedding my blood, and being stoned by them and being taken to the doors of death."[38]

Theodoret held office for thirty years, and was closely involved in the religious struggles of his time. His successor, John, was distinguished by his opposition to Peter the Fuller, and was expelled at the same time as his metropolitan, Cyr of Hierapolis, by order of the emperor Zeno in 489.[39] In 512, its bishop Sergius was present at

[36] Procopius, *De Oedif.*, 2:11.
[37] Theodoret, *H.R.*, *P.G.* 82, col. 1289 B.
[38] Ep 81; Azéma, 2:193.
[39] Devresse, *Le Patriarcat d'Antioche*, 67, n. 4; 284.

the consecration of Severus and signed a manifesto of the "Severan" bishops aimed against Julian of Halicarnassus. He was expelled by the emperor Justinus.[40] The last known orthodox bishop held the seat in the sixth century,[41] but the Syrian Jacobites kept a seat there whose titular even had the title of metropolitan.

However, the inhabitants of the diocese seem to have largely been opposed to Monophysitism. Philoxenus, metropolitan of the provincial capital, wrote after his banishment that he had succeeded in escaping only with great difficulty when he went to Cyr to find the body of Mar Bassos, a local martyr.[42] He erased the name of Theodoret from the diptychs in the church of Cyr, and abolished his commemoration.[43]

Finally, after the expulsion of Sergius I in 519, the priest and "defender" Andronicos and the deacon George placed an image of Theodoret on a chariot, and entered the town with great pomp, singing hymns. When Sergius II took possession of the bishopric, he recognized the two "culprits" as clerics and celebrated a *syntaxis* for Theodore of Mopsuestia, Diodorus of Tarsus, Theodoret, and a "martyr Nestorius" who seems to have been Nestorius the former patriarch of Constantinople.

Emperor Justinus assigned the "magister militum" Hypatius to make an investigation into the affair. Sergius II, found guilty, was deposed and excommunicated in 520.[44]

Apamaea

Apamaea in History

The site of "Pharnakea," later named Pella by the Macedonians, was renamed by Seleucos Nikator as "Apamaea."[45] The ancient city

[40] Ibid., 285, n. 1; Honigmann, *Évêques et évêchés Monophysites*, 68ff.
[41] Michel le Quien, *Oriens Christianus* (Paris, 1740), 2:930.
[42] Philoxenus, *Lettre aux moines de Senun*, 44; Honigmann, *Évêques*, 69.
[43] Honigmann, *Évêques*, 69.
[44] Ibid., 70.
[45] For Apamaea see: Pauly-Wissowa, *realenc.*, s.v. "*Apamée*"; Dussaud, *Topographie*, 165–233; Devresse, *Le Patriarcat d'Antioche*, 179; Honigmann, *Évêques*, 54ff.; for the cult of Bel, cf. Renan, *Mission de Phénicie*, 105.

stretched to the north of the fortress *Qal'at-al-Moudiq*, on a plateau
one hundred meters above the right bank of the Orontes. Encircled
with strong attractive walls, it was also protected by the course of the
Orontes, and by an immense lake which formed marshes and pastures
for herds of horses and oxen.

In 1929 a Belgian expedition including Mayence and Lacoste carried out excavations, which have yielded interesting archaeological
and architectural results. Unfortunately, many of the documents
were destroyed during World War II.

Enlarged and consolidated, Apamaea became the Seleucid
revenue office and a military center. It was the capital of the Syrian
region of Apamaea and later, in Byzantine times, the metropolis of
Syria Secunda. The Belgian excavations have demonstrated the great
extent of the town in Roman times, about 250 hectares. Apamaea
boasted 117,000 citizens in the census of Sulpicus Quirinus, the
legate over Syria in the years 6–7 of our era (Luke 2:1-2). Cumont
concluded that the census term *homines cives* included neither
slaves, plebeians, nor the rural proletariat; and consequently the
total population of all the district of Apamaea must have reached
about 500,000 souls.[46] The Seleucids established a stud farm with
500 elephants, 30,000 mares and 300 stallions.

Being at the intersection of the routes that passed through Homs
from Judea and the south, from the north through Cyr and from
Asia Minor, from the east through Berea (Aleppo) and from the
Mediterranean through Antioch and Seleucia, the Greco-Syrian city
was open to every influence. The work of the Belgian expeditions
allows a much clearer idea of these influences. The city underwent
rapid development on both the political and cultural levels in the
second century AD under pagan domination, and only at the end
of the fourth century did Christianity definitively prevail, to remain
preeminent throughout the fifth and sixth centuries.[47]

Apamaea had been hugely important in the history of Hellenistic
philosophy: it was Posidonius's hometown. At the end of the second

---

[46] The inscription is now acknowledged to be authentic. Dussaud, *Syria*
(1935), 116:13; Cumont, *Journal of Roman Studies* (1934): 187–90.

[47] R. Mondésert, *Inscriptions grecques de la Syrie*, in *Studia Patristica*, Conference
of Oxford, 1955 (Berlin, 1957), 1.1:652ff.

century, Numenius the Neo-Pythagorean was born and taught there. Plotinus praised Numenius's work, which was found in the libraries of Origen, Eusebius of Caesarea, and Theodoret of Cyr.[48] One hundred years later, the city was a center of attraction for the first generations of Neo-Platonists. Amelius withdrew there around 270, and a little later, Iamblichus established his famous school there. A native of neighboring Chalcis, he himself called Apamaea "his beloved city." Perhaps the presence of Iamblichus and the influence of his school in the beginning of the fourth century helps to explain why Christianity took more time to develop here than elsewhere.[49]

Apamaea was also a point of contact for many other influences, especially Jewish and Christian. Jews were found in Apamaea, as everywhere in the Seleucid kingdom. The Jewish community was, nevertheless, less important here than elsewhere. In spite of being greatly Hellenized, it maintained regular relations with Jerusalem.[50]

Apamaea and Christianity

The earliest known bishop of Apamaea was Alpheus, who attended the Council of Nicea and the Synod of Antioch (341).[51] Alpheus was succeeded at Apamaea by a series of bishops renowned for their orthodoxy, whose zeal for a well-defined religious policy was later approved by Theodoret of Cyr. These bishops were the following:

1. Uranius, who attended the Council of Antioch in 363 presided by Meletius (the bishop of Antioch elected to put an end to the divisions which troubled the church in Antioch following the exile of Eustathius).[52]

---

[48] H. Ch. Puech, "Numérius d'Apamée et les theologies orientales au second siècle," in *Mélanges Bidez* (Bruxelles, 1934), 745–78.

[49] J. Bidez, "Le Philosophe Jamblique et son école," *Revue des Études Grecques,* 32 (1919): 32–35.

[50] *Encyclopedia Judaica,* 2, col. 1128.

[51] Devresse, *Le Patriarcat d'Antioch,* 4, 5, and 180.

[52] Ferdinand Cavallera, *Le Schisme d'Antioche* (Paris: Alphonse Picard, 1905), quoted by Festugière, *Antioche païenne et chrétienne, Libanius, Chrysostome et les moines de Syrie* (Paris, 1959), 248–57.

2. John, ordained by Meletius himself. He was present at the Council of Constantinople in 381.[53]

3. Marcel, who paid with his life for his zeal in destroying pagan relics.

4. Agapetus, disciple of the anchorite Marcian, and founder of one of the monasteries of Nikertai near Apamaea. He was the bishop of Nikertai while Flavian, Meletius's successor, governed the church of Antioch (around 381). We know of him only through Theodoret.[54]

5. Polychronius, brother of Theodore of Mopsuestia, the famous head of the school of Antioch. He seems to have occupied the seat of Apamaea between 428 and 431. Literary history has retained memory of his work. We also know him through Theodoret.[55]

6. Alexander, who accompanied John of Antioch and Theodoret of Cyr to Ephesus in 431.

7. Finally, Domnus, who was represented by Meletius of Larissa at the Council of Ephesus in 449 and of Chalcedon in 451. Theodoret wrote him his letter n. 87. So it was during the episcopate of Domnus that Emperor Marcian had the monastery of Maron built in 452.

From the end of the fifth century to the beginning of the sixth century, the city of Apamaea, metropolis of Syria Secunda, was, together with Cilicia Prima and Tyre, a center of Chalcedonian opposition to Monophysitism in general and to Severus of Antioch in particular.[56]

In 512, the monks of Syria Secunda followed Flavian, the patriarch of Antioch (491–518), who himself came from a monastery situated in a district of Syria Secunda called Tilmongnon. Only a

[53] Devresse, *Le Patriarcat d'Antioche*, 129 and 180.

[54] Ibid., 180; Theodoret, *Hist. Eccl.*, 5:27, 1 and 3; for Marcel, see Theodoret, *Hist. Eccl.*, 5:21, 5, 15.

[55] Theodoret, *Hist. Eccl.*, 5:39; Bardenhewer, *Gesch. D. alt. Lit.*, 3:322–24; omitted by le Quien (or cited?).

[56] Honigmann, *Évêques*, 38, 45, and 65.

few monasteries in that province adhered to Monophysitism, but their members were persecuted by the majority. About one hundred monks from the monastery of Torgas or Torags, expelled by Flavian from one of the villages of the Apamaea region, went to Palestine, where they were welcomed by Severus (512–18), who was still head of the monastery of Romanos. This was before 508.[57]

Taken by the troops of Chosroes I in 540 and then by those of Chosroes II in the beginning of the seventh century, Apamaea disappeared from the scene little by little until it became no more than a huge "tell" or mound.[58]

Apamenia

Apamenia, a continental territory with the Apamaea region at its center, is difficult to define.[59] Starting from the rural district of the town of Apamaea, we possess a fairly clear idea of the extent of its territory. Tchalenko is certain that the rural district of Apamaea was greater than that of Antioch. It included toward the west the great plain of Ġāb, now marshy.

In the south, there is a plateau, watered by abundant springs, that extends to the bend of the Orontes river, as far as Larissa (Schaizar), whose ruins command an important crossing of the Orontes where the massacre of 350 of the Chalcedonian monks of Syria Secunda took place.[60] To the east, the vast vineyards and plains where cereal crops were grown extend to Khān Šeikhūn, Tell Minnis, and Maʿrrat-en-Noʿman. *It is between Khān Šeikhūn and Maʿrrat-en-*

---

[57] Ibid., 55ff.

[58] Michel Le Syrien, *Chronique*, ed. Chabot, 2:312.

[59] Among the cities that surround Apamaea, Strabo mentions Larissa, Kasiana, Megara, and Appolonio. Another whole series of towns of the same satrapy appear in the epitaphs left by Syrians in diverse regions, such as Varna, Rodosto, Rome, and in several regions in Italy and Gaul up to Treves. Specialists such as René Dussaud and Ernest Honigmann know very well the difficulty inherent in the identification of these sites. We will content ourselves in our study with marking out globally the region named Apamaea while noting with particular interest some names that have a direct relation with our subject; cf. Dussaud, *Topographie*, 200–201, n. 8.

[60] The survivors unanimously declared that the ambush was set up on behalf of Severus of Antioch by his agent, Peter of Apamaea (see below).

No*man that the ancient site of "Ḥirbet Mairūn," now abandoned, is to be found. It figures also on the map drawn and printed by the Department of Geography of the French Army in 1945. Tchalenko considers it to be one of the archaeological regions of the limestone massif.[61] Is it possible these ruins are those of the great monastery of Maron described by al-Masʿūdī?[62]

In the north of Apamenia, the olive groves of Gebel Zawiah stretch out to the hill of El-Bara. Tchalenko identifies the ancient Nikertai[63] with one of the two villages, *Qarrutiye and Qirata*. These are on the southern slope of Gebel Zawiyé, six kilometers northeast of Apamaea, that is, in the proximity of Ḥirbet Mairūn. With a fairly high population density, this territory reached its peak in the fifth and sixth centuries, a period during which it became the site of great building activity. This demographic and economic development is due essentially to the development of the olive trade. During this period, the prosperity of Apamaea does not seem to have been affected by the religious and political disputes, despite the potential for great harm.[64] This provides an idea of the extent of richness and prosperity of the extensive land of Apamenia in the fifth and sixth centuries.

Marcian and His Disciples:
The Cenobitic Life in Apamaea in the Fourth and Fifth Centuries According to the *Religious History*

The Religious History[65]

The *Religious History* is a basic document for our knowledge of monasticism in northern Syria from the beginning of the fourth century to 444. It is also our unique source for the life and the

---

[61] Tchalenko, *Villages*, vol. 2, 1. 23, "Region archéologique du Massif calcaire." See Map II.

[62] Al-Masʿūdī, *Kitab*, 153–54.

[63] Tchalenko, *Villages*, 3:3-B – XIII-15 and 3-B- XIII-14 (plate numbers).

[64] Ibid., 1:430, n. 1.

[65] Migne, *P.G.*, 82:1283ff.; Schiwietz, *Das morgenlandische Moenchtum*, vol. 3 (1938); Peeters, op. cit., 94–107; Festugière, *Antioche*, 245ff.; Vööbus, *History of Asceticism*, 3:13ff.; Draguet, *Les Pères du desert, Textes choisis* (Paris, 1949); Canivet, *Théodoret et le monachisme syrien avant le C. de Chalcédoine*, in *Théologie de la vie monastique* (Aubier, 1961), 241–82.

characters of Saints Maron and Marcian, and of their respective disciples. The book is composed of a prologue and thirty chapters. The first twenty are dedicated to ascetics who were already dead at the time the author wrote. The last ten are, on the contrary, dedicated to those then living. Many of these chapters are dedicated to hermits, most often to recluses who had been or were still living in the vicinity of Cyr, and whom Theodoret knew at the time of his episcopate (423 to 449). These are chapters 14 to 20 of the first series and chapters 21 to 25 of the second series. To these chapters, we should add chapter 3, which deals with Marcian, a native of Cyr, and chapter 30, which celebrates the virtues of Saint Domnina who was herself from Cyr. These notes provide us with many details about the life of the first Syrian anchorites, their lodging, food, ascetic practices, and reputation for miracles.

The book is coherent, although it deals with seventy-five different subjects and their diverse ways of life. It is integrated by Theodoret's desire to present a picture of the ascetic way of life through representative individuals. It is effectively a mosaic of examples for the edification of the reader and the glory of God.[66] Theodoret intended to eulogize his subjects without sacrificing accuracy. For as he says, it is not a eulogy in accordance with the traditional rule, where one should allow for the customary hyperbole. In our case he is particularly sincere and his brief notices have a very special authority: the author described to his contemporaries the life of hermits, some of whom they knew very well, and even had often visited. To anticipate the doubts of the skeptics, Theodoret declared in the prologue that he would speak only about the monks "who have shone like stars in the Orient, and whose rays have reached the boundaries of the universe," about things he has seen himself, or learned from trustworthy eyewitnesses. As has been observed, he often hesitates when telling wonders.[67]

Theodoret was concerned to give eyewitness testimony where possible. However, we cannot consider this book as a history in the

[66] For a development of this idea, see Canivet, *Théologie*, 243.

[67] Theodoret, *H.R.*, 1892D, 1385B 5-8, 1448D-1449A; also Canivet, *Théologie*, 242; Schiwietz, *Das morgenlandische Moenchtum*, 33–34; on Theodoret's effort to be objective, see also Vööbus, *History of Asceticism*, 12.

modern sense of the word; it is rather a series of documents which
are useful to historians. If Theodoret establishes the authenticity
of events, he does not do it systematically, and his topographical
and chronological data are generally insufficient.[68] Moreover, his
biographies are never complete. They are more a matter of quite
personal recollections of the author, observations made on the spot,
descriptions of the monastic life in all its variety and—one might
almost say—in its contradictions, without ever showing preference.
As has been noted, he praised equally the strictest anchoritic and
the most open cenobitic life, voluntary poverty which followed
the rule of living only on charity, and poverty which accepted
nothing not earned by work. "There emerges from diversity an
impression of paradisiacal anarchy (sic) that is strange to the point
where Theodoret avoids discussing the defects of the monks or their
deviation."[69] We shall, in the next chapter, inquire as to Theodoret's
aim in writing his history.

Saint Marcian the Anchorite

Life

Marcian, to whom Theodoret dedicated the third chapter of his
Religious History, was a native of the town of Cyr, born into a rich
and noble family of patrician standing. From early youth, he had
led a life of ease, "surrounded by all the advantages of the court,
where he made a brilliant appearance, as much by his tall stature
and beauty with which the Author of Nature had been pleased
to adorn his body as by the prudence and wisdom with which
He had enriched his soul" (1324D). The precise date of his birth
is not known but it is not difficult to deduce from Theodoret's
text that Marcian was born during the first quarter of the fourth
century. Lebon has established the approximate date of his death
as somewhere between 380 and 390.[70]

[68] Canivet, *Théologie*, 243.

[69] Ibid.

[70] J. Lebon, *Le moine Marcien*, in *Miscellanea historica in honorem Alberti de Meyer*
(Louvain-Brussels), 1:181–93. His life is found in Theodoret, *H.R.*, *P.G.* 82, 3:1324ff.

In his early youth, he retired into the depths of the desert
(1324D) of Chalcis ad Belum.[71] There, he led at first a solitary life:
"He built a very small hut, which was barely as large as his body
and he surrounded it with a fence, which was scarcely any more
spacious. He lived there away from any human contact" (1324D).
Later, he received two disciples, Eusebius and Agapetus (1325C),
and because of the small size of his hut, he allowed them to build
another nearby, and a third hut some little distance away to house
others. Eusebius was made their superior (1328 B2-5).[72]

Marcian remained a monk all his life, refusing priestly ordination
when the bishops who came to visit him wanted to ordain him (1331
A-B). His reputation for saintliness was so great that people walked
four days to come and visit him. People came in great numbers
from all directions, including leading prelates and magistrates. The
great Flavian, former leader of the Meletian community and bishop
of Antioch, came to Marcian with Acacius of Berea, Eusebius the
bishop of Chalcis, Isidore the bishop of Cyr, Theodotus the bishop
of Hierapolis (Membej), and other magistrates and personalities to
listen to the words of the saint (1332B).[73]

While Marcian was still alive, chapels were built in his name: one
in Cyr with the help of his nephew Alypius, another in Chalcis with
the help of a rich and noble lady called Zenobiana, and many more
in other places (1336D).[74] People were eager to acquire his relics after

[71] Theodoret, *Hist. Eccl.*, ed. Parmentier (Berlin, 1954), 4:28, n. 1. Theodoret
describes the desert of Chalcis as a great center of monastic life under the
reign of Constans (337–50). But it is difficult to locate the "desert." Theodoret
states in another part of the book that Berea (Aleppo) is four days' walk from
Marcian's residence, whereas the distance between Berea and Chalcis is only
twenty-seven kilometers or eighteen miles to the southwest of Aleppo. The site
of Chalcis is clearly defined by Peutinger's table and Antonin's Itinerary, so
that we may identify it with Qinnisrin, a place located at eighty-nine kilometers
east-southeast of Antioch, twenty-seven kilometers southwest of Aleppo and
eighty-six kilometers from Apamaea. Many ruins of monasteries are still found
there today; cf. Mouterde and Poidebard, *Les limes de Chalcis*, 7–38; Mattern,
Villes mortes, Tchalenko, *Villages*, 1; Festugière, *Antioche*, 252, n. 7; Dussaud,
Topographie, 476.

[72] Festugière, *Antioche*, 311.

[73] Ibid., 252, n. 6.

[74] Azéma, 3:66, n. 3.

his death, so as a result, according to an already classical theme, Marcian made his disciple Eusebius swear to bury him in a secret place and to reveal the site to no one (1336D-1337). In fact, when he breathed his last, Eusebius came with two of his monks and laid the body in the ground. Thus, his body remained hidden for fifty years until it was reinterred in one of the chapels, in a stone coffin.

Literary Works

Theodoret does not mention any book written by Marcian, but his name is known to patristic literature: the catalogs and the Greek and Syriac manuscripts mention it. Baumstark knew of him, but he came into the limelight only with the publication of *Florilegium Edessenum Anonymum* written by J. Rucker,[75] then the publication of two articles written by Joseph Lebon,[76] who developed and completed Rucker's data; the work of Father J. Kirchmeyer,[77] who argued that the Marcian of *Florilegium Edessenum* was not the Marcian of the *Religious History* but one from Bethlehem, and finally with Muylderman's research into the Syriac tradition of Evagrius of Pontius.[78]

The problem of identity is still quite complex. Only a study of the content of the theological and spiritual works transmitted by the Syriac manuscript tradition can offer a satisfactory answer to the problem.[79]

Disciples and the Monastic Movement of Apamaea

Theodoret mentioned that Marcian was the author of an eloquent literary work on the practice of monastic asceticism, his disciples,

[75] Baumstark, *Geschichte der syrischen literature* (Bonn, 1922), 90 and 165; Ignaz Rucker, *Florilegium Edessenum Anonymum*, in *Sitzungsberichte der Bayer Akademie der wissenschagten phil. Hist. Abt.* (Munich, 1933), fasc. 5. 127.

[76] Lebon, *Le moine Marcien*, 181–93, n. 67.

[77] Joseph Kirchmeyer, *The Monk Marcian (of Bethlehem)*, Oxford Conference, 1959 (Berlin, 1962), 5.3:341–59.

[78] Joseph Muyldermans, *Evagriana Syriaca* (Louvain: Publications universitaires, 1952), 82ff., and 109–14 (translation and text).

[79] Lebon, *Le moine Marcien* (Louvain, 1968).

and the monastic movement in Apamaea (1325C-D).[80] It was only
several years after his withdrawal into the desert of Chalcis that
Marcian received Eusebius and Agapetus as disciples. In addition to
the building of huts which we have described, Marcian demanded
that they live apart, praising God, praying and reading the Holy
Scriptures. (1328A-B). Eusebius succeeded him in his hermitage
(1325C). Agapetus brought Marcian's "angelic laws" to Nikertai
(1325C-13-14) near Apamaea.[81] There he founded two monasteries,
one of which bore his name and the other that of the monk Simon,[82]
who lived in it for fifty years (1325C-D). Theodoret wrote:

> Today, there still live in that Monastery more than four hundred
> monks who are paragons of virtue, lovers of piety and who
> through their sufferings reach paradise. However, those who es-
> tablished their rule were Agapetus and Simon, who themselves
> had received it from the great Marcian. From these foundations
> there arose many other places of monastic retreat too numerous
> to count that are subject to the same rule. Of all these establish-
> ments, the first author was this divine man who disseminated
> and planted them and, since he gave this divine seed, he has
> to be considered logically as the author and the cause of all the
> good that it has produced. (1325D-1328A)

This transfer from Chalcis to Nikertai and the founding of
two monasteries must have taken place around the year 381, for
Agapetus, the founder of one of these monasteries, was bishop of
Apamaea while Flavian governed the church of Antioch, and Flavian
was ordained bishop after July 381. Moreover, since Christianity was
not definitively established in Apamaea until the end of the fourth
century, we can only conclude that this foundation was, if not the

[80] Festugière, *Antioche*, 252 and 316.

[81] For the diverse attempts of Arab authors to identify Nikertai and Nikera-
tôn Kômé with Deir-en-Naquira and Deir Sim'ân, and on the location of these
two sites, see Dussaud, *Topographie*, 184–85; Honigmann, *Topographie*, nn. 327
and 328; Jean Sauvaget, *La Poste aux chevaux dans l'empire des mamelouks* (Paris:
Adrein-Maisonneuve, 1941), 90, n. 345; De Sourel, *Notes d'épigraphie et de topographie sur la Syrie du Nord*, in *Annales archéologiques de Syrie*, 3:83ff.

[82] One of the numerous Simons apart from Simon Stylites; and also from
Simon the Elder (*H.R.*, chap. 4), Festugière, *Antioche*, 253, n. 1.

first in the region, at least among the earliest. This partly explains
the preeminence of these two monasteries in Syria Secunda until
the founding of the monastery of Maron by the emperor Marcian.[83]

The foundations are all the more interesting for they represent the
transition from the eremitic life to the cenobitic life, and transmission
from Chalcis to Apamaea. Was the motive perhaps a missionary one?
Or should the transformation be attributed to the Apamaean origin
of these two disciples of Marcian, especially, perhaps to Agapetus,
future bishop of the town? The question remains open. One thing
only is certain: these foundations were to contribute effectively to
the maintaining of orthodoxy in these regions of Syria Secunda.
It was one of these two monasteries of Apamaea that the young
Theodoret had chosen for his retreat when, as a brilliant student, he
felt attracted toward monastic life. According to Festugière, it was
from the oral tradition of this Apamaean monastery that the author
of the *Religious History* drew his information about Marcian's life.

In time the monasteries developed into a religious confederation.
Theodoret wrote about "several places of retreat subject to the
same rule and almost beyond counting," but he mentions only
four, which the most important are probably (1) a monastery in the
desert of Chalcis that Marcian allowed to be built some distance
away (1328B) without himself leaving his hut (1325CB); (2) and
(3) the two monasteries in Nikertai near Apamaea to which we
have just referred; (4) the monastery of Seleucobelus or Seleucia ad
Belum,[84] which was certainly near Apamaea, though its location is
unknown. It was founded by Basilius, also a disciple of Marcian
(1337C 2-5). This grouping of monasteries "subject to the same
rule" still existed and flourished in the sixth century. Honigmann
estimates the number of these monks "at more than a thousand."[85]

Chalcedonian Orthodoxy

This monastic grouping was henceforward characterized by its
attachment to the doctrine of Chalcedon and its opposition, even

---

[83] Vööbus, *History of Asceticism*, 251ff.

[84] Dussaud, *Topographie*, 155ff.

[85] Honigmann, *Évêques*, 61.

its hostility toward the Monophysite doctrines, especially those of Severus of Antioch and Peter of Apamaea. This is established by documents, known principally through the Acts of the Council of Constantinople held under Patriarch Menas in 586.[86] Of the documents presented to the Synod of 518, only those which were cited eighteen years later before the assembly of 536 were kept. The authors of the documents produced in 536 did not take the trouble to establish a rigorous and clear chronology of events. They enumerated at random the infamies of Severus and Peter, and often contented themselves with making simple allusions:

1. One document, which can be dated with some probability to the autumn of 517, is a letter from the archimandrites and monks of Syria Secunda to Pope Hormisdas. These abbots and monks explained that, as they were approaching the cell of Saint Simon *pro causa ecclesiae*, the followers of Severus and Peter, who were waiting in ambush near the main road, attacked them without warning, killed 350 of them, injured some, and massacred others in addition who had taken refuge near the altars. They also set on fire several monasteries. The letter bears a long series of signatures of monastic notables, archimandrites, priests, and deacons. Only the first signature can be identified: "I, Alexander, by the divine mercy priest and archimandrite of the Monastery of Maron."[87] The other signatures cannot be identified because the topographical indexes that identify them have been omitted by the writer, as they were of little interest to the Roman readers.[88]

2. The same events were described in a letter (*libellus*) written by the monks of Apamaea (i.e., of Syria Secunda) to their own bishops in 517. According to this document, the reason for the trip was "peace and union in love." The letter bears also a long series of signatures, indicating the topographical indications that allow their identification and their comparison with the other signatures of the first letter. From this comparison it appears that the first and

---

[86] ACO Coll. *Sabbaitica*, ed. E. Schwartz, vol. 3 (Berolini: de Gruyter, 1940).

[87] Vööbus, *History of Asceticism*, 2:251ff.

[88] Coll. Avellana, Ep 139; 2:565ff. The pope answered on 10 February 518; see appendix, Documents I and II.

second places had been reserved respectively to Alexander, the archimandrite of the monastery of the Blessed Maron, and to Simon, the archimandrite of the monastery of the Blessed Agapetus. Then followed the names of twenty-four other archimandrites, of whom sixteen are priests and eight are deacons.[89]

3. Another letter, a petition written by the clergy and monks of Antioch "to Patriarch John and to the Synod held by him" in 518, tells how Severus took over the seat of Antioch regardless of the canons. It also bears a long series of signatures. The first signature after those of the Antiochian clergy is that of *"Joannes, the monk from the Monastery of Blessed Maron."* Then come the signatures of "Simon, the monk from the Monastery of Blessed Agapetus," and "Sergius, the monk from the Monastery of St Simon."[90]

Vööbus remarks that the monastery of Agapetus had a leading role in respect of the other monasteries of Syria Secunda, second only to that of Maron. This latter, which came first in precedence, had played a significant role in the region and became the "headquarters" of the Maronites but its origin and its history have been lost in oblivion.[91]

4. In the council of 536 mentioned above, the delegate of the monastery of Maron represented the other monasteries of Syria Secunda. He signed as follows: *"Paul . . . , Apocrisiary of the Monastery of blessed Maron, Exarch of the monasteries of Syria Secunda."* The expression "Exarch of the monasteries" means that this monastery had a certain power over the others. This primacy had been conferred by the Council of Ephesus on the monastery of Dalmatia in Constantinople. We do not know exactly when it had been conferred on the monastery of Saint Maron near Apamaea.[92]

---

[89] ACO, ibid., 109ff.; see appendix, Document III.

[90] ACO, ibid., 62; on the monastery of Saint Simon, see Peeters, *Hypatius et Vitalien*, 30, n. 3 in *Mélange*, H. Grégoire, vol. 2 (Bruxelles, 1850).

[91] Vööbus, *History of Asceticism*, 2:251f.; see appendix, Document IV.

[92] Placido De Meester, *De Monachico statu* (Vatican: Typis Polyglottis Vaticanis, 1942), s.v. "exarque"; G.W. Lampe, *Patristic Greek Lexicon* (Oxford: Clarendon Press, 1961), fasc. 2:493 s.v. "exarque"; Festugière, *Les Moines d'Orient* (Paris, 1961), 2.2:41; Pargoire, *Dict. d'archéologie chrétienne*, vol. 1, cols. 2741 and 2746; Lammens, *Le Liban*, 2:91.

5. At a conference held in Antioch around 592, between the "orthodox party" and the "sectaries of Peter of Callinices," a Jacobite patriarch from 578 to 591, the monks of Beit-Maron, partisans of the Council of Chalcedon, represented the "orthodox party." Their monastery then enjoyed an indisputable preeminence over the other monasteries of Syria Secunda. Nau found this precious text in a manuscript from the eighth century kept at the British Museum, Add. 12155, fol. 163ff.[93] It comprises a letter written by the monks of Beit-Maron to the Jacobites, together with their response following the conference of Antioch. The Maronites' letter includes a series of questions of Chalcedonian, or rather neo-Chalcedonian, tendency (there are several Dyophysite expressions, and the word *hypostasis* is used to mean "person"). The writers require an answer "according to the chosen scholars and saints concerning whom there is no problem either between you and us or for any Christian."[94]

Theodore of the monastery of Beit-Abaz wrote them a long answer which is of particular interest for our thesis concerning the circumstances of the founding of the monastery of Saint Maron. Nau says, "The answer is rich in insults that now turn into the glory of the Maronites . . . since the Jacobites do not accuse them of any error except that of not professing their own (Jacobite belief)." *[This response is addressed to the Maronite monks:]* "To the plant of the Chalcedonian vine, to the offspring of the root of Leo, to the acid germ produced by the vine of Theodoret and, to say it in a few words, to the sons of the great and principal schism to have taken place in the church [Chalcedon, 451], which scatters the members of the Messiah and divides his body into many parts."[95]

Further on, in a part that has not been translated by F. Nau and that we have personally consulted,[96] the writer declared that Dioscoros,

---

[93] F. Nau, *Les Maronites inquisiteurs*, in *Bulletin de l'Association de Saint Louis des Maronites*, n. 97 (January 1903), 343ff. See appendix, Document V.

[94] Ibid., 367. The writers of the letter are thinking here of Cyril of Alexandria, concerning whom there was a dispute between the Chalcedonians (in this context, the Maronites) and the anti-Chalcedonians (the monks of Beit-Abaz).

[95] Cf. Document V, section 2 in appendix.

[96] British Museum, Add. 12155, from fol. 166b, col. 1, line 47, to fol. 167b, col. 1, line 15.

the Monophysite "scholar," had removed the "nonsensical" and "fantastical" Eutyches. As for the Maronites, they always support Theodoret and Ibas, for, according to the writer Theodore, the anathema hurled by the Fifth Council after so many years against these impious people (Theodoret and Ibas) and the other chiefs of their (Chalcedonian) party by this very fact also affects the "Maronites and their mother, the Chalcedonian assembly." The anathema is an allusion to the Council of 553 under Justinian (527–65). Theodore also suggested to them that, if they want to free themselves from this anathema, they must renounce these "blasphemers" and support the orthodox (Monophysites). This proves that up to 592, that is to say some forty years after the Council of 553 was held to find a solution for the dispute of the Three Chapters, the Maronites were considered as the leaders of the Eastern-Chalcedonian party and the faithful friends of Theodoret of Cyr.

Finally, the same Theodore expressed surprise at the ignorance of these Maronite monks who were the advisers and theologians of Patriarch Ephrem of Amid (529–45) and at the way in which they allowed themselves to ask such very clear and simple questions. He says, "I am surprised at your ignorance. How could you, who are the scholars of Ephrem, be ignorant of that . . . . [I]f however you want a demonstration of these things, which are so well-known and evident, address yourselves to Saint Cyril on the subject about which for us [the Monophysites] there is no controversy."[97]

Thus, in the sixth century, the monastery of Maron enjoyed preeminence over all the other monasteries of Syria Secunda. *Vööbus does not conceal his astonishment at the rapid development of this monastery to surpass in authority other, more ancient monasteries,* such as those of Agapetus and Simon, to such a degree that the

---

[97] Ephrem of Amid, patriarch of Antioch from 529 to 545, harsh persecutor of the Monophysites and one of the eminent representatives of the neo-Chalcedonian theological movement that attempted to reconcile the diverse christological formulas. See Lebon, *Ephrem d'Amid,* in *Les Mélanges d'Histoires offerts à Charles Moeller* (Louvain-Paris, 1914), 1:213f.; and *Restitution à Theodoret de Cyr,* in *La Revue d'hist. eccl.* (1930), 26:535; M. Richard, Review *Mélanges des sciences religieuses* 3 (1946): 156 and his comments on the quality of the attempted compromise; Michel Le Syrien, *Chronique,* ed. Chabot, 2:181–85; Héfélé-Leclercq, *Histoires,* 3:15 ff., 194, 207.

monasteries which had not followed the Monophysite movement
found in it "a fortress of orthodoxy."[98]

Ascetic Doctrine: Marcian's Rule (1325D)

Writing on the economic and social history of Syria, Rostovtzeff
warned that "there is a danger of generalizing and considering
the whole of the Syrian territory as a single unity."[99] This is also
valid for the history of Syrian monasticism. In fact, early Syrian
monasticism did not emerge as a monolithic phenomenon: it had
several "founders" and no single Pachomius, Basil, or Theodore
Studite. Syrian monasticism was distinguished from other forms by
a great scope for originality in personal piety and acts of penance in
the eremitic and cenobitic lives, which always existed as two aspects
of Syrian monasticism. What held these ways of life together was,
even in the early period, an exterior organization and legislation,
which developed over time.

At first, this organization was more a spirit, a tradition founded
on the Scriptures and the fathers, than a "written rule." But the
influence of the founders and elders was also a regulating influence,
which became defined when the disciples gathered around a monk
whose way of life they wished to share. This monk became their
master and educator, and his example and his spirit became for
them a law and a rule of life.

We have too little direct information on Marcian to give a detailed
description of his spirit, let alone to draw from it the elements
that constituted his rule and so marked the monastic movement
of Apamaea. But in Theodoret's account, we can isolate total
renunciation, a love of contemplation, and assiduity in prayer and
reading Holy Scripture. Theodoret insisted, above all, on Marcian's
prudence and wisdom.

---

[98] Vööbus, *History of Asceticism*, 252. This monastery, he wrote, was praised
not only for its orthodoxy but also for its rigorous ascetic discipline, as appears
from a text of the Syriac manuscript kept in the National Library of Paris, Ms.
Par. Syr. 234, fol. 442b.

[99] Michael Ivanovitch Rostovtzeff, *Social and Economic History of the Roman
Empire* (Oxford: Clarendon Press, 1926), 244.

Prudence

In the *Religious History*, Theodoret presents the monk Marcian
not as a hermit given to great and rigorous penances, but as a model
of moderation, prudence, and balance. The early monks attached
great importance to fasting and penance. We know well their feats
of endurance: one would eat only once every two days, and another
once in every three.

As for Marcian, his food was meager, but he ate once every day,
in the evening, and never to repletion: "One should always feel
hungry and thirsty and give one's body only what is necessary
for its survival . . . it is better then, he used to say, to eat every
day but never satisfying one's appetite, for true fasting means
continuous hunger. Such is the law which this divine man always
laid down" (1325B-C). And such was the rule handed on by his
disciples Agapetus and Simon to the monasteries of Nikertai.[100]

With regards to shelter, Marcian preferred the life of a recluse to
that of a "hypethrite" (ascetic living in the open air). He built a cell,
which was designed to cause him continuous torment (1328A6-13).
Prudence, moderation, and balance allowed him to dominate the
wildest passions and to remain composed while facing dangers
and temptations. Theodoret related as characteristic of Marcian
an anecdote that a monk named Avitus one day visited Marcian
who was, as usual, cooking vegetables and making a salad. Avitus
apologized for not being able to break his fast. Marcian, conscious
of his duty as a host, pretended that on that day because of a certain
weakness, he could not wait until the evening to eat. Avitus again
refused the invitation. So Marcian said with a sigh: "Here I am
completely discouraged, struck to the heart. What! You have taken
such pains to see a 'philoponos' (friend of work) and a 'philosophos'
(friend of wisdom), and all you see is an innkeeper and a libertine!"
Avitus protested vehemently and agreed to eat some meat rather
than believe such a thing. Marcian assured him then: "I shall do
as you do; I respect fasting more than food, which we usually eat
only in the evening . . . but charity is more pleasing to God than
fasting because charity is his commandment to us, while fasting

---

[100] Festugière, *Antioche*, 316. See also Cassian, *Inst.*, 5. 9; and *Conf.*, 2. 22–24.

depends on us and on our will. Thus, we should undoubtedly respect God's commandments much more than our austerities and labors" (1333A-B).[101]

Wisdom

Such anecdotes, and Theodoret related many, illustrate Marcian's prudence and wisdom. It is that wisdom which Saint John Chrysostom[102] and Theodoret of Cyr called "philosophy," describing it as simply the ardent love of Christ, illuminating, inspiring, and supporting. As Canivet explains, for Theodoret the "real philosopher" is one whose moderation is his dominant quality, a virtue that, while helping the monk in his ascetic effort, makes him avoid exaggeration, and establishes harmony between the passions, resulting in "reconciliation between the soul and the body." Theodoret analyzed this Platonic expression in *Thérapeutique*: it corresponds more or less to "tranquility," the term which other spiritual men preferred to employ.[103] Moderation is a simple human quality, but can be raised to a spiritual virtue, a wisdom that illuminates and inspires the monk.

Theodoret approves Marcian's perfect orthodoxy, and opposition to heresy: "He loathed the crazy doctrine of Arius which sprang up like a flame due to the effect of imperial power. He abhorred the insanity of Apollinarius. He struggled valorously against the partisans of Sabellius, who confuse the three hypostases (persons) into one. He totally repudiated the people named Euchites, who under the monastic habit suffer from the evil of the Manicheans" (1336B).[104] The wisdom of orthodoxy guides the footsteps of the

---

[101] Festugière, *Antioche*, 302, n. 4; about the spirit of competition among the monks, see also Festugière in *Hermés*, 73 (1955): 272–77.

[102] *Homil.*, 162D-E (Gaume 186); Festugière, *Antioche*, 391.

[103] Canivet, *Théologie*, 262, and n. 130, where he describes "a very stable attitude found between two extreme solutions under the sign of reason and common sense . . . it gives behavior a gentleness that makes virtue attractive." Theodoret preferred moderation, and perhaps interprets Marcian's behavior in the light of his own philosophical culture.

[104] Canivet conjectures that the monks of Nikertai were especially warned against this danger (*H.R.*, 1324–40; *Hist. Eccl.*, ed. Parmentier [1954], 4:28, 1–2,

hermit along the safest path, that traced by the hierarchy of the church and its councils:

> So burning was his zeal for the ecclesiastical decrees that he even had a justified quarrel with an admirable and divine man. There was in the desert of Chalcis a certain Abraham, a white-haired old man, with a soul whiter still, shining with every virtue and who never ceased weeping tears of compunction. However, at first, driven by a kind of natural simplicity, this hermit had accepted to celebrate Easter as was done earlier;[105] unaware as it seems of the decrees of the Fathers of Nicea on this point, he preferred to follow the old custom. . . . The great Marcian had often attempted, using many arguments, to bring the old Abraham back to the common practice of the Church. As he saw him obstinate in his refusal, he openly broke off his relationship with him. But later this divine man rejected his folly and cele- brated the holy feast in accordance with the Church. . . . This happy result was achieved due to the teachings of the great Marcian (1336D).

This orthodox wisdom was also characteristic of Maron, and was also transmitted by his disciples to the monasteries of Apamaea.

Theodoret particularly insists on orthodoxy, which led Marcian's visitation by Flavian, former chief of the Meletian community and, from July 381, bishop of Antioch.[106]

268; 5:27, 3, 329; cf. Festugière, *Antioche*, 252); it may be speculative to state that Theodoret had been warned against the ideas of the Messalians in that monastery. Cf. Canivet, *Théodoret et le Messalianisme*, in *Revue Mabillon*, 51 (1961): 26–34.

[105] Festugière, *Antioche*, 254ff.

[106] For the circumstances of this visit, see Festugière, *Antioche*, 253–57: "Under its benign aspect this edifying conference, between Marcian on the one hand and Flavian and his friends the bishops and the magistrates on the other hand, perhaps hides more precise intentions." Festugière concludes: "Thus, from 381 to 398, the old Bishop Flavian was the object of many attacks and of all sorts of bad conduct. It is very natural under these conditions that with the neighboring bishops who happened to be his friends he should go one day to the hermit Marcianus asking for his help and support. We do not know the date when this conference was held. Marcianus must have been very old already in 381. We may suppose that during the early difficulties in his episcopate, Flavian

Prudence, moderation, and wisdom are the fruit of contemplation and of a thorough reading of Holy Scripture by the light of a strong faith. Theodoret described the requisite qualities thus: reading Scripture "which requires a soul that is pure of every stain, and a winged thought capable of embracing the things of God and which dares to enter the domain of the Holy Spirit." With respect to Marcianus, Theodoret related that one night, Eusebius his disciple saw him transfigured by a celestial light, which gave him an exalted understanding of Scripture. Theodoret concluded: "His reading was a real conversation with God, whose voice he heard, since he was convinced that Holy Scripture is the word of God" (1325A4, B4, 1238 B13-C6).[107]

Maron and His Disciples: The Eremitic Life in the Region of Cyr in the Fourth and Fifth Centuries

The Anchorites of Cyr[108]

Toward the end of the fourth century and the beginning of the fifth, that is to say, some time before the period of Theodoret, Cyr became a center of fervent religious devotion. On the mountains surrounding the town, the anchorites who were scattered all around

---

went to visit the hermit. It would have been more useful to know about the discourses of the pontiffs on that memorable day. Unfortunately according to a process that is dear to the hagiographers, Theodoret tells only about the humble protestations and the polite remarks exchanged between these saintly men. One thing, at least seems certain. If Flavian and his colleagues traveled the desert of Chalcis, it was on the one hand because of the problems faced by the bishop of Antioch and on the other hand because of the prestige of Marcianus, a prestige great enough for them to wish with all their might to win the hermit to their cause. Moreover, it is by no means absurd to think that, as formerly in the case of Julian Sabas, they came to ask him to come to Antioch to reinforce Flavian's position."

[107] See also Canivet, *Théologie*, 268ff.

[108] For this part see particularly Festugière, *Antioche*, 291–310; Canivet, *Théologie*, 244–74; Canivet, *Mission en Syrie*. O. Hendriks, *La Vie quotidienne du moine syrien*, in *Orient Syrien*, 5 (1960): 294ff.; Dussaud, *Topographie*, 450ff.

"shone like stars and their rays reached the limits of the universe" according to an expression used by Theodoret himself. Appointed bishop in 423, Theodoret did his best, by his zeal, example, and prayers, to increase this fervent devotion and to broadcast it. He wrote to Pope Saint Leo: "I have been endowed with the pastoral charge of eight hundred churches where, thanks to your prayers, not a single trace of heresy has remained."[109]

Filled as he was with an admiration for the heroes of Syrian asceticism, Theodoret did not content himself with encouraging them through his assiduous and paternal visits but he also conceived of a plan to make the Christian heroism and the philosophy of these simple men, peasants who were sometimes misunderstood and despised, known and admired as they deserved to be. "What excuse would we have, were we not to honour even in writing their remarkable lives?" Around the year 444, when Theodoret wrote his *Religious History*, he dedicated fourteen of its thirty chapters, almost half the book, to illustrating the life and the deeds of the anchorites of his diocese.

In chapter fourteen, Theodoret, passing from the anchorites of Antioch to those of Cyr, stated: "I will go now to the sacred pastures of Cyr to consider these lovely flowers whose fragrance equals that of the finest perfumes and whose beauty and excellence I shall describe as best I can." Theodoret had known most of these ascetics, with the exception of some of the older ones such as Maisymas (chap. 14), Acepsimas (chap. 15), Maron (chap. 16), Abraham (chap. 17), and Zebinas (chap. 24).

Maisymas, the first of these, was a parish priest of a village in the region of Cyr. Acepsimas, like Maisymas, became famous during the reign of Valens (364–78). Around the year 370, he enclosed himself in a cell, in which he remained for sixty years (chap. 15, 1413D). He was ordained a priest only a few days before his death. Abraham (chap. 17) was a hermit at first and then became bishop of Carrhae (Ḥarran) in Mesopotamia. Eusebius (chap. 18) lived at first in a monastery and then embraced the solitary life on the crest of a hill near the important township of Asikhas (1425B; cf.

---

[109] Ep 113; Azéma, 3:63.

Dussaud, 471). There, having chosen the state of a monk living "in the open air," he built at first a "thrinkion," a low wall as high as a man which forms a small unroofed enclosure where the hermit is invisible to others but not protected from bad weather. He refused all communication with people. "I alone," said Theodoret, "had the privilege of enjoying his gentle voice so dear to God. Every time I got up to leave he used to keep me a long time, talking to me about heavenly things. He fought this battle for more than ninety years and then died extremely weak" (1428A-B).

Salamanes (chap. 19), a native of Capersana on the left bank of the Euphrates (Dussaud, 459), crossed the river and enclosed himself in a cabin with neither doors nor windows (1428C-D). Maris (chap. 20), a recluse from the town of Omeros near Cyr (Dussaud, 471), enclosed himself in a cell and lived in it thirty-seven years until his death (1429B). "I have often talked to him," says Theodoret. "The moment I entered he used to embrace me and make me long speeches on the monastic life."[110]

There were then in the region of Cyr many recluses but the greater number of anchorites in this region were "hypethrites," that is to say, monks who lived in the open air. We know of them today only because Theodoret had personally known a great number of them and had written about them.

The Hypethrite Monks

Saint Maron the Anchorite

The founder of this life "in the open air" (*hypethritism*, 1417B) seems to have been Maron.[111] Theodoret said of Maron: "Dissatisfied with ordinary practices, Maron invented others so as to accumulate all the riches of wisdom." (418-c). Maron lived in the open air near

---

[110] One day, as he had been wanting for a long time to attend the sacrifice of the Eucharist, Theodoret came and celebrated Mass at his place. There was no altar and the bishop had to present the offerings on the outstretched hands of the deacons. The hermit was filled with spiritual joy as if he had seen heaven itself and declared that he had never experienced a similar exhilaration (1429D).

[111] Thus Festugière, *Antioche*, 299.

the site of a former temple. He erected a tent there, but only rarely used it to avoid extremes in the weather.

In the introduction to the life of Baradatus (chap. 27, 1484D), Theodoret, in defining the different ways of life among the Syrian ascetics, described this open-air ascetic life. "In his wish to destroy the human race," he says,

> the common enemy of men has found many types of vice. Similarly, the sucklings of piety have invented many different ladders to go up to heaven. . . . Many, of whom I have mentioned a few, decided to live neither in a grotto nor a cavern, hovel, or hut, but exposed their bodies to the open air, enduring the contrasting conditions of the seasons, sometimes frozen by the severity of the cold and at other times burnt by the blazing sun. These anchorites had different practices. Some remained standing continuously, while others stood at equally spaced intervals during the day, sometimes sitting and sometimes standing. Some others stayed confined in an enclosure with a small wall without wanting to communicate with anyone, while others refused such a screen and exposed themselves to the eyes of whoever wanted to see them. (27, 1484-D, 1485-B)

Theodoret considered the ascetic Maron to have been the initiator of this mode of living in the open air, and also the organizer and founder of the entire monastic movement around Cyr. "It was he," says the bishop of Cyr, "who planted for God the garden which is blossoming now in the region of Cyr" (1420A). It was also thanks to Maron that one could contemplate "today this spiritual paradise," since Jacob and others, who had been effective missionaries, were Maron's pupils (16, 1420). Although Theodoret was renowned for his balance and reserve, he here demonstrated a preference for this monastic movement which had been especially important in his diocese.[112]

For Theodoret, these two forms of monastic life, reclusion and life in the open air, were not opposed, but rather were complementary. In fact, as Festugière remarks, the state of the monk living in the

---

[112] In his notes from his mission to northern Syria during August and September 1965, Canivet expressed the view that Parsa Dăğ, where Maron probably withdrew, "was the starting point of a monastic movement."

open air is more difficult than that of a recluse. One starts as a "recluse" and then one becomes a "hypethrite." Jacob, for example, began as a recluse, and later became a hypethrite: "Having thus come to this mountain . . . he exposed himself to all comers, for as I said, he lives neither in a cave, nor a tent, nor a hut nor behind a low wall, nor a dry stone wall. He remains always visible while praying, resting, standing, or sitting and whether he is feeling well or suffering from some pain. Every spectator can see him fighting his battle continuously" (31, 1433B).

The lives of these ascetics made a tremendous impression on their contemporaries: "His only roof is the sky and he remains exposed to all the bad weather. One day he is drenched to the skin by heavy rain, another day frozen by frost and snow, and another day burnt and devoured by the rays of the sun" (31, 1432C-D).

Limnaius, at first a disciple of one Thalassius, who had founded a place for ascetics on a hill near Tillima,[113] later came to Maron, with Jacob his fellow disciple (1453B). Thence, he possessed a summit overlooking the village of Targala, without cell, shed, or hut, just a low wall of dry stones placed without mortar. The door was plastered with clay to exclude visitors. Only on Theodoret's arrival did Limnaius allow the door to be opened. The locals, sensing their opportunity, crowded around in the hope of finally entering the hypethrite's enclosure (22, 1453B-C).

The same manner of living was followed by Eusebius (25, 1464C), and by Baradatus, (27, 1484D), entirely cut off from the world, living in the open air;[114] and most spectacularly by Simon the Stylite (26, 1469B-D), who after three years of reclusion, began to lead the life of a "stylite" in the village of Telanissos, today Deir-Simᶜān. The first stylite, he climbed upon a pillar (the "style"), thus living exposed both to people and to weather.[115] According to Theodoret, choosing to live in the open air was, adhering to the school of Maron, opting for the most difficult path of detachment, sacrifice, and mortification.

Thus Saint Maron founded the monastic movement in the region of Cyr. Theodoret did not meet Maron but often spoke with his

[113] Dussaud, *Topographie*, 471.
[114] Festugière, *Antioche*, 296.
[115] See ibid., 309–10.

disciples. His few words on Maron were nonetheless significant and unequivocal.[116] The biographical details are meager in the extreme, especially concerning Maron's childhood and youth, for Maron, Theodoret said, had never belonged to this earth. Theodoret began his treatment of Maron with the ascetic's death, stating that Maron had already "increased the number of saints in heaven." However, if what Theodoret did say about Maron was accurate, the subject of his spirit and example fills a considerable part of the *Religious History*.

Maron lived high on a mountain in the region of Cyr. He retired "to that summit, which the pagans formerly considered as holy, and consecrated to God the temple which the demons had possessed; he came there having erected a small hut he rarely used" (1417B-C). As we have seen, Canivet thinks it was a pagan temple, today transformed into a "Wali." "The information in literary sources," he noted, "is not sufficient to identify the Parsa Dāğ with the place where Maron withdrew to live. Moreover, it is at least possible that the Parsa Dāğ with its temple might have been the summit that Maron chose, since up until now no other mountain in the region of Cyr seems to bear any similarity to that described by Theodoret except the Parsa Dāğ."

Within a short period of time, this anchorite became the spiritual master, not only of a small group of disciples, hermits, and anchorites living in the open air but also of the Christian people of the region of Cyr: "God," says Theodoret, "bestowed upon him fully the grace of healing the sick. . . . But Maron," continues the bishop of Cyr, "not only cured the sickness of the body but he also cured that of the soul, putting an end to the greed of one and to the anger of another, instructing one in the rules of temperance and giving another precepts for living according to justice, controlling the incontinence of this person and fighting the laziness of that one."[117] Theodoret is emphatic regarding the wisdom, saintliness, and spiritual gifts of Maron, and also, perhaps even above all, his remarkable natural gifts: a deep knowledge of the human soul and a certain culture.

[116] Tillemont, *Mémoires*, 12:412–26.

[117] For the translation, cf. *Vies des Pères du desert*, ed. Grasset, n. 4 (Paris, 1961), 219.

Such affirmations are said to have been commonly used by ancient historians. This is true, but this does not mean that they were always false. Theodoret intended to persuade through veracious testimony, and the brevity of his writing on Maron indicates his discretion. "Critics as severe as the Bollandists," Professor Pierre Canivet once wrote to me, "have acknowledged the historical value of the work (*R.H.*) and Schiwietz, the historian of the monks of the East, has trust in him. As for myself," continues Canivet, "I intend to publish an article on the stories of the miracles written by Theodoret and I shall show the discreet and moderate character of the author."

Maronite tradition, as related by the learned patriarch Al-Douaihi (1630–1704), states that the friendship between Maron and John Chrysostom goes back to the time when they were students in Antioch.[118] If this was all that we had, we would suspend judgment. However, it is not: letter 36, written by John Chrysostom from his exile in the Caucasus to "Maron, the priest and solitary," will confirm this tradition if critical study can ever establish that it was sent to the same Maron as that of the *Religious History*. Schiwietz and Canivet are doubtful but Tillemont, on the contrary, sees only this Maron as the one to whom the letter could have been written, and it is difficult to see why the Maronite tradition should be allowed no weight whatsoever.[119] Indications are not lacking to support Tillemont's opinion that John Chrysostom had known Maron in Syria before 398, but they are far from conclusive:

1. Maron was still alive and well known in 405, the probable date of the letter. He had just received two eminent disciples, Jacob and Limnaius.

2. Chrysostom was particularly interested in Syrian monasticism and had during this particular period a great nostalgia for it. His biographies usually provide an excellent summary of Syrian monastic life. If the Maron in question is a Syrian, he can only be the Maron of the *Religious History*.

---

[118] E. Al-Douaihi, *Histoire de la communauté Maronite*, ed. Chartouny (Beirut, 1890), 19–20.

[119] Tillemont, *Mémoires*, 412.

3. No other Maron is known to have been identified as the recipient of this letter.[120]
4. Maron's austerity and gift of miracles gave him great renown. Crowds swarmed to him, seeking his prayers, advice, and aid, and sharing his discipline.[121]

The popular devotion to Maron went as far as their literally stripping him in their zeal for relics, and their desire for his corpse. After his death, a great dispute broke out among the inhabitants of the neighboring villages. Some from a "densely populated" village managed to seize Maron's body by force, and place it in a temple a considerable distance away from Cyr, and probably also from Apamaea (16, 1420). Unfortunately, Theodoret does not indicate the town where this temple stood, but implies that it was very important and some distance from Cyr. In any case, it is hard to imagine it in Apamaea because of the great distance separating the two regions.[122] Such an occurrence of body snatching is frequent in the *Religious History*: Jacob, the disciple of Maron, was stripped even before he breathed his last breath (1436).[123] This reveals, however, the great veneration that the people had for these saintly anchorites. In the case of Maron, one particularity is to be noted: this great saint was still "honored publicly and solemnly" thirty years after his death (1420).

The dates of the birth and the death of the saint have not yet been fixed. Tillemont thinks that Maron was either a disciple or an emulator of Acepsimas, who as we have mentioned had become famous under the reign of Valens (364–78) around 370. We know,

[120] Festugière, *Antioche*, 329–46, and 392ff.; Chrysostomus Bauer, *Der Heilige Johannes Chrysostomus and seine zeit* (Munich: M. Hueber, 1929); Anatole Moulard, *Saint Jean Chrysostôme, sa vie, son oeuvre* (Paris: Procure Générale du Clergé, 1949).

[121] Even Jews visited him. The story of the tame lions, which on the order of Simon (4) led lost Jewish travelers to the right path, was told by the Jews themselves to Maron in the presence of Jacob (21:1432c), who in turn told the story to Theodoret (1360A-9).

[122] Lammens, *Le Liban*, 79 and 92, thinks that the temple was on the southern frontier of Cyr. Canivet thinks that the temple was rather in the Azaz region.

[123] *H.R.*, cols. 1391, 1415, 1434, 1435.

on the other hand, that Jacob and Limnaius, after having visited
Maron, lived in the open air for thirty-eight years. Thus, if we accept
that the *Religious History* was written around 444–45, we have to
conclude that Maron was still alive around 406–7. His death must
have been after 407 and before 423.

The Disciples of Maron

After having related, at length, features of the lives of Jacob
and Limnaius, Maron's two most illustrious disciples, Theodoret
lists ascetics in Cyr who embraced the same way of life as Saint
Maron. There was John (23), who chose an abrupt ridge, which
was windy and exposed to the north, where he stayed "25 years
until the present day, enduring the various torments of the climate"
(1456C). Also Moses, who lived on a summit which dominated the
village of Rama, and the aged Antiochus, who in his senile body
fought as valiantly as did the young. "And," continues Theodoret,
"I can name many others in our regions, on the mountains and in
the plains, so numerous that it is difficult to count them" (23, 1457,
A7-8). Another anchorite, famous in Cyr, was Zebinas (24, 1457B),
"a contemporary and a friend of Maron . . . . All those who ever
saw him celebrate his virtues until this day." Maron admired him
greatly and urged those who came to see him to visit Zebinas and
receive his blessing. Zebinas first gave Jacob the monastic habit
(1457D). Moreover, before he died, Maron expressed the desire to be
buried next to Zebinas, but the affection of the people for his relics
prevented his disciples from carrying out his final wishes. Zebinas
had other disciples but they do not seem to have taken part in any
independent monastic movement.[124]

In Cyr, this way of life was not practiced by men alone, although
Theodoret limits himself to writing about the life of the "saintly and
admirable nun Domnina, an emulator of Maron, who sheds tears
unceasingly because of her sins." Theodoret had wiped them away
himself (30, 1493A). In emulation of Maron's way of life, she built
a small thatched-straw shed in her mother's garden, and allowed

---

[124] Festugière, *Antioche*, 304ff.

The Maronites

all—male and female alike—to see her, without herself looking anybody in the face. Indeed, as she wore a habit which totally covered her, and was always bending, no one ever saw her face. There is legend of two other nuns, Marana and Kyra, who followed this same way of life in the region of Berea (Aleppo), although as Abdo Badwi notes, these three may be the same person, with her name given in Latin (Domnina), Syriac (Marana), and Greek (Kyra). While some women ascetics pursued a solitary life, others lived together. One community, which numbered about 250, shared their food, slept on mattresses, and occupied themselves with spinning and singing hymns.

Theodoret makes no mention of any monastery named after Maron. Relying, therefore, on the only source that refers to Maron and his disciples, we may conclude that during his lifetime, Saint Maron only had disciples who lived in the open air, and that up to 449—a date suggested as a deadline for the writing of the *Religious History*—there was no monastery bearing the name of Maron or following his discipline. There was only a temple in which the venerable remains of the saint were laid to rest (16, 1420).[125]

Characteristic Traits of the Syrian Anchorites

Such were the monks of Cyr who lived in the open air, simple, humble, of a rudimentary culture, who often spoke only Syriac and who were filled with the love of Christ. They were virtuous to the point of heroism, completely consecrated to the contemplation of God and the sanctification of their souls, ignoring entirely all other considerations, obeying the ecclesiastical hierarchy, imitating their masters, Maron in particular, by leading one of the most austere ways of spiritual life, above all remarkable for their love of contemplation, sometimes excessive penances, and complete submission to the hierarchy.

[125] In phrase 16 (Maron) 1420 A 1/3 (πολλὰ φυτὰ φιλοσοφίας ἀπέφηνε . . .), monasteries are not the issue, as A. Festugière explains. In any case, the two hospices for blind people founded by Limnaius (22:1456B 13 SS) cannot be counted as monasteries.

Love of Contemplation

These solitaries were essentially contemplatives as may easily be seen from their search for solitude and love of it, and from their discomfort on receiving numerous visitors. Jacob bears with extreme annoyance those who come to bother him during his time of prayer. Hardly do they leave in obedience to his order than he returns to his prayers. Theodoret describes how difficult Jacob found it to put up with long visits, which he sometimes used to cut short abruptly to the great disappointment of the faithful who had not been able to receive his blessing. To Theodoret himself who pointed this out to him, he answered: "It was not for their sakes that I came to this mountain. It was for mine. Covered as I am with the ulcers of my many sins . . . would it not be absurd and foolish to break the thread of my supplication for conversation with men?"[126]

These ascetics possessed a deep sense of their misery. According to Festugière: "The same regard that turns the contemplative towards God makes him discover the immense abyss between himself and God. This is what these holy people, so virtuous and pure, call their indignity."[127] They wept unceasingly for their sins, by day and by night, seeking forgiveness in the love and contemplation of the beauty of God. Hence Theodoret, in speaking of the anchorite Jacob, mentions what other spiritual men call "the memory of God."[128] As Theodoret wrote: "It is the peculiarity of lovers to ignore all else and to be attached to the person they love and cherish, to dream about that person at night and think of the individual all day long" (1452C2-5). This contemplation was nourished almost uniquely by the recitation or the reading of Holy Scripture: "Prayers followed the chanting of the Psalms or the hymns and the reading of Holy Scripture followed the prayer (1328A), by day and by night." Limnaius, when a number of the blind had come to him,

---

[126] Festugière, *Antioche*, 306.

[127] "Contemplation thus becomes, with fidelity to the practical lessons of the spiritual master, one of the main practices of the ascetic life. With the singing or the recitation of the Psalms and the reading of the Holy Scripture, it constitutes the essence of the monastic life" (Festugière, *Antioche*, 306).

[128] Canivet, *Théologie*, 371ff.

had shelters built for them on each side of his hermitage, where he had them engaged in continuously singing the Psalms (1456-BC).[129]

The Practice of Penance

In addition to their life in the open air, which in itself was a very great penance, these ascetics wore iron chains whose weight bent their bodies to the ground (11, 1396-A; 4, 1344-D), hair shirts, and heavy iron belts (4, 1352). Theodoret gives the example of Jacob who, exhausted from his acts of penance, fell ill. Theodoret, who went to see him, persuaded him to lie down: "I put my hand under his habit to try to gently rub his back . . . . I then felt he had heavy iron chains around the small of his back and round his neck." (21, 1436-BC).

In their practice of extreme poverty, food and clothes were reduced to the strict minimum. Some lived only from the produce of the land; others were supported by the charity of the faithful. Others like Domnina, perhaps wealthy, regularly supported a great number of anchorites. Jacob of Cyr deprived himself of fire and refused anything, even to drink, that was prepared by fire (1441C). Another Jacob, also a hermit in the vicinity of Cyr, lived in a hut but used neither fire nor artificial light (1464C 10-11). Jacob the open-air anchorite even buried himself in the snow so that nothing could be seen of his clothes until the inhabitants of the neighboring villages dug him out with spades and hoes. Others wore yokes and chains and attached their feet to a wooden post or suspended themselves in an openwork cage. Rarely did these anchorites lack ideas to make themselves suffer.

Total Submission to the Hierarchy

The total submission to the hierarchy in general and to the bishop in particular is a clear and remarkable fact for those who read the *Religious History*. Theodoret not only emphasizes the complete harmony between the hierarchy and the ascetics but still more

[129] For the Holy Scriptures as a science, and the Syrian tradition, see Canivet, *Théologie*, 267ff. and nn. 164 and 165.

their mutual love and respect. The anchorite Zenon refused, out of deference, to give his blessing to Theodoret, suggesting rather that he should ask a blessing from the young lector. Theodoret insists emphatically on the respect and submission shown by the ascetics to the bishops. Limnaius never opened the door of his enclosure to visitors; it was only upon the arrival of Theodoret, bishop of Cyr, that he gave permission for it to be opened (1451 B-C). It will be seen, says P. Canivet, that a great number of these cases were to be found in Theodoret's diocese.[130]

Conclusion

Given their importance in our study, in the first part of this chapter we intentionally omitted certain developments to highlight in detail certain notions of history and physical and human geography concerning this part of northern Syria between Cyr and Apamaea, Antioch and Berea. To this region, Tchalenko gave the name "the Limestone Massif of Belus." However, this massif manifests a certain archaeological unity, which could only have been established by frequent and easy relations along its two principal axes:

1. Cyr-Chalcis-Apamaea, which goes from the north to the south; and

2. Antioch-Chalcis-Hierapolis (Membij), which goes from west to east and which joins the Orontes to the Euphrates.

Was there a cultural, religious, or even ascetic unity which corresponded to this archaeological unity? Was there in fact an interdependence between the two monastic centers of Apamaea and Cyr respectively studied in the second and third parts of this chapter? The two monastic movements seem to differ in their ways of life; one in fact is cenobitic, moderate, and open while the other prefers rigid and austere eremitic existence.

---

[130] Canivet, *Théologie*, 281–84. We shall return to this point in the following chapter.

But while Theodoret makes no mention of frequent relations between the "hypethritic" (open-air) monks around Cyr and the cenobitic monks of Apamaea, he does mention that the founding of the monastic order in Apamaea was due to two solitaries from Cyr, Agapetus and Simon, who were both disciples of Marcian, a contemporary of Maron and probably a native of Cyr. This relationship, one of origin and perhaps spiritual dependence, was to be consolidated and strengthened with the passing of time and the impact of many factors, especially political and religious. Although the specific ascetic practices were different, the goal, spirit, and doctrine were the same, namely, a continuous concern for sanctification and orthodoxy according to the Antiochian way.

Agapetus later became bishop of Apamaea. He was succeeded by Polychronius, brother of Theodore of Mopsuestia, head of the school of Antioch. Finally Theodoret, who was a monk in one of the two monasteries of Nikertai, from 423 on tended the diocese of Cyr. He greatly admired Maron and his disciples and had a particular affection for Marcian and the monks of Apamaea. He was involved very directly in the christological debates of his time, and when it was no longer possible for him to stay in his diocese, he retired to Nikertai near Apamaea, as we have seen.

Why did Theodoret choose Apamaea? It was probably because in Theodoret's mind Apamaea offered a better chance for orthodoxy than all the other centers of Syria. It had a more homogeneous population than that of Antioch and the other big towns, and was the Syriac-language capital of northern Syria. Also, thanks to a succession of orthodox bishops, it had from the beginning adopted the religious policy preferred by Theodoret. The following chapter will establish on a balance of probabilities that it was probably due to this great bishop that the unity of these two monastic centers was effectively achieved.

It would otherwise be a remarkable coincidence that Theodoret was the only historian of these two monastic movements from northern Syria!

Chapter Three

Theodoret of Cyr and the Patriarchate of Antioch after the Council of Ephesus (431-452)[1]

We learned from Theodoret's *Religious History* that there existed two monastic centers in northern Syria, one in Cyr, due to the inspiration of the hypethrite Maron, and another in Apamaea, which followed the rule of the ascetic Marcian but was founded by two solitaries from Cyr, Simon and Agapetus. In the previous chapter, we contended that the connection with Cyr may have led to a relationship of dependence and origin between the two movements. We shall now see that documents from the sixth century concerning the christological debates in northern Syria mention a real religious confederation in Syria Secunda, centered on the monastery of Maron near Apamaea. Thus the connection we have postulated certainly did come into existence, even if we cannot prove that it was present from the founding of the Apamaean monasteries. The most likely thesis, however, is that the connection was original, and was later consolidated, for if we

[1] For this chapter, see particularly Augustin Fliche and Victor Martin, *Histoire de l'Eglise* (Paris, 1934), 4:163–240; L. Duchesne, *Histoire ancienne de l'Eglise*, 3:313ff. Devresse, *Le Patriarcat d'Antioche*; Ernest Stein, *Histoire du Bas-empire* (Paris: Desclée de Brouwer, 1959); P. Th. Camelot, *Éphèse et Chalcédoine*, in *Histoire des conciles*, n. 2 (Paris, 1961); C. Bihlmeyer H. Tuchle, *Histoire de l'Eglise*, vol. 1 (Paris, 1962); Marrou, *Nouvelle Histoire*, vol. 1.

cannot prove the antiquity of the connection, neither is there any evidence of its specific establishment at a later point, and in favor of such a connection we have the facts that (a) Agapetus and Simon were themselves from Cyr; (b) in 452 a new Apamaean monastery was named after Maron, the ascetic of Cyr; and (c) Theodoret, once a monk in one of the two original monasteries of Nikertai in Apamaea, was tremendously impressed by Maron.

Thus, when Theodoret gives Maron credit only for the movement in Cyr, he must be taken to mean "directly responsible through his personal pupils." The question of spiritual influence is a different issue. This all strongly supports the notion that from its very inception the ascetic movement in Apamaea was conscious of and acknowledged the movement in Cyr; indeed, by naming an early monastery after Maron, it blazoned its connection with the latter movement.

We know that this monastery does not seem to have existed before 449, otherwise Theodoret, who had a particular interest in this monastic movement, would have mentioned it. Its foundation is indicated in only the single document we have already studied, and through which we know that it was founded in the year 452 under the emperor Marcian.

In the sixth century, the Maronite monks and their followers were considered by the Monophysites to be "the fruit of the Chalcedonian vineyard, the fruits of Leo, bitter seed produced by the vineyard of Theodoret, son of the great schism (Chalcedon)." The Monophysites considered them to be one with Theodoret of Cyr, so that the anathema against him at the Third Council of Constantinople in 553 touched them directly together with "their mother the assembly of Chalcedon."

Major events marked the history of the church in general, and the patriarchate of Antioch in particular, between 449 and 452. What were the repercussions of these events on the monastic groupings of northern Syria? Can we identify the personage who was behind the founding of this monastery of Maron in Apamaea?

It could not have been the emperor Marcian directly as Abū l-Fidā would have us believe. It is true that the founding of a Chalcedonian monastery in such circumstances could gain the support and the favors of the court. However, did the civil authority have sufficient knowledge about the deeper feelings of these monastic circles of northern Syria?

Only one personality seems to satisfy the conditions for being able to suggest and encourage such a foundation. It is Theodoret, the bishop of Cyr, the former monk of Nikertai, the chief of the Eastern party, the indefatigable champion of Antioch, the author of the *Religious History*, the great victor at the Council of Chalcedon, and the friend both of the emperor Marcian and of Bishop Domnus of Apamaea.

Thus, it is very natural to devote to him this chapter, the central point and the core of our thesis. The chapter comprises three main sections:

1. Theodoret: his life, monastic education, and activities

2. Theodoret and the christological debates

3. Monasticism and the hierarchy during the christological crisis

It is not our intention to write a new study of the religious history of this period, but rather to focus on Theodoret and his role and relations with the monks of northern Syria during the christological crisis that dominated the fifth and sixth centuries.

Theodoret of Cyr:
Life, Monastic Formation, Activities[2]

Childhood

Theodoret was born in Antioch around 393, at the end of the reign of Theodosius I (379–95). It seems that for several generations

---

[2] For Theodoret, see Gennadius Massiliensis, *De Scriptoribus ecclesiasticis*, c. 89 in *P.L.* 58, c. 1112B- 1113A; Jacques Sirmond, *Beati Theodoreti episcopi Cyrensis Opera omnia*, 4 vols. (Paris, 1642); *Dissertatio de vita et scriptis Theodoreti* in *P.G.* 80, c. 35A-56B; P. Garnier, *Beati Theodoret episcopi Cyri*, vol. 5 (Paris, 1684), in *P.G.* 84; Le Nain de Tillemont, *Mémoires*, vol. 15, *Théodoret, Evêque de Cyr*, 207–2040, and the notes, 868–78; N. N. Glubokovskij, *Blazennyi Feodorit episkop Kirrskie. Ego Jizn literaturnaia diéiatelnost. Tserkoivno istoritchcheskoe izlidovanie*; Le BX, "Théodoret, Bishop of Cyr, his life and his literary activity," research paper on ecclesiastical history, 2 vols. (Moscow, 1892); John Henry Newman, *Historical Sketches* (London, 1876), 2:303–62; G. Bardy, *Dict. De Théologie Catholique* 15.1

his family, a Christian one, had led a life of ease and luxury, at least on his mother's side. It belonged to the upper class of Antioch, and owned much property. His father, married for many years without any children, regularly visited the solitaries living in the neighborhood of Antioch, begging them to intercede for him in this regard. His mother, married at the age of seventeen, was at first worldly and given more to coquetry than piety according to the judgment of her austere son. However, after she was cured of acute ophthalmia by the prayers and intercession of Peter of Chalcis, a saintly hermit in the nearby region,[3] and after a long discourse from the hermit, she was inwardly converted (9, 1384B).

Furthermore, she was concerned about her childlessness. Following the advice of another solitary, Macedonius, she took a vow to consecrate her child to God if she conceived. She did conceive, and when Theodoret was born, his mother was thirty years old and had been married for thirteen years. She fell seriously ill during birth, and seemed about to die, when she was cured through Peter's prayers. Theodoret was still very young when she took him to the hermit Macedonius to be blessed.[4] She told her young son about Saint Simon the Elder (6, 1358-1363). When he reached adolescence, she took him to see and receive the instructions and blessing of Aphraates.[5] She also took him every week to receive the blessing of Saint Peter of Chalcis. Theodoret was still in Antioch when he visited for the first time Saint Zenon (12, C1395-1399). These many visits to monks, and their influence, were clearly significant to Theodoret, who related them. They illustrate his state of mind, profound spirituality, and deep dedication of mind and heart to God.[6]

---

col. 299–326. See also the thesis of Yvan Azéma, *Théodoret de Cyr d'après sa correspondance. Étude sur la personalité morale, religieuse et intellectuelle de l'évêque de Cyr* (Paris, 1952) (unedited); Canivet, *Histoire d'une enterprise opologétique au V*e *siècle* (Paris, 1957); Theodoret De Cyr, *Thérapeutique*, ed. Canivet, introduction; *Théodoret de Cyr Correspondence*, ed. Azéma, introduction.

[3] Theodoret, *Thérapeutique*, 12–13.

[4] *H.R.*, 13:1409C 14-15; Tillemont, *Mémoires*, 214.

[5] *H.R.*, 13:1373 B 5-11.

[6] These details may seem insignificant but were piously mentioned by Theodoret. They illustrate his childhood but also his entire life. His sensitivity

Education

Thus, for his religious education, Theodoret had powerful models in his parents and especially the monks around Antioch. However, Theodoret made no mention of his secular education and upbringing, or the Antiochian milieu.[7] Concerning his theological studies, we have no lack of information. He stated that his "masters" were Diodore of Tarsus and Theodore of Mopsuestia. It is not difficult to believe that he had received instruction from Theodore, who died only in 428 or 429, but one can scarcely believe that he was instructed by Diodore, who died about the time when Theodoret was born. However, there are several ways in which one can be, or consider oneself to be, the student of an eminent teacher and author.

Was he the student of Saint John Chrysostom? Or was he the fellow student of Nestorius and John of Antioch? The hypothesis is not improbable but it is far from being proved. Theodoret was about fifteen when the great bishop of Constantinople died. It is conjectured to be most unlikely that he did not know of the piety and talented oratory of Chrysostom, who had been in Antioch.[8] Later in life, Theodoret would reveal a particular respect for Chrysostom.

Destined by his parents, even before his birth, to the monastic life, Theodoret very likely remained in Antioch until the time of their death. He was then twenty-three years old, and a church lector.[9] Being the sole heir, he distributed his riches to the poor, and retreated to one of the two monasteries of Nikertai; as we have seen, this was three miles away from Apamaea, seventy-five miles from Antioch, and 120 miles from Cyr.[10]

---

bears, perhaps, the influence of his "blessed" mother, as he likes to say, and his spirituality reflects the monks "whose examples had touched his imagination as a child and whose prophecies had traced his destiny." *H.R.*, 4:1364 D 6-7; Theodoret, *Thérapeutique*, 1:12.

[7] As Canivet states, we are reduced to conjectures: *Histoire d'une entreprise apologétique au Ve siècle*, in *Bibliothèque de l'Histoire de l'Église* (Paris, 1957), 21.

[8] Azéma, 1:14.

[9] *P.G.* 82, col. 1325.

[10] Ep 119; Azéma, 3:77.

The Monastery of Nikertai, 416(?)–423

In this monastery where Syriac culture was flourishing,[11] Theodoret spent seven years. We lack significant documents for this period; only a few allusions and scattered details have survived in his writings. It is clear that for these seven years in Nikertai young Theodoret followed Marcian's rule. He considered monastic life to be an imitation of the life lived in heaven (1285C 12-19); it was the existence of the angels themselves that David the Igumen (Superior) proposed to Theodoret and his friends (1348C 2-5). The monastery Agapetus built in the region of Apamaea, and in which our young monk lived, followed the rule of the angels (1325C 13-14). The monks of Teleda imitated the celestial life (1348B4) as certainly did those of Egypt whom Theodoret had heard about.[12] Once they died, they expected, like Theodosius, Aphraate, and Maron, to occupy a place awaiting them among the choirs of angels, which also received Marcian (1392D; 1377 C2; 1420, 1496C). Theodoret wished to join this angelic choir in his turn.[13]

As for vows, we know that Theodoret had a great admiration for chastity and poverty. In *Thérapeutique*, a book written during this period, he praised virginity, admiring the ascetics, male and female alike, who fought the body, avoiding even legitimate physical relationships. Indeed, he wrote a treatise on virginity, a true preparation for future life since "the person who professes virginity liberates his soul from superfluous and useless preoccupations as much as he can." The notice dedicated for the nun Domnina is one of the most beautiful passages that he ever wrote on chastity (1493D).

Concerning poverty, Theodoret recalled in a letter to the consul Nomus that during his episcopate he remained faithful to the monastic virtues, which he professed before becoming a bishop, especially regarding poverty: "I have received neither alms nor clothing. Nobody in my house has received a piece of bread or a single egg. Apart from the rags that I wear, I have wanted nothing.

---

[11] Peeters, *Tréfonds*, 90.

[12] Fliche-Martin, *Histoire de l'Eglise*, 4:21, 5–8, 247.

[13] Canivet, *Théologie*, 252–54.

With my ecclesiastical revenues I have erected porticos."[14] In a letter
to Pope Leo (113), he proudly declared "that not content during
such a long episcopate with having acquired neither house nor
field, nor pittance, nor tomb, I spontaneously embraced poverty
to the point of distributing all the riches inherited from my parents
immediately after their death. All those who live in the Orient know
that."[15] Theodoret felt that these declarations were necessary at
a time when he was misunderstood and was being slandered.[16]
During his seven years in Nikertai he mastered Greek, Syriac, and
probably Hebrew; studied Holy Scripture; and read apologetics of
Clement and Eusebius of Caesarea.[17]

In Nikertai, Theodoret made the acquaintance of David the
Igumen (4, 1345 D). According to Schiwietz, Theodoret went to
visit the monastery of Saint Eusebius near Teleda in the diocese
of Antioch from Nikertai. "One day," he said, "that I wished to
go and see this group, I went with some companions on the road,
men who had embraced the same kind of life as I had." During
this visit, Theodoret came to know several other solitaries.[18] From
these visits to the many monasteries of Cyr, whether near or distant,
Theodoret drew the material which he later used in the *Religious
History*. It may even be that the trip to Jerusalem mentioned in the
Thérapeutique took place at this time.[19]

Theodoret's first literary works are often dated to this period.
Canivet believes that Theodoret had written the *Thérapeutique*, his
most important apologetic work, while still a monk in the region of
Apamaea, contending that it bears the mark of a monastic milieu.[20]

---

[14] Ep 81; Azéma, 2:197.

[15] Ep 113; Azéma, 3:57ff.

[16] Canivet, *Méssalianisme*, in *Rev. Mabillon* 51 (1961): 31, says that, by devoting
the episcopal revenues to the public good, he applied the rule that the Third
Council of Carthage had laid down in 419 for the benefit of bishops "deprived
of riches," that is to say, monks. Since he also took care of the orphans in his
diocese, he anticipated what the Council of Chalcedon was soon to define for
bishops.

[17] Theodoret, *Thérapeutique*, 1:15.

[18] *P.G.*, 82:1349ff.

[19] Theodoret, *Thérapeutique*, 15, n. 4.

[20] Canivet, *Entreprise*, 40–41.

Marcel Richard argues that Theodoret could not, in less than two years, have acquired his reputation as the best theologian of the patriarchate of Antioch during the Council of Ephesus (431).[21]

But why did Theodoret choose for a place of retreat one of the monasteries of Nikertai and the monastic rule of Marcian? A native of Antioch, he might naturally have chosen one of the numerous monasteries which surrounded it,[22] or one of the religious communities of Teleda, founded by "the great Eusebius" and his disciples.[23] There Saint Simon, later known as the Stylite, attracted by the great reputation of this monastery, remained for ten years (1468B 13C).

It is impossible to ascertain the personal reasons determining Theodoret's choice, but hypothetical explanations can be advanced, even if they are subject to strong reservations. It may have been that he wished to be away from his familiar surroundings and acquaintances, to devote himself completely to a life of meditation, prayer, and solitude. Another reason, not mutually exclusive, might have been his admiration for Marcian's moderate monastic rule. Theodoret, while loving virtue in all of its forms, personally preferred the moderate ascetical life, striving to lighten what he considered were excessive penances. For example, later, as bishop of Cyr, he hastened from Berea to persuade Jacob to accept lighter penances (1433B-1440A).[24] He condemned, just as Marcian did, "the Euchites, who under the monastic habit, suffer from the evil of the Manicheans" who rage against the body (1336B-D).[25]

Theodoret must have opted for a monastery where intellectual life was possible. He was in fact able, thanks to a moderate rule, to pursue his studies, develop his knowledge, and write his *Thérapeutique*. Moreover, we know that intellectual life was possible in the later monastic confederation of Apamaea: the monastery of

---

[21] Richard, *L'Activité littéraire de Théodoret avant le concile d'Ephèse, R.S.P.T.,* vol. 24 (1935): 85–106.

[22] Festugière, *Antioche,* 314–16.

[23] *H.R.* 4:1340 D 9-10; 1352 A12 BI; 26:1368 A11-12, and for Eusebius, 1340 D-1344 A.

[24] For a comparison between the different rules of the monasteries of northern Syria, see Festugière, *Antioche,* 316–18.

[25] On Theodoret's moderation, see Canivet, *Théologie,* 252–53.

Saint Maron, part of this confederation, had a well-organized and well-managed library, with two monks in charge of its organization.[26] Lastly, and perhaps not least, the guarantee of orthodoxy offered by these monasteries may have been critical for him. Theodoret insists on Marcian's orthodoxy,[27] and, as will be seen later, he retired to this same monastery of Nikertai after the "council" at Ephesus in 449, when it became impossible for him to stay in his diocese.

Bishop of Cyr, 423–466(?)

Activities

While working in peaceful solitude, with the monastic aims of perfecting his soul and enriching his spirit, Theodoret was called from his monastery to shepherd the diocese of Cyr. He reluctantly left a life which seemed to suit his nature and his studious temperament very well.[28] The leading role was probably played by the metropolitan of Hierapolis (Mabboug) and the bishops of his synod. In 423 or soon after, he was, against his will, raised to the episcopal seat of Cyr.[29]

Once he became bishop, he followed the example of the anchorite Abraham. Theodoret wrote of Abraham that "being forced to change his surroundings—as appointed bishop of Ḥarran—he did not reduce his monastic austerities and up until his death was continually engaged in the hardest chores of solitary life with the greatest responsibilities of episcopal life" (1419).

Theodoret seems to have united in his person the love of tranquility and solitude with an intense, multidimensional ministry. But many apparently sincere passages declare that, left to himself, Theodoret would have preferred to continue in the monastic life. For example, letter 18 to a commander of the soldiers spoke of his love of peace, and stated that the ministerial duties were costly to him. Theodoret often reflected on the satisfactions of the monastic

[26] Ms. British Museum, add. 17, 169; Nau, *Bulletin*, 344–45.

[27] Canivet, *Messalianisme*, 26–27.

[28] Ep 81; Azéma, 2:193. Canivet, *Thérapeutique*, 16, n. 3.

[29] Peeters, *Tréfonds*, 90.

life: "When I lived in the monastic state, I preferred the tranquility prescribed by the rule to all the goods of this earth." In general, it is enough to scan through his letters to find abundant testimony to his love of solitude and peace.[30]

Such assertions, and similar ones, pointing to a fundamental trait of his personality, are found constantly in his writings. He frequently tells us about the "pleasant fruits of tranquility" (ep 140), and the "pleasure of enjoying a life free from worries" (ep 146). Later, when the "council" of Ephesus of 449 was being prepared, Theodoret declared to Irenaeus: "It is not with a view to temporal good that I act in this way nor to attach myself to this charge loaded with trouble, which I scruple somewhat to call an ordeal. My conscience is my witness. For if it were up to me, I would have given it up long ago, did I not fear God's judgment."[31] When, on the eve of the "council" of Ephesus in 449, he was threatened with exile, he requested to be allowed to retire to his monastery in Apamaea.[32]

When he was sent into exile, he protested against this new sanction (ep 113) not because the exile in itself was a burden to him, for he experienced an inner joy in having thus found calm and peace, but because an injustice might prevail, since his enemies sought to make mileage from his exile.[33] Once the storm had calmed down, Theodoret recalled with evident joy "the calm and limpid waters,"[34] and said that of all things, tranquility had most value. He dreamt of "fleeing from the worry of business and hastening back to live that (monastic life) so dear to us," once the slanders had been refuted, and truth reestablished.[35]

During this period, his activity, his writings, and especially his correspondence are eloquent. Assigned by God, as he says, to be head of this city, he considered the act of abandoning any of the

---

[30] Ep 18; Azéma, 1:56; 89.

[31] Azéma, 2:56, n. 2; 2:62, n. 1.

[32] Ep 119; Azéma, 3:81.

[33] Epp 113, 139, 140; Azéma, 3.

[34] Ep 133; Azéma, 3.

[35] Epp 134, 137; Azéma, 3. Many other texts show his love for solitude and his desire to return to monastic life: Azéma, vol. III, ep. 113, 141, 146, 124; *ép. à Nestorius*, 208 (Syn. 120).

many and diverse activities that presented themselves to him as treason. In addition, he was the Builder Bishop,[36] the defender of the common interests of his people,[37] the director of consciences,[38] the comforter of the afflicted, the redoubtable adversary of heresies, the indefatigable apostle of the Syrian countryside, the zealous orator, the alert theologian,[39] the talented writer, and one "of the most creative among the Church Fathers."[40] It is difficult to establish the complete list of his writings. Some of them have disappeared; others are probably now known only by a pseudonym. Given the condemnation of the Council of 533, we are fortunate that for some of his texts the consequences were not more serious.[41]

Frequentation of the Solitaries of Cyr

Immersed in this intense and multifaceted obligation, and dedicating himself to all sorts of activities, Theodoret temporarily lost at that time direct contact with his monastery, but his love and respect for the community did not diminish. When toward the year 444 he wrote his *Religious History*, he dedicated a long chapter to Marcian, the charismatic founder of this flourishing monastic movement.

In his bishopric, Theodoret had other contacts with other monks who, although having chosen an asceticism which was harder and more austere than that of Marcian's rule, were no less agreeable and attractive. He had a great love and particular esteem for them; of the thirty notices in his *Religious History*, thirteen chapters are devoted to them. Upon his arrival at Cyr, he found, in his own words, "a blooming garden" prepared by the anchorite Maron (16). Among

---

[36] Epp 81, 79; Azéma, 2; Epp 113–15, 116; Azéma, 3.

[37] Epp 29, 30, 36, 52, 70; Azéma, 2.

[38] Epp 8, 9; Azéma, 1. Epp 3, 77, 78; Azéma, 2. Epp 110, 112; Azéma, 3.

[39] Epp 16, 21, 82, 83; Azéma, 3. Epp 104, 109, 121, 130, 144, 146; Azéma, 3.

[40] Canivet wrote: "His literary work is one of the most important of the fourth and fifth centuries with those of Saint John Chrysostom and Saint Cyril of Alexandria. It embraces all the issues that a bishop might deal with and is dominated by the requirements of the apostolate; it expresses one of the most characteristic tendencies of the spirit of Theodoret, his intellectual curiosity and his taste for positive and erudite studies." Canivet, *Thérapeutique*, 1:24.

[41] See Bardy, *D.T.C.*, 15.1, cols. 303–17; Canivet, *Thérapeutique*, 1:24, n. 1.

his various duties, the new bishop had care of this "garden," and of each individual plant. He was interested in the lives of these monks, in all their diversity, without showing any preference.

Here we shall confine ourselves to the particular affection that Theodoret had for one of these solitaries, the anchorite and hypethrite Jacob. For Jacob alone, who still lived in the district of Cyr when Theodoret wrote his *Religious History*, did Theodoret begin with the words "the most famous and illustrious Jacob since he precedes in time and surpasses with his works those who, in imitating him, do such extraordinary and marvelous things." He had then already led the hypethritic life for thirty-eight years (1456C), living on a mountain thirty stadia from the town of Cyr.[42]

Of the seventy-five persons who illustrate this "gallery of monastic celebrities," Theodoret reserves the first place for this "illustrious Jacob," to whom he applies the words of the prophet: "the righteous will flourish like palm trees; they will grow like the cedars of Lebanon."[43] In considering the *Religious History*'s treatment of Simon the Stylite, Peeters remarked that the portrait of Jacob took a "more penetrating turn because one feels that it is linked more closely with the life and the personal experience of Theodoret."[44] Jacob, he said, was his Isaiah: "I go to Isaiah to obtain through his intercession the help and the assistance of God" (1440D). Theodoret was invariably by his side in sickness, providing for his care. As stated, he persuaded Jacob to accept some relaxation of his rule (1433B-1440A). He intervened vigorously to oblige the public to withdraw when the anchorite suffered from colic (1434D7-1436C15). Theodoret emphasized the mutual affection existing between them: "This saint could not resist my insistence, having no charms more agreeable than the prayers of a friend."[45]

---

[42] According to Honigmann, the place where Jacob withdrew was 5.5 km from the town of Cyr. Honigmann, *Studi et testi*, 97, n. 173; Dussaud, op. cit., 472, n. 1; Martin Hartmann, *Das Liwa Haleb, Zeitschrift der Gesellschaft für Erdkunde* (Berlin: Druck von W. Pormetter, 1894), 480, 484; Canivet, *Mission en Syrie*, 11ff.

[43] This is also Honigmann's view, *Studi et testi*.

[44] Peeters, *Tréfonds*, 95–96. Jacob is found in *H.R.* 21:1400–1452.

[45] *H.R.*, 1433 B-1440A, story of the sickness of Jacobus, Festugière, *Antioche*, 299–301.

Moreover, Jacob confided to Theodoret his most intimate secrets, his revelations.[46] Jacob prayed on behalf of Theodoret's efforts to eradicate the Marcionite heresy: "I would have torn you to pieces," said the spirit to Theodoret, "but for the troop of martyrs and Jacob whom I saw were guarding you" (1440D). Theodoret prepared a tomb for him, where, according to Theodore the Lector, Jacob was in fact laid to rest.[47]

Jacob enjoyed a great prestige, and a particular reputation for sanctity. Theodoret took pleasure in invoking his name in letters written to the highest dignitaries to plead the cause of his diocese crushed by taxation, as in letter 42 written to the prefect Constantine[48] or letter 44 written to Patrices Senator.[49] Letter 28 of Theodoret's correspondence "to Jacob priest and monk" is not to the anchorite Jacob,[50] but to Jacob of Syria, the miracle-worker.[51] According to Honigmann, Theodoret's Jacob was certainly the same "Mar Yacob Rêsh Dairâ (Reverend Jacob Superior of the monastery) of Kaphrâ Rehimâ" mentioned in two letters forged by the Monophysites. The first one attributed to the famous Stylite is addressed to "Mar Yacob of Kaphrâ Rehimâ," and in the text Jacob is called "Resh Dairâ = archimandrite." The second letter is attributed to Alexander of Hierapolis and to Andrew of Samosata

---

[46] Tillemont, *Mémoires*, 227.

[47] *H.R.*, 1444 BC; Theodorus Lector, *Hist. Eccl.*, 1, 2; *P.G.* 86A, 172b.

[48] Ep 42; Azéma, 2:113. On Constantine, see Azéma, 1:51.

[49] Azéma, 2:118. On Senator, see Azéma, 1:48.

[50] Azéma, 1:43.

[51] It is to him "that the emperor Leo wrote in 457, also to Simon the Stylite and to Baradatus to learn their opinion about the Council of Chalcedon and Timothy Elures, the usurper of the seat of Alexandria. These three illustrious saints wrote back to him in 458. It was this same Jacob who together with Simon and Baradatus interceded to persuade Theodoret to join John of Antioch after the signing of the Act of Union." Cf. *Coll. Sangerm.* 1.11, ACO, 2, 5:23, 13–15, n. 19–21; see Honigmann, *The Monks Symeon, Jacobus and Baradatus, Patristic Studies*, in *Studi et testi*, 95s, n. 173. "All three answered the emperor," Baradatus's answer to the emperor, dated 27 August 458, is still preserved among the encyclia. Therefore, it is true of all three of them what Duchesne remarks with regard to the famous Stylite alone: "Simon, simple man as he was, was treated as though he were a council." Duchesne, *Histoire*, 3:312.

concerning Simon the Stylite and "Mar Jacob of Kaphrâ Rehimâ (Agreeable Village)."[52]

Theodoret and the Christological Debate From 431 to 451

"No list of the activities of Theodoret will be complete if it fails to acknowledge the important role played by the bishop of Cyr in the debates of his time," said Newman, in what he termed "the trials" of Theodoret. This period of his life, which started in 430 with the Nestorian crisis and ended in Theodoret's rehabilitation and triumph of his terminology in Chalcedon (451), is significant for our thesis concerning the circumstances of the founding of the monastery of Maron after that council.

It is essential to start by affirming that Theodoret was a Syrian: "one of his admirers who has, however, studied him deeply, thinks it is essential for his glory that he should be a pure Greek."[53] This is just one of the distortions caused by Hellenocentric misconceptions. "Theodoret must be given back to Syria," states Peeters.[54] Theodoret was Syrian Antiochian not only by origin, birth, and language but above all by feeling and thought. He is a worthy representative of the school of Antioch, the defender of Diodoros and Theodore, two bishops who held the patriarchate of Antioch with distinction.[55] Theodoret was fully aware of the patriarchal policy of Alexandria, and he knew the story of John Chrysostom too well to be forgetful. He knew also that the patriarchate of Antioch was threatened by the ambitions of the patriarchs of Alexandria, and also by the development of imperial authority over that of Constantinople.[56]

---

[52] Honigmann, ibid. Letters of Simon the Stylite, Brit. Mus., *cod. Syr.* 860-Add. 12154, saec. 9, fol. 200r, 201r (Wright, *Catalogue*, 2:986), the second also in Cod. 857-Add. 12155 (saec. 8), fol. 229v (Wright, *Catalogue*, 2:951), ed. C. C. Torrey, *Journal of the American Eastern Society*, 20 (1899): 262–63. English trans., ibid., 265ff. Torrey, 271ff. English trans., 272.

[53] Glubokovskij, *Blazennyi Feodorit*, 1:4.

[54] Peeters, *Tréfonds*, 89.

[55] Canivet, *Entreprise*, 24, n. 6; Bardy, *D.T.C.*, c. 304.

[56] P. Goubert, *Le rôle de Ste Pulchérie et de l'ennuque Chrysaphios dans das Konzil von Chalkedon*, A. Grillmeier, H. Bacht (Echter-Verlag-Woerzburg, 1954–59), 1:309.

The Council of Ephesus

We know nothing of the first seven years of Theodoret's episcopate. He comes into view only in 430 when John of Antioch received letters from Pope Celestine and Cyril of Alexandria concerning Nestorius. Following the advice of his bishops, among whose number was Theodoret, John of Antioch wrote to Nestorius an affectionate letter "in which he urged him to do what the Pope was asking him to do and to abandon his opposition to the term Theotokos."[57] Some believe that this letter was written by Theodoret.[58] Nestorius's reply was in the same irenic tone. "Thus, thanks to the good sense of the Orientals and to the concessions made by Nestorius, the debate moved towards a pacific ending. The anathemas of Cyril came to disturb these good dispositions."[59] John of Antioch found an Apollinarist inspiration in them, and asked Theodoret and Andrew of Samosata to write a refutation of the anathemas.[60] This revealed Theodoret's standing and intellectual authority in the Eastern Church. As has been observed, Theodoret had been educated in the methods of the Antiochian school, and insisted on the reality of Christ's divine and human natures. He also had personal links with Nestorius. Accordingly, immediately before the opening of the Council of Ephesus, he revealed himself a redoubtable adversary of the Alexandrine theology.[61] Having traveled to Ephesus with its metropolitan Alexander and John of Antioch, Theodoret seems to have played a particularly important role. This is why when Theodosius summoned the delegates of the two parties to Chalcedon to reach a compromise, the Easterners carefully chose Theodoret as spokesman of their delegation.[62]

The Act of Union

Around the end of the summer of 432, serious negotiations began between Antioch and Alexandria, with the tribune Aristolaus

---

[57] Mansi, 4, c. 1061; also 5, c. 753, cited by Duchesne, *Histoire*, 3, n. 1.

[58] Tillemont, *Mémoires*, 15:246.

[59] Duchesne, *Histoire*, 3:42.

[60] This refutation is known only from the replies of Cyril, *P.G.* 77, c. 316–85.

[61] Points made by Azéma, 1:18–19.

[62] Duchesne, *Histoire*, 3:364.

presiding. Summoned by his patriarch, Theodoret participated during the month of September, meeting behind closed doors, to determine what proposition should be made to Cyril. Six formulas were proposed. Aristolaus chose the most moderate [Syn. 147 (58)],[63] and carried it to Alexandria with a letter from Acacius of Berea. Cyril's reply to the old bishop [Syn. 145 (36)] was most disappointing. Theodoret was the only one in his province who did not hesitate to declare it orthodox [Syn. 149 (60)]. He tried even to make Metropolitan Alexander of Hierapolis adopt his point of view, but this only resulted in bringing about his enmity. Alexander went so far as to accuse Theodoret of treason in the presence of Helladius of Tarsus, who in turn alerted Himerius of Nicomedia. Theodoret had to defend himself [Syn. 15-161 (170-172)], and the three letters he then wrote show how deeply grieved he was by such a lack of understanding.

Meanwhile, Paul of Homs went to Alexandria on a peace-making mission, which proved to be successful. John of Antioch wrote to Theodoret informing him that peace was achieved [Syn. 174 (86)], insisting much on Cyril's concessions, without mentioning those required on his part. But Theodoret had heard that this "peace" might not hold. Thus, his reply was full of apprehension:

> If it is only an illusion of peace . . . those who concluded it did nothing but offer to God a peace that is odious to him and unworthy of every pious man: however, it is exactly that kind of peace which according to us is being concluded. It would be in fact, neither honest nor good for us to annul the depositions and condemnations which are just, to accept illegal ordinations and to grant forgiveness to these people who have turned everything upside down, while on their side they commit with a clear conscience acts of hostility and chase away from their churches those of us who are most distinguished. May Your Holiness write both to the Emperor, the friend of Christ, and

[63] *Synodicon*: Latin version of the acts of Ephesus and Chalcedon by Rusticus, in Migne, *P.G.*, 84, c. 565–863; Schwartz, ACO, 1:4. For further details, Camelot, op. cit., 241; Bardy, *Fliche et Martin*, 4:163–64. We are much indebted to the remarkable article of Marcel Richard, *Théodoret, Jean d'Antioche et les moines d'Orient*, in *Mélanges de science religieuse* 3 (1946): 150ff.

to the powerful judges, to make it clearly known that not for anything shall we agree to accept this peace and to embrace their communion as long as those who were with us during the time of the quarrels have not been given back their churches since it is advisable for Your Holiness to prepare for the churches a peace without stain, which does not harm pious souls more than the battle itself did. [Syn. 175 (87)]

However, John penned a triumphant encyclical to his suffragans, announcing the reestablishment of peace [Syn. 77 (2)] and telling of the documents exchanged between Cyril and himself. This letter provoked diverse reactions: there was a state of panic in the bishoprics of Cilicia and Euphratesia. The consequent revolt was led by Alexander. Yet, despite his views as stated above, Theodoret offered a respectful yet determined opposition: he did not wish to act precipitously. In his opinion, the letter of Cyril was satisfactory in that it showed that no dogmatic problem separated Syria from Egypt any longer [Syn. 176 (88)]. In these circumstances, he added, the condemnation of Nestorius, who had always taught the doctrine now accepted by Cyril, was an absurdity to which he would not subscribe. He had the satisfaction of gaining to his point of view his colleagues of the province of Euphratesia during a synod held in Zeugma. Alexander of Hierapolis, foreseeing what would happen, refused to attend. The synod delegated Andrew of Samosata and Theodoret to write to John of Antioch. They did so with the greatest moderation [Syn. 183 (95)].

This success did not last. Alexander, who was most dissatisfied, incited against Theodoret the bishops of Cilicia, who had just adopted his uncompromising attitude and broken off their relations with Antioch. Theodoret again had to defend himself against his friends. He asked Helladius of Tarsus the reason for his coldness [Syn. 198 (110)]; to Nestorius he affirmed that if he considered Cyril's letter to be orthodox, he would be ready to suffer rather than abandon the Alexandrine victims.[64]

On his side, John was losing patience due to the procrastination of the bishops of Euphratesia. He decided to take the offensive.

---

[64] Richard, *Théodoret, Jean d'Antioche*, 150ff.

For reasons not clear, without even telling the old Metropolitan Alexander, John deposed two bishops of his province. This provoked regrettable incidents and, sometime before Easter 434, the synod of Euphratesia, presided this time by Alexander, broke off relations with John [Syn. 211 (123)]. Theodoret approved this decision.

The emperor, alerted by John, decided to intervene. He sent to the bishop of Antioch a decree which was intended especially for Alexander of Hierapolis, Helladius of Tarsus, Maximinus of Anazarbes, and Theodoret, and of which we have only the first lines [Syn. 228 (140)].

They tried at first to negotiate. Bardy captures the human side of these endeavors. Theodoret, he wrote, "was the first to be chosen because of his saintliness, knowledge and influence. All possible means were used to persuade him to make peace with John of Antioch, the prayers of the most influential monks of the region, Simon the Stylite, Jacob the disciple of Maron, and Baradatus, the supplications of his people; the more or less threatening measures of the imperial officers and the letters of his colleagues. Theodoret hesitated for a long time and a moving correspondence between him and Alexander of Hierapolis shows his anxiety and his distress."[65] Finally, he met John. He entered into communion with him, signed the act of union, and wrote to Cyril to show him his agreement. Out of consideration for him, he was not asked to condemn Nestorius.[66] This reconciliation brought the expected happy results: numerous bishops from the two Cilicias and Isauria rejoined the church, and the two who did not were ousted from their churches.

There remained the case of Alexander, metropolitan and friend of Theodoret, now aged but inflexible and not softened. He resisted approaches from Theodoret and many others.[67] Theodoret vainly tried to convince him that entering into communion with John did not at all imply abandoning the essential principles the Antiochian episcopate had defended at Ephesus. "It is because I know this situation," he wrote to him, "that I ask you to think in a general way about the interest of the Churches. I see clearly that our obstinacy

---

[65] Bardy, *Théodoret de Cyr*, 201.

[66] Duchesne, *Histoire*, 3:382.

[67] Ibid., 3:283.

far from bringing any solution will beget nothing but trouble for the Churches and deliver to the wolves, avid for raw flesh, the people of whom we are the shepherds. We know very well those who are waiting for our departure and who will be here to replace us. Thus, it is to be feared that this excessive rigor of ours needs to be expiated before God if we are thinking only of that which concerns our own persons and do not consider the good of the greater number" [Syn. 239 (151)]. In a further letter written the day after his meeting with John, Theodoret stated: "We have even found a way to satisfy the purity of your conscience, one capable of preserving it from every hesitation" [Syn. 254 (168)]. Theodoret elsewhere declared [Syn. 256 (168)] that he was on his knees begging him to "approve the decisions which have been taken in common" with the bishops of the two Cilicias and Isauria who had already entered into communion with John.

It is obvious this submission of Theodoret's was not an act of surrender. He himself mocked the "versatile ones," the "chameleons." He, more than anyone else, was personally and fully engaged both by his ideas and by the eminent role he played at the time of the council. Thus, if anyone had reason to be reticent about the negotiations destined to render reconciliation possible, it would have been he. However, Theodoret, deeply pious, was conscious of his deficiencies. He put aside his pride in his wish to put an end to a conflict which bitterly divided the church. Theodoret wrote that "if he did not intend to renounce the ideas he had defended at Ephesus as well as at Chalcedon, in the presence of the Emperor, and was very much determined not to do anything in contradiction with his past attitude, it is also incontestable that he did not at all want to risk hindering the negotiations by his actions in any way whatsoever" [Syn. 183 (95)]; [Syn. 149 (60)]; [Syn. 150 (61)].

From 438 to the Council of Chalcedon

The peace thus reached more or less held up until 446. A first serious threat occurred in 438 when Cyril, following the agitation provoked in Armenia over the writings of Diodoros of Tarsus and Theodore of Mopsuestia, published a book against them which today is lost. Theodoret, charged with replying, wrote a work in which he took up in detail the argumentation of Cyril and endeavored to demonstrate the fundamental orthodoxy of the two Antiochian doctors.[68]

A few years passed, during which there was a change of generations; the protagonists of the Nestorian crisis disappeared one after the other. In Rome, Saint Leo succeeded Sixtus III in 440. John of Antioch died in 441 or 442 and was replaced by his nephew Domnus. Cyril of Alexandria died on 27 June 444.[69] He was succeeded by Dioscoros, a controversial figure. Although he was possibly raised to the See of Alexandria because he was Cyril's nephew, he was not in Cyril's class for knowledge, wisdom, and sincerity.[70] Proclus died in 446, and was replaced in the See of Constantinople by Flavian, whom Bardy considers, probably correctly, to have been a "calm and moderate man . . . who wished only for peace and the good of the church. The most we can say is that he was more inclined to the formulas of the Orientals than to those of Cyril. In any case, was it not those of the former rather than of the latter that had in a certain sense consecrated the edict of the union of 433?"[71] Nestorius was now forgotten in his distant exile.

Of all the players in the Nestorian crisis, only Theodoret remained active and prominent.[72] The situation of the Eastern churches was now appreciably better than it had been after the Council of Ephesus, or even after the peace of 433. The government had rid them of Nestorius, and had thus done them a very great service, whatever their opinion of the matter might be. The divisions between them had come to an end. All the Syrian bishops were gathered around Domnus, the patriarch of Antioch who was inspired by the ideas of his uncle John, but was more determined. It seems that the circumstances allowed this. Edessa no longer supported Cyril's position, since its bishop Ibas (Hiba) held the same views

[68] Azéma, 1:21ff.

[69] See Duchesne, *Histoire*, 3:390.

[70] Camelot, *Éphèse et Chalcédoine*, 85; Duchesne, *Histoire*.

[71] Bardy, *Théodoret de Cyr*, 4:209.

[72] Camelot, *Éphèse et Chalcédoine*. See the complaints written by the clergy of Alexandria and presented at the 3rd Session of Chalcedon; Bardy, *Théodoret de Cyr*, 208, n. 2.

as Theodoret, views expressed in writing after the peace of 433.[73] Theodoret was now considered to be the greatest theological authority of the East; having inherited the mantle of Diodore and Theodore, he purged it of elements that could not be assimilated, and maintaining an impartial attitude, seeking only the vindication of what he considered to be the true Christian tradition.

Theodoret set the tone around him. Even if there were unresolved tensions between Alexandrine formulas and Eastern applications, the Easterners had come closer to the ideas which were to prevail in Rome. Theodoret's theological accomplishments were indisputable. He possessed a great intellectual culture, eloquence, and consequent popularity in Antioch.[74] Another sign of the state of minds and of the security in this region was the elevation of Count Irenaeus, Nestorius's old friend, to the episcopal dignity and to the position of Metropolitan of Tyre.[75] Moreover, relations between the Easterners and the bishop of Constantinople were excellent. Friendly exchanges provoked the annoyance of the patriarch of Alexandria, ever jealous of the privileges of his seat. He strongly reproached the Easterners, saying: "You are betraying the rights of Antioch and of Alexandria."[76]

When Proclus died in 446, he was replaced by Flavian, who, as we have seen, was more inclined than Proclus to the Eastern formulas, and so, perhaps for this reason, was deeply disliked by Dioscoros. There was relative calm until 448 when Eutyches, an elderly monk of Constantinople, archimandrite of a monastery of over three hundred monks, who remembered Ephesus, and was of the anti-Nestorian and pro-Cyril party, challenged Theodoret's orthodoxy. Theodoret was first to raise the alarm, in the three books of his *Eranistes*.[77] However, Eutyches was powerful: he was popular in the

[73] Duchesne, *Histoire*, 3:393; see also autobiographical details in Ep 81; Azéma, 2:193–94.

[74] Marcel Richard, *Notes sur l'évolution doctrinale de Théodoret*, in *R.S.P.T.*, 25 (1936): 459–81.

[75] Azéma, 3:38–39, n. 1; on Irenaeus, see Azéma, 1:29–30; Tillemont, *Mémoires*, 15:263–68; and Pauly-Wissowa, *realenc.*, 5:2136; *D.T.C.*, 7, c. 2533ff.

[76] Ep 86; Azéma, 2:231. Duchesne, *Histoire*, 3:395.

[77] On the "Eranistes," see Camelot, op. cit., 87–88; Bardy, *D.T.C.*, 15:1, col. 305; Saltet, *Les sources de l'Eraniste*, in *R.H.E.*, 6 (1905): 289–300, 513–36, and 741–54; Richard, *R.S.R.*, 14 (1934): 57.

monastic world, and had Alexandrine contacts, being the sponsor of the eunuch Chrysaphios, who since 441 completely dominated the weak Theodosius, and directed the affairs of state. Dioscoros saw in Eutyches an ally in his struggle against the Easterners. Theodoret paid dearly for his work, being severely admonished by the imperial government, and seeing two decrees issued against him. One ordered him to stay in his bishopric on the pretext that he organized too many synods in Antioch,[78] while the other forbade him to attend the planned council. As for the seat of Tyre, Irenaeus was replaced by a certain Photius.[79] Eutyches, believing that Rome would not oppose them, wrote to Pope Leo to incite him against what Eutyches described as reborn Nestorianism, but was disappointed in Leo's noncommittal reply.[80]

Then, in an unexpected turn of events, Eutyches, denounced by Eusebius of Dorylaea, was declared a heretic and deprived of the priestly state in a synod presided over by Flavian on 22 November 448. The emperor, partisan to Eutyches, now called a council which was prepared by Eutyches's friends. Theodoret was told not to take part,[81] while his notorious adversary, the Syrian Archimandrite Bar Sauma, was expressly requested by an imperial letter of 14 May to represent the archimandrites and monks of the East. Dioscoros was appointed president of the council.

The council adopted some rather questionable tactics, stealing the papal document "tome to Flavian," intimidating some and silencing others. As a result, Eutyches was rehabilitated, while Flavian, Eusebius, and Theodoret of Cyr, and with him the main representatives of the school of Antioch, were all deposed as being Nestorians. The council solemnly accepted Cyril's anathemas.[82] Theodoret, meanwhile, was personally safe. Ironically, in his faraway see, he was out of reach of the hostile monks. Soon, however, Pope Leo spoke in his favor.[83] Theodoret, never indifferent

[78] Epp 79–82; Azéma, 2.
[79] Duchesne, *Histoire*, 3:402, n. 1.
[80] Letter of 1 June 448, ibid., 402.
[81] ACO, 2, 1.1:68–69.
[82] Marrou, *Nouvelle Histoire*, 1:394–95.
[83] Duchesne, *Histoire*, 3:420; Canivet, *Thérapeutique*, 1:22, n. 2.

or inactive when something important happened in the life of the church, did the only thing he could: he wrote.

Deposed at Ephesus on 22 August 449, Theodoret was only reinstated in October 451 by the Council of Chalcedon. During the intervening twenty-six months, he resided mostly in his monastery in Apamaea, in exile, but sent letters all around the world. Unfortunately, we have only thirty-five letters from this period. Never was his firmness, courage, perseverance, and tenacity, sometimes even ardor, so clearly in evidence.[84] He acted, he wrote, from "an acute sense of duty," "a great love for souls," and a passionate concern for truth and justice.[85] After the death of Theodosius, Theodoret wrote to Romulus, bishop of Chalcis (ep 135) that he was "a fighter who does not stop fighting before the triumph of what he believes to be the truth. . . . What one must not do is to alter one's speech according to circumstances, for one must always stick firmly to the truth." As Azéma states, that which expresses the condemnation of opportunism appears in his letters as the constant rule in his actions and in his life.[86] He was, in short, a man of principle.

"This truth," wrote Theodoret in 448 to Flavian, bishop of Constantinople, "is stronger than anything because it can triumph even with weak means." He firmly believed that the "injustice plotted against him by the enemies of truth" was capable of "erasing the numerous stains caused by his sins."[87] Theodoret considered himself to be struggling selflessly for the truth. This sustained him, for the struggle bore its own reward. As Saint Paul understood, the truth generates inexhaustible energy and passionate zeal: "even if those who struggle for piety are not given any reward, the truth in itself shall be enough to persuade those who love it to embrace with the greatest joy the perils which they face for its sake."[88]

[84] Ep 146; Azéma, 3:199.

[85] Epp 133, 146; Azéma, 3.

[86] Epp 3, 77, 78, and 57; Azéma, 2. Azéma studied Theodoret's personality in depth: from it we have drawn much of our information about the personality of Theodoret.

[87] Ep 82; Azéma, 2:227–33 and n. 1.

[88] Ep 21, 71; Azéma, 2 (referring to Rom 8:18). Energy and zeal were needed to struggle endlessly against heresies, lies, informers, slanderers and against

Convinced of the rightness of his cause, and acting in self-defense, Theodoret appealed to the pope after the death of Theodosius, and the palace revolution. Theodoret also called for the convocation of a new council, believing that it would undo the work of the "robber council" of 449, and restore his standing.

Far from being content with the banishment of Eutyches and the change in religious politics favoring the Eastern party, Theodoret wrote to three influential notables in the early months of 451: the patrician Anatoles,[89] the patrician Aspar,[90] and the master of the Vincomal offices.[91] Letters 138, 139, and 140, the last we have of Theodoret, deserve to be attentively studied, since they deal with Theodoret's later role at the Council of Chalcedon. In fact, nothing is left to us of his correspondence after the Council of Chalcedon except some passages from the letter to John of Egaea.[92]

These letters can be studied together not only because they are contemporary (dating from the early months of 451) but also because they bear the same objectives of first, seeking the convocation of a new council to erase the stains of the first, and second, thanking "the glorious Emperor and friend of Christ" and Pulcheria, "the very pious Augusta," for having interceded with Marcian. Through their intercession, justice was done to Theodoret and the imperial order exiling him was lifted.[93]

It is to be noted that these personages were among the most influential of the period: Aspar was the strong man of the empire,

---

those who, driven by mania or wickedness, sought to mislead others. Ep 59–60; Azéma, 1. Ep 21, 81; Azéma, 2. Ep 104, 109, 113, 143; Azéma, 3.

[89] Azéma, 1:48ff., n. 1; on Anatoles, see ACO, 2: 1, 2, 69, n. 1; Pauly-Wissowa, *realenc.*, 1:2072.

[90] Azéma, ibid.; Theophanes, *P.G.*, 1.108, c. 249 B.C.; on the Arianism of Asparsee Theophanes, ibid., 239, A.

[91] Azéma, 1:51, n. 6.

[92] In the fourteenth century Nicephorus Callistus could still read more than 500 letters of Theodoret. Today there only remain 231, not even half the collection! Almost all date from the years 431–37 or the years 444–51, which shows the enormous gaps in our documentation. The most regrettable loss is certainly the correspondence after the Council of Chalcedon. Of the letters that he wrote at this time tradition has preserved four short fragments of the one he addressed to the Nestorian John of Egaea, Richard in *R.S.P.T.*, 30 (1941–42): 415ff.

[93] Bardy, *Théodoret de Cyr*, 226.

the patrician who made Marcian and Leo emperors.[94] Although
Aspar was an Arian, he recommended Theodoret's cause to his
friend Marcian when he came to the throne. Anatoles, the first
imperial commissioner to the Council of Chalcedon, the "magister
militum" and the "magister praesentalis," had been Theodoret's
friend for a while. Finally Vincomales was master of offices and the
fourth imperial commissioner named in the Acts of the Council of
Chalcedon.

In his letters, Theodoret forcefully laid down the conditions the
new council would have to fulfill. It should not again be composed
of argumentative and factious persons, and in particular, not with
those who "have formerly caused trouble and provoked a scandal
in Ephesus."[95] Theodoret here was referring not only to Dioscoros
and his acolytes, but also to the monks of Constantinople and Syria
who were the principal authors of the disorders in the assembly.
On the contrary, it should be composed of "judges . . . who attach
great importance to divine issues and who consider the truth more
valuable than all the riches of this world . . . of peaceful Bishops
who are instructed in divine matters, of men who strengthen
the doctrine of the Apostles and reject impure beliefs that are
contradictory with the truth . . . (and) of those who are enamored
of the truth, men who are willing to support the teachings of the
Apostles and to publicly reject this new heresy." Theodoret added
that if the authorities wanted to restore the church to its former
peace, they should implore the pious to attend the debates in order
to demonstrate by their presence that the truth will not encounter
any obstacles, and that the churches themselves will examine the
facts and decide whether the doctrine proposed was truly apostolic.

Finally, he declared, the only thing he wished for was an official
acknowledgement of his orthodoxy, and a condemnation of the
errors of his adversaries. This concern for the triumph of the truth
was indisputably of primary importance for him. Around the end of
450 or the beginning of 451, at a time when his hope of entering Cyr
promised to become an imminent reality, he wrote to John, bishop of
Germanicia, in clear precise terms that in spite of intending "to run

[94] Azéma, 3:148, n. 1.
[95] Azéma, 3:147.

away from the worries caused by these affairs," he would not do
so "unless the lies are refuted and truth triumphs."[96] Once more we
see that Theodoret was not a man who believed in half-measures or
in equivocal situations when high interests of faith and the respect
of truth were at stake. In fact, several months later the Council of
Chalcedon abrogated the work of the Council of Ephesus of 449,[97]
and fulfilled Theodoret's proposed conditions. Wishing to attend
the debates of the council in person but occupied with affairs of
state, the emperor Marcian decided to move the council already
announced to take place at Nicea in Bythinia to Chalcedon, so that
even if public business kept him in the capital, he could be present
at the sessions. Measures were taken to ensure that the followers
of Eutyches and other agitators would not create any trouble.[98]

The Council of Chalcedon

In the first session, Paschasinus, representing Pope (later Saint)
Leo, declared, on Leo's instructions, that "Dioscoros should not
have a seat in the Council and if he tried to find himself one, he
should be expelled from the session."[99] Thus Dioscoros, no longer
judge, but now the accused, left his place to come into the middle
of the assembly, and legal proceedings began against him. The letter
of Theodosius II, forbidding Theodoret from attending the Council
of Ephesus, was exhibited. When the secretary read it, he added:
"Things have changed since then, our pious Emperor Marcian has
ended the exile of the most reverend Bishop Theodoret and, at his
request, the Most Holy Pope Leo has given him back his title of
bishop; thus he can be present here." The imperial commissioners,
among whom were Anatoles and Vincomales, offered Theodoret
a seat in the assembly. When he entered the basilica to take his
seat, a tumult arose in the assembly: the followers of Dioscoros,
that is to say, the bishops of Egypt, Illyria, and Palestine, cried out:
"Mercy! The faith is lost! Get out of here master of Nestorius." The

---

[96] Ep 134; Azéma, 3:129.
[97] Marrou, *Nouvelle Histoire*, 1:395.
[98] ACO, 2, 1:1, 29–30 (22 Sept.); Camelot, *Éphèse et Chalcédoine*, 120–21.
[99] ACO, 2, 1:1, 65.

Easterners and the bishops of Pontus, Asia, and Thrace replied with a cry: "Get out of here Dioscoros, it is the assassins of Flavian who should be expelled." Dioscoros, standing up, roared as he pointed to Theodoret: "He has anathematized Cyril; is Cyril to be cast out now?" The commissioners tried to calm them but the tumult grew even stronger. The Easterners shouted: "Theodoret is worthy of attending this assembly." "We all demand," shouted the Egyptians, "for the sake of religion and of orthodox faith, that you chase away one man and we shall all listen." The commissioners replied negatively and remarked that these "plebeian" shouts were not worthy of bishops nor helpful for the parties in question.[100] This alone indicates the great influence that Theodoret was to have on the Council of Chalcedon. Subsequently, Dioscoros would be deposed, and Theodoret proclaimed "master of orthodoxy."[101] From the acts of this council, two salient facts are of interest: the similarity of views between the Easterners and the Roman Legates, and Theodoret's influence in the elaboration of the dogmatic definition.

The Identity of Views between the Easterners and the Legates

Following the question of attendance, attention shifted to the doctrinal divergences which divided the assembly: should it be said that Christ is "*of* two natures" or "*in* two natures"? Palestinians, Egyptians, and Illyrians were opposed to the theology held by both the Easterners and Pope Saint Leo, as disclosed in his letters. At the beginning of the fifth session, the patrician Anatoles asked that the formula of faith elaborated at the patriarchate of Constantinople be read. The majority applauded, but objections were heard from among the Eastern bishops, supported by the Roman legates.[102] Paschasinus put an end to the equivocation: there should be a clear pronouncement on the two natures.

The assembly from then on became tumultuous, and angry shouts were heard: "Go away Nestorians," meaning the bishops of the East.

[100] Duchesne, *Histoire*, 431.

[101] ACO, 2, 1:1, 66–70.

[102] Canivet, *Thérapeutique*, 1:57; Camelot, *Éphèse et Chalcédoine*, 152–54. Duchesne, *Histoire*, 440–41; Camelot, *Éphèse et Chalcédoine*, 1:132–34.

It was announced that Leo agreed with Cyril and that all should cling to the text proposed. It was a dramatic moment. The representative of the emperor proposed the setting up of a commission composed of six bishops from the East, three from Asia, three from Pontus, three from Illyria, three from Thrace and the Roman legates. Upon the invitation of the emperor, the designated bishops retired to the oratory of Saint Euphemia to finalize the definitive writing of the formula of faith. The task was difficult but the legates and the Easterners insisted on using clear terms. The difficulty resided in the fact that they were opposed to the general sentiment favoring ambiguity and equivocation, and only the Easterners of ancient style or Nestorians, as it was commonly said, supported them wholeheartedly. The like-mindedness of the Easterners and legates was even more marked when it came to the condemnation of the "robber council" of Ephesus (AD 449), and the rehabilitation of Domnus, Theodoret, and Ibas.[103] When the commission entered the basilica, the seated bishops listened in silence to the solemn definition which had been elaborated with such difficulty. It contained the clear and precise formula, "one person *in* two natures."

For Msgr. Duchesne, this was a victory for the Easterners and a consolidation of their union with the See of Rome. Thus, he says, the Eastern term "two natures," strongly repugnant to Cyril, was not only tolerated but imposed as a rule of faith. Nestorius's old friends, particularly Theodoret and Ibas, who figured among the leading adversaries of Cyril, were welcomed, reinstated, and reintegrated in the sees from which Dioscoros's sentences and Theodosius II's police had driven them.

"What can be clearer?" concluded the Monophysites. "Nestorius has taken his revenge. The bishops of Chalcedon and their instigator Pope Leo are no more than Nestorians. What a comedy! They anathematized Nestorius and canonized his doctrine."[104] The legates attested this union between the Roman legates and the Easterners, particularly Theodoret, "although Theodoret had expressed his opinion and signed," says Tillemont, "in favor of Constantinople (canon 28 of Chalcedon); this was entirely opposed

---

[103] Duchesne, *Histoire*, 444–45.
[104] Ibid.

to the sentiments of the legates of Saint Leo, but they did not fail to maintain a favorable opinion of him."[105] Once they were back in Rome toward the end of April 452, these same legates expressed to the pope the good opinion they had formed of Theodoret. Leo wrote him a long letter, expressing his esteem, adding that the only form of gratitude the Roman church asked of him for his reinstatement was his continuing defense of the whole church with the same purity and courage for which he had been and was still admired, and to strive to extirpate what remained in the East of the heresies of Nestorius and Eutyches. However, we know very little of what Theodoret did after the Council of Chalcedon.[106]

The Influence of Theodoret in the Elaboration of the Dogmatic Formula of Chalcedon

Theodoret played a dominant role in the Council of Chalcedon, insisting on precision in the christological vocabulary. Analyzing the sources of the formula of Chalcedon, Camelot noticed that the first part of the definition is taken in its entirety from the letter of John of Antioch to Saint Cyril (said to have been written by Theodoret) and that Cyril himself had copied it in his reply to John. This letter was read and approved by the council, and so came to be included in the definitive document. On the other hand, the second part is less homogeneous, comprising a collection of passages from Saints Cyril and Leo, from Flavian and Theodoret.[107] Charles Moeller, who agrees with M. Richard, sheds more light on the elaboration of the formula of Chalcedon. This defines the faith by the expression "two natures inseparably united in one prosopon and one sole hypostasis."[108] By expressing itself this way, the council draws on

---

[105] Tillemont, *Mémoires*, 15:211–12.

[106] ACO, 2:4, and 78–81, n. 71, Leo epist. 120 J.K. 496. *Nuovi studi*, in *Gregorianum XII*, 373 s, 567ff.; also *Textus et Documenta*, P.V.G., n. 20, Pars secunda, 169ff. and introduction, 34. Schwartz reproduced this letter of Saint Leo in his critical edition. C. Silva-Tarouca has cast doubt on its authenticity.

[107] Camelot, *Éphèse et Chalcédoine*, 141.

[108] Richard, *La lettre de Théodoret à Jean d'Égées*, R.S.P.T., n. 30 (1941–42): 415–33. For the wording, see ACO, 2, 1:3, 129; Mansi, *Sacrorum conciliorum*, 7, c. 116; Bardy, *Théodoret de Cyr*, 235.

the two traditions, Antiochian and Alexandrine, for the expression
"two natures inseparably united" was certainly Theodoret's. It
is also found in the critique of the anathemas quoted by Cyril
himself.[109] But the addition of the final term "one sole hypostasis" is
not of Antiochian inspiration and seems to be deliberate, "since the
text of the Tome of Leo, which served as a basis for the discussions,
speaks only of 'two natures, two substances and one person.'"[110]
The council thus officially consecrated the coming together of two
traditions.[111]

In order to prove the definition of Chalcedon was not uniquely of
Antiochian and Roman inspiration, Charles Moeller has recourse to
the letter of John of Egaea, who, being scandalized by the addition
of the term "one sole hypostasis," refers to Theodoret, who was
indisputably the greatest theological authority in the East. Through
his reply, Theodoret unmistakably implied that he was behind this
concession from the Easterners, and that he well understood the
theological significance of this new terminology.

John of Egaea was a strict Dyophysite of Nestorian tendency. He
saw in the word "hypostasis" an ambiguity implying the confusion
of natures. The reply of Theodoret, of which a part is conserved, is
the first known theological explication of the formula of Chalcedon.
John thought φύσις meant ὑπόστασις: "What is then the unique
hypostasis of the flesh and the divinity, tell me? Is it simple or
compound, visible or invisible, of the same essence (οὐσία) or of
a different one? Or is it obvious that it is composed and that it is
composed of natures which are not similar to one another?"[112]

In his reply, Theodoret affirmed that the unity of the hypostasis
does not beget the unity of nature or of essence (οὐσία) but means
only the unity of the person (πρόσωπον). It seems that, in order to

[109] *P.G.*, 76:437C; Bardy, *Théodoret de Cyr*, 191, 195–96; Charles Moeller, *Ne-phalius d'Alexandrie* 1 in *R.H.E.*, 11 (1944–45): 111–12.

[110] Moeller, *R.H.E.*, 114, n. 3; Bardy, *Théodoret de Cyr*, 220, n. 1.

[111] Even before the Council of Chalcedon we found the formula of the one
sole hypostasis, of the hypostatic union, and even of a conscious bringing
together of the essential formulas of Cyril and of Theodoret. Richard, *R.H.E.*
38 (1942): 303–31; Moeller, *R.H.E.*, 113, n. 1, 2, 3; 114, n. 3.

[112] See the excellent article of Richard, ibid.

justify in Dyophysite Christology this similarity between the terms (ὑπόστασις-πρόσωπον), he appealed to Trinitarian terminology.[113]

Moeller summarizes the position thus: "We see then in Theodoret two things which were soon to become the basis of neo-Chalcedonianism: the equivalence of prosopon–hypostasis and the spreading of the Trinitarian terminology to Christology, the whole in a Dyophysite system. Theodoret was the initiator of these two new ideas: we consider this one of his finest titles deserving our respect. This fact dissipates all the doubts which might still hang over his orthodoxy."[114]

If the actual formula μία ὑπόστασις seems to be unknown to Theodoret himself and to the school of Antioch during the period of Chalcedon, Theodoret maintained, however, that the definition of 451, of which he was one of the authors, imposed a broadening of the terminology. In this, Theodoret revealed the same broad-mindedness as Cyril. By bringing together hypostasis and prosopon, and explaining nature through essence by means of the Trinitarian terminology, Theodoret pointed to a path, which was to be taken by all Chalcedonian and neo-Chalcedonian Christology.[115] His attitude here is analogous to that which he had maintained in 433 toward Cyril: without admitting himself the Alexandrine terminology, he knew how to acknowledge the same faith under a different vocabulary. But here he goes even farther since he acknowledges the formula "one sole hypostasis" and explains it.[116] Of this, Richard opined: "Theodoret knew how to break, when he deemed it necessary, with the narrowness of tradition without however adopting a contemptuous attitude towards those who found it difficult to do so. In this is undoubtedly the act of a great theologian."[117]

---

[113] Moeller, *R.H.E.*, 115, n. 4. One of the tasks of the neo-Chalcedonian theology was precisely to achieve the total unification of terminology, at Alexandria as well as among the Antiochians. The identification made at Chalcedon between "person" and "hypostasis" which led to this unification is explained by Theodoret.

[114] Ibid., 116–17 and n. 2.

[115] Charles Moeller, *Le Chalcedonisme et le néo-chalcedonisme en Orient de 451 à la fin du VI s.*, in *Daz Konzil von Chalkedon*, 1:659.

[116] Moeller, *Nephalius*, 116–17.

[117] Richard, *Notes sur l'évaluation doctrinale*, 1 in *R.S.P.T.*, 25 (1936): 481.

The Monks and the Hierarchy During the Christological Crisis[118]

The Monks and the Hierarchy

Initially, monasticism was no different from the perfect Christian life. The Christian trained himself to lead a more perfect life in the world, and then he began seeking solitude, often attracting disciples who were then organized into a community. Separation from other Christians seems to have occurred very slowly, and the question of special monastic education and theological studies was raised only later. Consequently, monks had frequent contact with people who, admiring their heroic acts of mortification, and their complete detachment, held them in high esteem.[119] But this prestige and esteem did not always guarantee good results, especially during the christological quarrels when some of these monks took advantage of their standing. As mentioned above, being mostly drawn from the people and without any serious theological education, they were not especially qualified to intervene in such complex and delicate problems as those which were then being debated on the subject of the incarnation.

Following the lamentable Nestorian crisis, in Syria as in Egypt, the monasteries and the hermitages were the most ardent centers of this agitation. In them, one was for or against the sentence of the

---

[118] For this part, see Festugière, Antioche; H. Bacht, *Die Rolle des Easternischen Mœnchtuns in den kirchenpolitischen Auseinandersetzungen um Chalkedon* (431–519), in *Das Konzil von Chalkedon* (1951–54), 2:193–314; O. Hendriks, *L'Activité apostolique des premiers moines syriens*, in *Proche-Orient Chrétien*, 8 (1958): 3–25; Eugène Matrin, *Les moines de Constantinople* (Paris: Victor Lecoffre, 1897); J. M. Besse, *Les moines d'Orient antérieurs au concile de Chalcedon* (Paris, 1900), c. 17, *les moines et les discussions théologiques*, 397–410.

[119] The principal texts will be found in Festugière, op. cit., 247–52, 287, 400, 410–23; Hippolyte Delehaye, *Les saints stylites* (Brussels: Société des Bollandistes, 1923), 67ff.: "People came from quite far away and in groups to hear what they had to say and to receive their blessing. Even princes bowed before them or consulted them. Similarly bishops recommended themselves to their prayers, came in delegations to their hermitages and asked for support in their struggle against heresies and maintaining the unity of the Church. In a word, these monks enjoyed great prestige as a result of their asceticism."

council and the anathemas of Saint Cyril. Passion was heightened by the fact that, given the inability to clearly capture the meaning of the theological formula, the conflict was effectively reduced to antagonism between persons.

At Constantinople, even before the meeting of the Council of Ephesus in 431, it was noticed that the local opposition rallied around the monks, for these had been ill-treated and humiliated by Nestorius.[120] They desired the proposed council and prepared themselves for it. When they were due to travel to Ephesus, Cyril provided the bishops with the escort of a considerable number of the lower clergy, and, above all, monks. Among these was the renowned Shnoudi, almost a centenarian who had come from his monastery in the Upper Nile. All were devoted body and soul to Cyril. After the council of 431, an anxious Cyril used all available means,[121] exploiting the prestige of the monks of both Egypt and Constantinople. Among the most influential monks of the capital was the abbot Dalmatius, who for forty-eight years had not left his monastery. From time to time, the emperor traveled there to see him. Dalmatius did not like Nestorius, and Cyril was well aware of his sentiments. A letter was sent to him in secret, informing him of the situation, and outlining the help which Cyril expected from him. Dalmatius left his monastery, and headed for the imperial palace followed by a large crowd of monks. The sudden arrival in the streets of the capital of this long procession deeply impressed the people. The presence of another monk of great renown was also noticed, namely, Eutyches, who was known to be a great friend of Cyril. By the time these monks left the imperial palace, Theodosius II had been won over to Cyril's cause.[122]

At Chalcedon, just as at Ephesus, the Easterners had to take into consideration the hostility of the clergy; for example, the monks of Rufinianes, led by their abbot Hypatius, demonstrated against

[120] The details of this treatment are to be found in the letter addressed to the emperors Theodosius and Valentinian by several monks of the imperial city. See Mansi, *Sacrorum conciliorum*, 4:1101–7; Héfélé-Leclercq, *Histoires*, 2:357–60; then Mansi, *Sacrorum conciliorum*, 5:725; Duchesne, *Histoire*, 3:342–43.

[121] Duchesne, op. cit., 3:344, n. 2; Bardy, *Théodoret de Cyr*, 188, n. 2.

[122] Mansi, *Sacrorum conciliorum*, 4:1429; Héfélé-Leclercq, *Histoires*, 2:393.

them. At Alexandria just as in Egypt and Palestine, monastic
opinion was hostile to the Easterners, and everywhere they were
taken for Nestorians. A crowning misfortune came in the hostility
of the Syrian monks, which began to take shape when Bar Sauma,
Eutyches's famous friend and another favorite of Chrysaphios,
entered the arena. On 14 May 449, Bar Sauma had received an
imperial letter inviting him to the council. He was known both
for his austerity and fanatical zeal against the Nestorians—but he
understood "Nestorians" to be those who did not share Eutyches's
doctrine. To a substantial degree, he had represented the monks
and the archimandrites of the East at the council of 449.[123] It was
quite significant that Bar Sauma, who was not a bishop, should
have been called to that council. He was perhaps requested on
account of his personal authority, but also perhaps because the
turbulent monks whom he was expected to bring with him might
influence the assembly, as they did. His escort of one thousand
monks was fearsome, brandishing sticks and swords rather than
books.[124] The letter inviting the monk Bar Sauma to the council of
449 had followed the letter forbidding Theodoret's attendance.[125]

In its turn, the Eastern party, and Theodoret in particular, were
sensitive to such matters. They tried, when they could, to attract a fair
part of the monastic opinion to their side. But it seems that the monks
who remained faithful to this party were either small in number,
badly organized, or insufficiently turbulent and aggressive alongside
those supporting Cyril, Eutyches, and Bar Sauma. Rather, the most
famous among them, upon the insistence of the emperor, used their
influence to persuade the chiefs of the Eastern party to deal with Cyril
of Alexandria. Thus, in September 432, the emperor Theodosius II
sent the tribune and notary Aristolaus to Saint Simon the Stylite to
ask him to intercede with John, the bishop of Antioch, to subscribe to
Nestorius's deposition and to the condemnation of his teachings.[126]

[123] ACO, 2, 1. 1:71.
[124] Camelot, *Éphèse et Chalcédoine*, 94 and 109, and especially nn. 1 and 2.
See also ACO, 2:78; 4:27.
[125] ACO, 2, 1. 1:68–69.
[126] ACO, 1, 4:91, 2; Honigmann, *Patristic Studies*, 94; Festugière, *Antioche*,
419, n. 3.

In the spring of 434, the emperor had used the influence of the Syrian monastic celebrities, Jacobus, Simon, and Baradatus, to bring recalcitrant individuals, especially Theodoret and Alexander of Hierapolis, back into communion with John of Antioch, as we have already seen. During this period, Theodoret one day saw at his door the tribune Eurycianus, bearing Count Titus's letters to Theodoret and to the monks, and letters from the monks to Theodoret. Troubled and shaken, Theodoret wrote to Alexander: "These letters threatened that if I did not agree to make peace [with John of Antioch], I would be deposed soon and another consecrated in my place. I laughed at these threats. But the holy monks deeply hurt me with their long petitions in favor of peace. It was as if they were accusing me. Full of anger and taking these missives with sorrow, I was ready to leave the town and the province to seek refuge in the monastic life. They were deeply saddened and promised to go with me as far as Gindaros and to persuade the bishop of Antioch to come there to meet me and to talk with me."[127]

Peeters[128] and A. J. Festugière[129] consider that Theodoret was deeply hurt by this intervention of the monks. However, like Richard, we have our doubts. The letter was written by Theodoret to Alexander of Hierapolis, his inflexible metropolitan, and Theodoret had probably decided to meet John. Certainly, Alexander had this impression. In any event, already anticipating what his reaction would be, Theodoret "must have been highly embarrassed about reporting these first discussions to his ferocious Metropolitan. Without accusing him of insincerity, it seems to us that he must have been very happy to insist on the pressure of the monks and his protests."[130] The intervention of these celebrated Syrian monks, far from causing difficulty between them and Theodoret, gave the latter an opportunity to get out of an embarrassing situation. Being accustomed as he was to the subtlety of correspondence, he wrote

---

[127] ACO, 1, 4:170/33–171/5, *Théodoret, lettre à Alexandre*, Coll. Casin., 2:234 (146) (synodicon), translation by Festugière, *Antioche*, 420; Honigmann, *Évêques*, 100.

[128] Peeters, *Tréfonds*, 99.

[129] Festugière, *Antioche*, 1.

[130] Richard, *R.S.R.*, 3–4 (1946–47): 155.

this letter so as not to compromise himself in the eyes of the rigid bishop of Hierapolis.

As the intellectual leader of the Eastern party, Theodoret took the initiative to remain in continual contact with the monks of his party to inform them of the great events taking place in the church, and, if need be, to seek refuge with them. He did not allow any occasion or means to pass to instruct them, revive their courage, raise their prestige among others, and make known their sanctity in order to buttress their position against the spokesmen of Egyptian monasticism who used all of their considerable reputation in support of Cyril's Christology.[131] This is probably why Theodoret wrote them so many letters of instruction, of which we now have unfortunately only a fragment. It was probably with the same aim in view that around 444 he wrote his *Religious History*.

Letters to the Monks of the East

Immediately following his return after 431 from a secret meeting held in Chalcedon after the Council of Ephesus, at which Theodoret had been chosen to represent the Eastern party, Theodoret wrote a letter "to the monks of Euphratesia, Osroene, Syria, Phoenicia and Cilicia," the title of which already gives an idea about the intention of the author. He painfully announced to them the final rebuff concerning the hopes the Eastern party had placed in the outcome of a contradictory debate. Cyril's delegation had refused any discussions concerning a doctrinal question which they considered as already settled. For his part, the emperor Theodosius II, in spite of the repeated attacks, had opposed the Easterners with an inflexible refusal. The only thing left was to return home, and to report (1432B). Theodoret wrote: "Having been unable, in spite of our efforts, to make them see the truth, we have come back to our Churches, discouraged but happy: happy because our conscience is clear and discouraged because the conscience of those whom we consider as our members is stained."[132] This was at the end of

[131] Peeters, *Tréfonds*, 101.

[132] A. D'Ales, *La lettre de Théodoret aux moines d'Orient*, in *Ephemerides theologicae lovanienses* (Louvain: Peeters, 1931). Tillemont speaks of another letter

431 or the beginning of 432, certainly before the opening of the negotiations which resulted in the signature of the Act of Union of 433.

Theodoret's other letters to the monks and archimandrites of Constantinople must have been written after 449. These were letters 128, 129, and 130, probably addressed from his monastery in Apamaea to Job, Candidus, and Magnus Antonius, all priests and archimandrites of Constantinople. He urged them to pray for him personally and for the good of the church. He showed his esteem for them because they had fought the good fight (ep 130) against impiety and for the doctrine of the Gospel (ep 138).[133]

Theodoret also wrote two letters to Marcel, abbot of the Acemetes, to whom he had never written previously, praising him for his devotion in favor of orthodoxy, especially on the occasion of his stand against Monophysitism at the Council of Ephesus in 449. Marcel had in fact struggled against Eutyches, participating in the councils at Constantinople in 448, at Ephesus in 449, and at Chalcedon in 451.[134] Theodoret also wrote to a monk in Constantinople named Andrew, whom he had never seen. He assured him that he deeply wished to meet him and receive letters from him because of all the good things he had learned about him. "Everybody admires the orthodoxy of your faith, the brilliance of your life, the steadfastness of your soul, the stability of your character, the appeal and the grace of your conversation . . . For your part, respond as soon as possible to my desire and give me the pleasure of a conversation by letter . . . You will not be writing to one who believes differently to what you do, but to a herald of the Trinity, not of the Quarternity."[135]

A final letter, by far the most considerable, was written to all the monks of Constantinople. In it, Theodoret gave an account of

addressed to the monks and composed around the same date, treating dogma and what had taken place in the councils and assemblies held at Ephesus, but it seems this letter is lost.

[133] Epp 128–30; Azéma, 3:107–11; shortly before this date, Pope Saint Leo had written a letter to this same Magnus, calling on him and the other abbots of the capital to remain true to the faith and united with the pastor Flavian, ep 51, *P.L.* 54:843–45.

[134] Epp 142, 143; Azéma, 3:153–59. On Marcel, see *D.T.C.*, 2:304–8.

[135] Ep 144; Azéma, 3:159–63. On Andrew, see Azéma, 1:39–40.

how he was condemned in his absence, falsely accused of sharing the errors of Arius, Eunomius, and Apollinarius. He explained in detail his doctrine of the incarnation of the Word and the unity of the person in Jesus Christ. His faith is that of all the fathers of the church, those of the East as well as the West, and particularly that of the "most holy Leo who now directs the great Rome, author of the tome to Flavian."[136] It is this unanimous chorus of voices heard simultaneously through time and space which represents for Theodoret the best guarantee for orthodoxy.

The Circumstances of Writing the Religious History[137]

The idea of writing an *apologia* for the monastic life as a perfect expression of the Christian life dated back to when Theodoret was a young monk in Apamaea.[138] But given the dramatic events which marked his life, the execution of this work may well have been tendentious. Therefore, Peeters, the eminent Bollandist, inquired as to the "end of the writing" of this work. Convinced of Theodoret's sincerity in his stated purpose of "having written for the glory of God and the edification of the Christian people,"[139] Peeters believed, however, that one cannot help conjecturing that some calculation must have been mixed with this zeal, a calculation perhaps responsive to special circumstances. The *Religious History* was in fact written around 444, that is to say, a relatively calm period requiring attentive vigilance. Cyril's days were numbered, for he died on 27 June 444. Of all the main actors of the Nestorian crisis, only Theodoret remained. Domnus, bishop of Antioch, had arranged for him a residence there, where he could feel at home, and freely meet his friends and faithful supporters.[140] Domnus had absolute confidence in this old fighter, and followed his advice so implicitly

[136] Ep 146; Azéma, 3:173–201.

[137] This has appeared under the title *Histoire des moines de Syrie*, ed. Pierre Canivet and Alice Leroy-Molingen, in *Sources Chrétiennes* 1:234, II:257 (Paris, 1977–79).

[138] Canivet, *Entreprise*, 40–41.

[139] Peeters, *Tréfonds*, 100.

[140] Glubokovskij, op. cit., 2 (Moscow, 1890), 412ff.

that later at the Council of Ephesus of 449, his enemies accused him of having totally abdicated his authority to Theodoret.[141] Everything seemed to favor Theodoret's religious policy, which was in the ascendant in the sees of Edessa (occupied by Ibas), Tyre, and above all, Rome. Pope Leo was known to entertain little sympathy for Cyril's terminology, least of all in the anathemas. In these favorable circumstances, Theodoret perhaps saw an opportunity to carry out his project of writing a "history" which would be at one and the same time an edifying work and a defense of Syrian monasticism.[142]

Greatly admiring these monks' heroism, Theodoret was an excellent candidate for writing such a book persuasively yet without ostensibly raising any controversial issues. All Theodoret had to do to promote orthodoxy was display these simple men as they were. Their works and fruits would do more than any overtly partisan tract. In doing so, he would assure these monks, so often misunderstood and belittled by comparison with those of Egypt and Constantinople, greater prestige and confidence in themselves and in their own value. To this end, the theater of exploits was limited to northern Syria, that is, the area between Cyr and Apamaea, the Euphrates and the Mediterranean.[143] Further, its heroes were chosen from those figures most famous for holiness, but above all for their orthodoxy, to the point where one may detect throughout the chapters of the *Religious History* a subtle line of Antiochian religious politics, as Festugière has demonstrated in the instance of Marcian. Significantly, Theodoret passed in silence over some famous monastic figures, ignoring some great figures in Syrian monasticism: this must have been deliberate. For example, Theodoret does not even mention Rabbula, who was a monk in Chalcis, then bishop of Edessa in 412, and one of the first to have laid down the monastic discipline. Theodoret's silence is eloquence itself: Rabbula was a serious adversary of the Antiochian theology after the Council of Ephesus, and promoted Cyril's theology in Syria. Neither does Theodoret mention Alexander, the founder of

---

[141] Ibid., 160–61, quoted by Peeters, *Tréfonds*, 100.
[142] Similarly, see Peeters, *Tréfonds*, 100.
[143] Festugière, *Antioche*, 255ff.; also Cavallera, *Schisme d'Antioche*, 215ff.

the Acemetes: he had quarreled with Flavian, bishop of Antioch.[144] Theodoret also failed to mention Jerome, who had been a monk at Chalcis but did not have a good word to say about his colleagues, who were all held in veneration by Theodoret.

Seen in this light, the book, simply through its subject matter, its laudatory uncritical treatment of those included, and its omission of others, was more than merely an *apologia*, although it certainly was that. It also promoted the claims of Syria against those of Egypt. So it is that in Theodoret's chapter on Simon, the apology concerning stylitism, which has surprised scholars, is no longer seen to be a pointless digression, if we consider that it was directed against the oracles of Egyptian monasticism, all zealous for Cyril's Christology. The overall tendency of the work is clearly shown in Theodoret's insistence on the "orthodoxy of Marcian," and his respect for "ecclesiastical decrees"; the complete detachment of the disciples of Maron, their spirit of mortification, of contemplation, and their noninterference in the affairs of church and of state, unless at the request of the authorities and for the sake of peace.

These various indexes are all of great interest. Only a few years separated this book from the Council of Chalcedon, and in Theodoret's assessment, monasticism needed to be brought back or be kept faithful to orthodoxy and to respect authority.[145] To Theodoret, the monk's path was clear: coenobitism, which had been noisily involved in the religious quarrels, needed reorganization. Above all, it needed new elements necessary for a true monasticism. When the time came, Theodoret would, we contend, think of gathering the disciples of Maron, who until then were still separated, and if not exactly disunited, did not possess the strength which an organizational unity would afford them. Theodoret in fact brought them out of obscurity, to make of their exemplary lives one of the most beautiful pages of the religious history of Syria; and Theodoret alone could bring them out of their

---

[144] After having founded a monastery on the borders of the Euphrates, Alexander, founder of the Acemetes, tried in vain to establish a second at Antioch. 15 January, 2 (Paris), c. 6:308.

[145] Canivet, *Théologie*, 282.

state of dispersal, grouping them together in a monastic community which would bear the name of their great master Maron.

Theodoret and the Monastic Legislation of Chalcedon

Monasticism and the Church according to Theodoret[146]

In his *Commentary on the Song of Songs* written at the beginning of his career as an exegete, Theodoret gives the priesthood a place of exceptional importance in the church: it is "the face of the Groom" (Christ). As for the monks, a certain ambiguity surrounds their situation because the author does not distinguish yet between a vocation based on precepts and one based on the counsels.[147] On the other hand, in the *Religious History* written around 444, Theodoret attached considerable importance to charismatic gifts, to the manifestation of the Spirit which acts freely in souls, outside any institution: this is the charisma of the anchorite monks "which finally also make of them apostles and living images of Christ. This is why, even while being laymen, they have considerable authority and intervene in private, civil and ecclesiastical affairs," but always in total harmony with the hierarchy and even at the request of authority. Theodoret emphasizes these traits without, however, marking out the opposition between Spirit and institution, for "whatever the place and the influence that Theodoret accords to the monks, the Priesthood which is the face of the Groom occupies the predominant place in the *Religious History*." However, since Theodoret hardly gave any indication of the monks' precise priestly functions, whether from the point of view of the liturgy, or jurisdiction, or even the ministry, the respective positions of the priest and the monk remained imprecise.

But if the respective positions of the priest and of the monk remained vague in Theodoret, the episcopate always held pride of place. In a page from *Discourse on Charity*, Theodoret, who had reluctantly become a bishop, justified the custom of choosing

[146] Ibid., 274–82.
[147] *In Cant.* (*P.G.* 81:60, B-C; 64, D; 80, C), quoted by Canivet, ibid.

bishops from among the monks, a custom which had grown from the end of the fourth century. He went so far as to write that, if it is for the better service of the church, one may aspire to the episcopate.[148] "We shall not be surprised then," says Canivet, "that Theodoret insists so much on the respect and submission that the ascetics . . . show towards the bishops. Before them, silence and the cloister give way."[149]

When there is a bishop among the crowd pressing around the pillar of Simon, the Stylite calls on the bishop to bless the pilgrims,[150] and a hermit asked for the blessing of Theodoret when the latter was still only a young lector.[151] Finally, a bishop can make himself obeyed when the superiors have failed, as happened in the case of an archbishop of Antioch with Simon Stylites.[152] Theodoret provided multiple examples of bishops who controlled the anchorites, imposing some modifications in their way of life.[153] It is as if Theodoret wished to discreetly vindicate the episcopate's authority of these virtuous and charismatic monks, who had an aura of inviolability, and seemed to belong to a category parallel to the priesthood. If Theodoret, for example, reported without any apparent reserve that monks performed exorcisms, he nonetheless implied that the custom of blessing the oil was an abuse; and it was soon to be forbidden to lay monks.[154] On many occasions, Theodoret stressed the monks' fidelity to "ecclesiastic discipline," and their devotion to the cause of orthodoxy, as we have seen above.

The texts collected and studied by Canivet in his excellent article "Theodoret and Syrian Monasticism before the Council of Chalcedon" shed light on Theodoret's conceptions on this point

[148] *Discourse on Charity*, *P.G.* 82:1508 D-1512 A, Canivet, ibid., 280, n. 242.

[149] *H.R.* 1428 A, 1461 C, 1464 VC, 1492 A.

[150] *H.R.* 1476 C.

[151] *H.R.* 1397 A.

[152] *H.R.* 1472 B-C.

[153] *H.R.* 1392 B; 1397D-1436, C; 1485 C. It will be noted, observes Canivet, that a good number of these cases occurred in Theodoret's diocese.

[154] "Whether one be priest, bishop or one vowed to the monastic life, one must submit to those to whom power has been confided." *Com. ad Rom.* 13:1, in *P.G.* 82:193 B, Canivet, ibid.; epp 141–42; Azéma, 3:153–59, to Marcel, Abbot of the Acemetes.

up until 444–45. But after Eutyches and his monks' intervention, and that of Bar Sauma and his monks, and the calumnies directed against Theodoret and Domnus, Theodoret, discreet and skillful as ever, was perhaps more inclined to stress the inherent opposition between Spirit and institution.

Theodoret wrote to the consul Nomus that personally he "really likes tranquility more than those who want to rule over the Churches while being in the monastic state."[155] To the consular and patrician Aspar, to the patrician Anatoles and to Vincomales, the Master of the Offices, he sent a request that they act in such a way that the new council should not be filled with "a bunch . . . of those who, being used to tumult, would trouble the assembly" as they had previously done at the Council of Ephesus of 449. He even asked the Roman legates to inform Pope Leo of the insolence of certain monks whose incessant preaching had troubled the church.[156] The pope took these observations into consideration. He wrote on 10 June 453 to Maximus, bishop of Antioch, asking him not to allow any monk or layman, no matter how learned, to involve himself in instructing and preaching, because there had to be order in the church and each member had to carry on his own function.[157] At the same time Leo wrote to Theodoret, telling him that he had already written about the subject to Maximus.[158] On 2 April 453, the pope wrote, making the same remark to Julian of Cos, his nuncio at Constantinople.

Prior to Theodoret, his friends had revealed a stronger and more categorical reaction. Nestorius complained strongly about the authority which Eutyches enjoyed at that time: "As he was not a bishop, he gave himself another role, thanks to the Imperial authority, that of the Bishop of Bishops. It was he who directed the affairs of the Church and he used Flavian (the Bishop of Constantinople) to execute the orders of the court. . . . He expelled as heretics those who did not share his opinion. As for those who helped him, he raised them up and gave them assistance."[159] More categorical and

[155] Ep 81; Azéma, 2:195.
[156] Labbe, *Concilia* (Paris, 1671), col. 6:627; Tillemont, *Mémoires*, 311.
[157] ACO 2, 4, n. 66; *Textes et documents*, P.U.G., n. 20, 2:108–12 (2, 6, 453).
[158] ACO 2, 4, n. 71; *Textes et documents*, P.U.G., 169–75.
[159] *Le livre d'Héraclide*, trans. F. Nau., 294–95; Camelot, *Éphèse et Chalcédoine*, 89.

expressive still is Alexander of Hierapolis's letter to Theodoret about
the intervention of the Syrian monks for reconciliation with John of
Antioch. "It is hard for me to bear the indiscreet interference of the
monks in our affairs," he wrote to Theodoret. "Were they to resurrect
all those who had died since the beginning of the world, I would
only ask that, if they agreed with us, they should pray for us; if on
the contrary they condemn us, may God spare them! For they do
not have more authority than the angels of heaven and the choir of
apostles whom Christ anathematized through the voice of Paul if
ever they dared to preach a Gospel other than his."[160]

Such was the conception of Theodoret and the state of mind of a
great part of the Eastern episcopate before the Council of Chalcedon.
This was undoubtedly to have repercussions, influencing the
monastic legislation of Chalcedon, especially after the incidents
of the fourth session and the arrival of Bar Sauma, who, in
disobedience, had stirred up all of Syria against their opponents.

The Legislation of Chalcedon

The assembly of Chalcedon, like that of Nicea, had not only to
resolve questions of faith, but also to take important disciplinary
measures completing the edicts which the emperor Marcian had
caused to be approved by the council at the end of the fourth session
on 25 October 451. Following the minutes of this *actio sexta*, the
Greek manuscripts of the Acts of the Council preserved under the
title of *actio septima*, a series of twenty-seven "ecclesiastical canons
pronounced by the Holy and Ecumenical Synod assembled at
Chalcedon."[161] We shall trace here the spirit, the meaning, and the
impact of the meaning and the measures taken regarding the monks.

[160] Festugière, *Antioche*, 422ff.

[161] The complete text of the canons of Chalcedon may be read in ACO, 2: 1,
2, 158–63; Héfélé-Leclercq, 2:2, 770–828, text and translation; Camelot, *Éphèse et
Chalcédoine*, 228–33, translation; for the legislation of Chalcedon, see Ueding Von
Leo, *Die Kanones von Chalkedon in ihrer Bedeutung für Moenchtumund Klerus*, in
Daz Konzil von Chalkedon, 2:569–676; Schiwietz, op. cit., 1 and 3; H. R. Bittermann,
"The Council of Chalcedon and Episcopal Jurisdiction," *Speculum* 13 (1938):
198–203; P. De Meester, *De monachico statu iuxta disciplinam Byzantiniam statuta
selectis fontibus et commentariis instructa* (Città del Vaticano, 1942).

The Historical Context

The legislation was passed to prevent quarrels such as those in Edessa, where some of the clergy had plotted against Bishop Ibas, or in Ephesus, where there was dissension between the bishops Bassianus and Stephen. Of greater concern were the violent protests over jurisdiction in Nicea or in Berytus (Beirut). There is no doubt that Chalcedon sought to strengthen the bishops' authority over these clerics.[162] Here, we shall limit our study to some of the more recent incidents which, according to most historians, were the direct inspiration for the measures taken at Chalcedon regarding the monks. However, the minutes of the fourth session of the council of 451 reveal that the fourth canon relating to the monks was a response to Eutyches and Bar Sauna, and their monks, who had withdrawn from the jurisdiction of their bishops, whom they accused of Nestorianism.[163]

During this session the Catholic archimandrites and those of Eutyches's party were brought before the council.[164] The presence of Bar Sauma among the latter provoked indignation. "There he is," said Diogenes, bishop of Cyziques, "this Bar Sauma, the assassin of Flavian." And all the bishops shouted: "He is the one who caused a revolution in all Syria, he is the one who stirred up against us a thousand monks. His name does not figure on the petition to the Emperor. Why did he come in here? Outside with you, you homicide."[165] In fact, Bar Sauma's name did not figure on the list among the archimandrites of Eutyches who signed the letter to the emperor Marcian.[166] This petition was signed by eighteen names followed by the title "most humble archimandrites." But after examination in a public session, it was determined that all signatories, except three, Carossus, Dorotheus, and Maximus, had usurped the title.[167] A letter was also read, in which eighteen

---

[162] Camelot, *Éphèse et Chalcédoine*, 158.

[163] Héfélé-Leclercq, *Histoires*, 3:104; ACO, 2, 1: 2, 116.

[164] ACO, 2, 2: 2, 115, n. 76; Mansi, *Sacrorum conciliorum*, 7:65; Héfélé-Leclercq, *Histoires*, 3:50.

[165] ACO 2.2. 1: 2, 116, n. 76; Mansi, *Sacrorum conciliorum*, 7:68.

[166] ACO 2, 2: 115–16, n. 76; Mansi, *Sacrorum conciliorum*, 7:65.

[167] ACO 2, 1: 2, 114–15, nn. 61–64; Mansi, *Sacrorum conciliorum*, 7:61–64; Héfélé-Leclercq, *Histoires*, 3:50.

Catholic archimandrites had written to the emperor, praising him for his zeal in favor of orthodoxy, and asking him to treat those monks who persisted in their errors with the strictness required by the monastic rule and to put their monasteries at the disposal of the orthodox.[168] After reading the letter, Carossus and Dorotheus wrote a petition in which the Eutychian monks sought Dioscorus's rehabilitation, declaring that if their request were refused, they would go into schism. This manifesto was perceived to be insolent and evoked a storm. When calm had been restored, Actius, the archdeacon of Constantinople, produced the canons of Antioch against those clerics, summoning them to condemn Eutyches and to accept the Tome of Leo. But they absolutely refused to condemn Eutyches and to profess "a faith other than that of their baptism and of the Council of Nicea." This same business took up another session on 20 October: "If within thirty days the monks in question do not submit to the decisions of the Council, they shall be deposed and excommunicated, and excluded from their rank, dignity, and the management of monasteries."[169]

Bar Sauma refused to submit. He left Chalcedon and returned to Syria, where he never gave up spreading the Eutychian doctrine.[170] Carossus and Dorotheus, upon Leo's request, were sent away from their monasteries.[171] To forestall recurrence of the troubles, the council laid down several canons to restore regular discipline to the monastic order by making the monks absolutely dependent on the bishops. Canons 3, 4, 5 were decreed by the council at the request of the emperor.

The Meaning

The aim meaning of this legislation, and particularly that of the fourth canon, was that the monastic life should be honored

[168] ACO 2, 1: 2, 119–20, nn. 101–5; Mansi, *Sacrorum conciliorum*, 7:76–77.
[169] Camelot, *Éphèse et Chalcédoine*, 131–32.
[170] *Kirchenlexicon*, art. *Bar Sauma*; according to Héfélé, Bar Sauma died in 454 in exile at Gangres in Paphlagonia, also Mansi, *Sacrorum conciliorum*, 6:293.
[171] Mansi, *Sacrorum conciliorum*, 1, ibid., 304, 305; epp 141 and 142, dated 13 March 455; Héfélé-Leclercq, *Histoires*, 3:153.

and respected, but on condition that it was authentic. This meant that the monks should keep the *hesychia*, that is to say, the calm and peace for which solitude and asceticism prepare the soul and so dispose it for contemplation; and in connection with this, remain in the place where they renounced the world, and dedicate themselves to fasting and praying. The monks were not to have secular responsibilities, not to wander in the towns, engage in the affairs of church and state, and were to be obedient to the bishop in every town or province.

Further, and significantly, the founding and building of new monasteries now required the authorization of the regional bishop. That bishop had a right to exercise the necessary oversight (*pronoia*) of all the monasteries of his bishopric.

No sanction was indicated in this imperial project;[172] however, the council took miscellaneous steps, and added: "if anyone transgresses this edict, he shall be excommunicated."[173]

The Import

It seems these measures went beyond the scope of a simple disciplinary legislation to take on the aspect of a monastic reform, one undertaken conjointly by the civil power and by the fathers of the Council of Chalcedon. In fact, the two phases of this reform are clearly expressed by Emperor Marcian in his discourse pronounced during the opening of the sixth session. The fathers later laid down these two phases canonically during the seventh session. The questions involved all concerned the purification of the religious life. They sought to expel those not devoted to the religious life, who troubled church and state, who visited the towns and built themselves monasteries. Monks were henceforth to meditate, fast, pray, remain in their monasteries, and become involved in ecclesiastical or secular affairs only when their bishop asked them to.[174] Following the example of Constantine, the emperors who succeeded him on the

---

[172] Mansi, *Sacrorum conciliorum*, 7:173, 360.

[173] Mansi, *Sacrorum conciliorum*, 7:176, 360–65; Héfélé-Leclercq, *Histoires*, 3:107–17; Camelot, *Éphèse et Chalcédoine*, 229–32.

[174] ACO 2, 1:2, 158ff.; Camelot, *Éphèse et Chalcédoine*, 229, c. 4.

throne of Byzantium claimed the right to interfere and decide in
theological matters that in no way involved the obedience due to
the civil authority. Marcian went so far as to interfere jointly with
the council in prescribing canonically measures that concerned
the civil police as much as they concerned ecclesiastical discipline.
Moreover, before the Council of Chalcedon, the founding and the
establishment of monasteries had not been regulated by law. As
this was outside ecclesiastical control, individuals or groups of
individuals had been free to act as they saw fit. It was at Chalcedon
that the church, supported by the state, for the first time undertook
to settle the question.[175] Seen in this light, this "legislation reform"
has a double interest: it efficiently contributed to maintaining order,
peace, and orthodoxy in the empire and particularly in Syria; and
it strengthened the bishops' authority, reserving to them the right
to authorize the foundation of new monasteries and to exercise
supervision over these.[176]

The foundation of monasteries, then, would henceforth be tied to the
approbation of the bishop, and also the consent and the liberality of the
emperor or the civil authority. Marcian considered himself responsible not
only for maintaining order and peace but also for upholding orthodoxy
and the decisions of the Council of Chalcedon, which may indeed have
been two aspects of the same thing.

The founding of the monastery of Maron near Apamaea, made necessary
by contemporary events and by the monastic reform, therefore, depended
on the will of the emperor as well as that of the bishop of Apamaea, as
was made clear by Abū l-Fidā. Domnus, the then bishop,[177] is known
to us through the signature of his representative Paul of Emesa
at the two councils of 449 and 451 and through a letter written to
him in 448 by Theodoret of Cyr.[178] Domnus was a member of the

[175] B. Granic, *L'Acte de fondation d'un monastère dans les provinces grecques du*
Bas-Empire au V et VI s, in *Mélanges Ch. Diehl*, 1 (Paris: E. Leroux, 1930), 101.

[176] Ibid., 102; for the monastery as a legal person and its juridical charac-
teristics in the law of the late empire, Knecht, *System iustinianischem Kirchen-*
vermogensrechtes, 50; CUQ, *Manuel des instituions juridiques des Romains* (Paris,
1928), 116; Salleiles, *L'Organisation juridique des premières communautés chrétiennes*
(1912).

[177] Devresse, *Patriarcat d'Antioche*, 181, n. 4; Azéma, 1:33, n. 3.

[178] Ep 87; Azéma, 2:233.

Eastern party but seems to have played a rather unassuming role. He sent a representative to the Council of Ephesus in 449 and to the Council of Chalcedon. At the first council, his representative, under pressure of the assembly, approved the condemnation of the chiefs of the Eastern party and of Theodoret. Ever since 448, Theodoret had been blaming Domnus for this passive attitude, writing around the summer or autumn of 448: "The law of brotherly love demands that at this time we should receive many letters from your piety. However, I have received none."[179] At this point, Theodoret was most in need of support. But the monks of his monastery had helped, having recently gone to see Theodoret in Cyr with the priest Elias of the monastery of Apamaea. Hence, the monks of Apamaea remained on friendly terms with Theodoret even in the most critical moment, when he was confined to his diocese and when the bishop of Apamaea was wary of intervening. This cannot have been a simple courtesy visit. At a time when most monks favored Eutyches and Bar Sauma, Theodoret could count on the fidelity of the monks of Apamaea and Cyr, despite the fact that until then the latter had lived separately and completely isolated from the others.

So, when Theodoret was obliged to leave his diocese, he went willingly into exile in that monastery which had received him when he was young. "Numerous" faithful friends left the town with him. Of these we know only the name of a priest-doctor named Peter.[180] In this solitude of the monastery of Apamaea, Theodoret spent, as we have seen, twenty-six months rich in controversy, after which he received the order to come to Chalcedon, where he was to play his significant role. *It was probably during these twenty-six months that Theodoret, the monks of Apamaea, and some disciples of Saint Maron conceived the idea of a new foundation having for its principal objective the sanctification of souls and the defense of what this old fighter believed to be the truth according to the Antiochian tradition and the Chalcedonian formula.*

Being fully and personally committed more than anyone else both because of his ideas and the eminent role he had played up till then,

---

[179] Ibid., 233–34.

[180] Ep 116; Azéma, 3:69: "but now that we leave the town, others also—and many of them—leave this town." See also epp 114 and 115.

Theodoret could not help but think seriously of providing a sound, stable, and sure element for the continuation of this role. Thus when the appropriate moment came, we conjecture, it was his first concern to suggest and support this idea. Such is the impression left upon reading the history of these events and the Monophysite and Maronite documents relating to the christological quarrels in the sixth and seventh centuries.

In addition, this was the impression made on the Bollandist P. Peeters, who was, however, guided by other concerns than ours. "Hostility to the Monophysite doctrines had old roots here [in the surroundings of Apamaea]. Two secluded from Cyr, Simon and Agapetus, had founded two important monasteries located approximately three miles to the south of Apamaea at a place called Nikertai, where they introduced the discipline and observance of their master Marcian. Afterwards Agapetus became Archbishop of Apamaea. Theodoret had lived there in his youth and it was there that he retreated when it became impossible for him to stay in his diocese. His spirit and his observance seem to have remained very much alive there."[181] Peeters was undoubtedly unaware of the document discovered and translated in part by F. Nau; otherwise he would have reached the same conclusion.

Almost around the same period, that is to say, at the beginning of 451, a time when the hope of returning to Cyr was becoming an impending reality, Theodoret declared to John, bishop of Germanicia, that "once the lies have been refuted and truth has triumphed, we propose to flee the worries of affairs [running of the bishopric] and return quickly to the quiet life that is so dear to us."[182]

Unfortunately, as so little evidence has survived from after the Council of Chalcedon, we have no idea of how and where this great man ended his days. Even the date of his death is not certain. Gennade of Marseille says that Theodoret wrote his ten books (we only have five) of the *Ecclesiastical History usque ad Emperium Leonis Senioris, sub quo mortuus est.*[183] We know that the emperor Leo reigned from 454 to 474. Canivet says that "after the Council of Chalcedon, Theodoret continued to write some books on controversies and

---

[181] Peeters, *Hypatius et Vitalien*, 26.
[182] Ep 134; Azéma, 3:129.
[183] *De scriptor. eccl.*, c. 89, in *P.L.* 58:113 B.

exegesis. But he gradually withdrew into obscurity. According to an allusion contained in the dedication of his Commentary on Genesis, which is one of his last books, his health deteriorated. He undoubtedly died between 458 and 466."[184]

---

[184] Canivet, *Thérapeutique*, 1, 23, n. 2; for his health troubles, *in Genesim* (*P.G.* 80:76 A 9-10).

General Conclusion

At the end of this study, which has run into so many diverse areas, we must consider whether the study admits of a coherent solution to our question of Maronite origins and the Maronite relationship with Antioch. Let us briefly retrace our steps, and seek a synthetic vision.

If at the time of the Crusaders, let alone the Ottomans, the Maronites had already succeeded in forming a structured dynamic ecclesiastical community, it was because their origins went further back in history. The first question is chronology: at precisely what date did the Maronite community take form? The second is interpretation: which factors played a decisive role in that community's appearance? Third is religious identity: how does the Maronite Church justify its individual existence within the church as a whole? What fundamental conviction, or theological principle, apparent or hidden, animates it? Is it the depository of a new mission, of a hitherto unannounced word that it is destined to proclaim?

Perhaps prior even to this, we must say a word about the historian's general methodological principles. It would be futile to study the present state of the Maronite community to find definitive answers to historical questions. As for religious identity, from the very fact of its constant evolution, the conclusion we draw today will probably be denied tomorrow. Thus, we are forced to abandon this shifting ground and to seek truths. According to Soloviev, "the idea of a nation is not what it thinks of itself in time but what God thinks of it in eternity!"[1]

---

[1] Vladimir Soloviev, *L'Idée russe* (Paris: Perrin et Cie, 1888), 6.

Such a conception is not incompatible with historical research; on the contrary, it helps us to better decipher the historical events. God, Maronites believe, has spoken to mankind both directly through his Son, and also indirectly, through prophets, Scripture, and the church, but also through historical events. Providence even uses human intrigues, making them all converge toward the realization of this plan. Being essentially theological, history is finally reduced to a continuous revelation in the sense that God's will and providence reveal his plan.

Such is our vision of history, and so we look for deeper causes, the causes for the continuing existence of the Maronites. This does not exclude, but rather includes, the norms of modern scholarship. Thus we have taken care to return to the most ancient sources which bear upon Maronite origins. The greater part of these documents have already been published but unfortunately not yet explored in a serious and thorough way. We mention in particular:

1. The *Philotheon Historia* or *Religious History* of Theodoret of Cyr (397–457?). This work, which we consider to be the prologue to the history of the Maronites, was published in the collection *Sources Chrétiennes*, no. 234 and no. 257.
2. The Correspondence of Theodoret of Cyr himself, already published in three volumes in the same collection, *Sources Chrétiennes*.
3. The Acts of the Council held between 431 and 536, namely, Ephesus I in 431, Ephesus II in 449, Chalcedon in 451, and the Synod of Constantinople in 536.
4. Some letters and treatises written or received by the monks of the monastery of Saint Maron in Syria Secunda in the sixth and seventh centuries. They were published by Nau. We have, however, insisted on consulting the manuscripts personally, to clarify certain points which have remained obscure until now.

To be both clear and precise, we have divided this conclusion into four sections.

I. First Section: The History of Monasticism in Northern Syria in the Fourth and Fifth Centuries

Between the years 370–80 two hermit anchorites, the monks Marcian and Maron, led a way of life which provoked the admiration of their contemporaries, the inhabitants of northern Syria. Marcian was distinguished by the moderation of his asceticism, prudence, and wisdom in the struggle to control his body, whereas Maron's celebrity was characterized by sacrifices without limit and extreme mortification. For Marcian, the ideal Christian life is simply an imitation of the life of Christ, who grew in wisdom and knowledge before God and men. Maron apparently could not imagine Christ except as crucified and suffering. His conception of Christ being such, Maron was inspired by it to impose upon himself a new way of life. He paved the way to "life in the open air" (*Bios hupaitros*) for all those who wished to practice asceticism: sleeping under the stars, with no mattress or blanket, supporting the rigors of the climate, the bitter cold of winter and the burning heat of summer. His only biographer, Theodoret of Cyr, wrote the following about him: "Being unsatisfied with ordinary practices, Maron invented others to accumulate all the riches of perfect wisdom" (1418-C). "He retired to a summit venerated by the pagans and he consecrated to God the temple that demons had possessed. There he settled near a small hut, which he himself had erected but rarely used" (1417 B-C).

Commentators unanimously consider Maron as the pioneer and the founder of ascetical life "in the open air." Saint Simon the Stylite later imitated this kind of asceticism. Maron's reputation for holiness brought him a great number of disciples, and made of him the spiritual master of a limited group of recluses, open-air anchorites, and all the Christians of Cyr. "It was Maron," says Theodoret, "who planted for God the garden which blossoms today in the region of Cyr" (1420A).

Marcian was no less famous, but by temperament he was more inclined to the missionary life. Thus, we see him sending his disciples, Agapetus and Simon, to Apamaea, entrusting them with founding in that region, which was not yet entirely Christianized, what we call today a religious order. Once more, Theodoret informs us of this. He states precisely that the two disciples went to Nikertai, not far from Apamaea, and brought there the angelic laws of

Marcian by building in fact two monasteries, which were to bear the names of Agapetus and Simon respectively (*H.R.* 1325 C-D). "There live today," wrote Theodoret around the year 445, "more than four hundred monks, athletes of virtue, lovers of piety, who through their sufferings will go to heaven. Those who established their rule were Agapetus and Simon, who themselves had taken it from the great Marcian; and from these monasteries there arose many other places of monastic retreat submitted to the same rule."

The question now arises as to the motives Marcian and his disciples had to install themselves in the region of Apamaea, which is about 150 kilometers from Cyr. Certain considerations were probably paramount. At that time Apamaea was known to be the metropolis of inner Syria, which was predominantly Aramaean. It was here, in this cultural and spiritual center, that the greatest number of Aramaeans were gathered, the original inhabitants of Syria. This fact made it more united and more Syrian than the capital Antioch. In fact, the cosmopolitan nature of Antioch resulted in the reign of Hellenic civilization there to the detriment of the Aramaic/Syriac culture. Recent archaeological research shows that it was only around the end of the fourth century that Apamaea was converted to Christianity. Until then, it was the meeting place for different cultures and civilizations coming from Judea and from the south through Emessa (Homs), from the north and from Asia Minor through Cyr, from the west and the Mediterranean through Antioch, and from the east through Beraea (Aleppo). During that time also, Apamaea had one of the most famous schools of philosophy, that of the famous Jamblicus, whose great influence was most probably one of the causes of the slow Christianization of these regions. The fact that the monastery of Nikertai was founded as a center of Christian mission is indicated by the fact that Agapetus, its founder, was afterwards appointed bishop of Apamaea. In addition, Polychronius, the brother of Theodore of Mopsuestia, who succeeded him as bishop, was one of the eminent founders of the school of Antioch, who was of great influence in the town of Apamaea.

The monastery and its congregation progressively developed. The number of candidates for monastic life steadily increased. Among these was the young intellectual Theodoret, who tells us that after the death of his parents, he sold all he possessed, distributed the money among the poor, and went to the monastery of Nikertai, near Apamaea. He remained there for seven years, from 416 to 423, following the community life and spending his time in prayer, meditation, and study in a community of more than four hundred monks. During his stay in Nikertai, Theodoret gathered documents and began writing his *Religious History.*

In 423, while he was working in peace and solitude, he was forced, as he says, to take in hand the poor and mountainous diocese of Cyr. The Bollandist scholar P. Peeters reports that the metropolitan of Hierapolis and the bishops of his synod, all of whom were Syrian, insisted on employing the exceptional talent of the young monk. As Theodoret's letters show, the episcopate did not suppress his nostalgia for the monastic life and the wonderful memories of his brothers. When he was excommunicated at the Council of Ephesus (449), his only wish was to go back to his monastery. Then when circumstances were favorable, he dedicated to Marcian and the monastic movement of Apamaea one of the most beautiful chapters of his *Religious History.*

In Cyr, during his episcopate, Theodoret met other monks, different certainly from those in Apamaea as regards their way of life, but no less agreeable and friendly. He recounts how upon his arrival in Cyr, he found "a blooming garden" planted and cared for by the anchorite Maron. As early as the first days of his new mission, he took the decision to be at the service of these monks, to take care of each one of them, to be their elder brother; in a word, to take over from Saint Maron. They needed a shepherd of his caliber, scattered as they were almost everywhere in the region of Cyr and having no link between them but their love of God and their attachment to their spiritual master Maron. To obtain an idea of the importance that Theodoret attached to these monks, it is enough to note that of the thirty chapters of his *History*, he dedicated to them no less than thirteen.

As he discloses there, Theodoret had not known Saint Maron personally. He learned about Maron's virtues and qualities from his disciples, particularly from the esteemed hermit Jacob, with whom Theodoret conversed often. Theodoret repeatedly said that to this great hermit the words of the prophet David could be applied: "The righteous will flourish like the cedars of Lebanon." Theodoret turned to Jacob every time he had to face difficult trials, and counted on his prayers when he defended the faith from the heretical Marcionites. Theodoret was in the habit of calling Jacob his Isaiah, that is to say, his guide. When Jacob fell ill—and this happened often to the anchorites living in the open air—it was Theodoret in person who tended him. Theodoret did not hide this particular affection, speaking openly about it in his letters. The regard was mutual.

Moreover, it seems that all Jacob's peers found in him an extraordinary person. His popularity had grown to such an extent that Theodoret himself made use of it every time he went to see the Roman governor to ask him to relieve his flock, which was being crushed by taxation. Furthermore, Emperor Leo himself wrote in 457 to Jacob of Syria, called "the miracle worker," to ask him his opinion about the Council of Chalcedon and about Timothy Elures, "usurper" of the see of Alexandria. Leo wrote similar letters to Simon the Stylite and to Baradatus. It should be stressed that these were disciples of Saint Maron. This same Jacob, assisted by Simon and Baradatus, intervened to persuade Theodoret to join John of Antioch after the signature of the Act of Union.

Here then are the main features of the first section. In view of their importance for the conclusions that we later drew, it is useful to state them again in more condensed form.

Around the end of the fourth century, there lived in northern Syria two hermits, Maron and Marcian. Maron was the promoter of the eremitic movement for life in the open air, which from Cyr, its center, spread through the dependent mountainous region. Marcian founded at Nikertai a coenobitic monastic order, the rule of which was distinguished by a moderation favoring harmony between intellectual work and eremitic asceticism. He did this, one might say, by proxy through the intermediary of his disciples Agapetus and Simon.

In 416, a rich and cultivated young Antiochian man named Theodoret became a monk in this order and spent seven years there. Afterwards, being appointed bishop, he had to leave his monastery and give up his solitude to join his diocese among the mountains of Cyr, doing so unwillingly and regretfully. There, he had the opportunity of making the acquaintance more intimately of the disciples of Saint Maron, whom he encountered everywhere in his diocese. It was not long before he made friends with them and had affectionate, intimate, and respectful relations with them. He was on particularly good terms with their most senior member, the ascetic Jacob of Syria. This first section covered the period from 370 to 431, the eve of the Council of Ephesus.

II. Second Section: The Doctrinal Divergences and the Political Competition between Syria and Egypt

Until the end of the third century, the great bulk of the early church understood and lived their faith. The prevailing belief was that Christ was both God and man, the son of Mary, of the lineage of David. He was at the same time the Son of God, the Word incarnate. To answer objections raised by their adversaries, Christian thinkers were obliged to study more explicitly the mystery of the unity of Christ. However, the two ways, which seemed to give access to the understanding of this mystery, went in opposite directions. The first, having transcendence as its starting point, heaven in other words, or the Word made flesh, as the Gospel of Saint John conceives it, is characterized by the predominance of the divinity over the humanity. It leads to what is called Monophysite Christology. The second starts from the immanence, the earth if we dare say so, from the man who is the son of Mary and David to the Son of God. It draws its inspiration from the Synoptic Gospels and seeks to explain how the humanity and the divinity of Christ are only one. We call it, nevertheless, dualistic Christology.

The two approaches are legitimate on condition that one acknowledges the sound basis of the other and does not seek at any price to promote one system at the expense of the other. The fathers adopted both methods in their interpretation of the Holy Scriptures. The "unitarian" theology was more widespread, especially among the anchorite monks, probably because it is easier to understand and is more suited to the mystical spirit. It was preferred particularly by the fathers of Alexandria, to such a point that it was considered as the Alexandrine system. Clement, Origen, Athanasius, and Cyril all used this system, which gives much place to symbolism and interprets the Bible according to the spiritual meaning. We hardly need to add the influential role that philosophy played in the spreading of unitarian Christology.

The dualistic Christology developed only where Christianity was deeply marked by Semitic thought, Hebrew and Aramaic. It was precisely the fathers of the church of Antioch who were its promoters and supporters. Being positive in their turn of mind, the interpretation that they proposed of the Holy Scriptures considered only the historical meaning to the exclusion of the mystical meaning. Diodore of Tarsus, Theodore of Mopsuestia, John Chrysostom, Nestorius, and Theodoret of Cyr were representatives of this dualistic Christology.

These two approaches remained in force and were considered equally valid until 361 with the appearance of the bishop of Laodicea, Apollinarius, on the scene. Although of Syrian origin, he devoted himself to destroying Antiochian Christology. He took advantage of the friendship of Athanasius of Alexandria to accomplish his mission. Instead of signing his writings with his own name, he used that of his famous and influential friend. He, therefore, put into circulation his famous formula on the nature of Christ, "the one incarnate nature of the Word of God." It was to this famous formula that Cyril of Alexandria gave his approbation without any hesitation, while attributing it to Athanasius. He used it as a weapon against the Antiochian thinkers, and it was against this formula that the latter directed their attacks. Knowing full well who its author was, they found it difficult to pardon Apollinarius, their compatriot, for having deserted their camp.

Among the patriarchates of the Orient, Alexandria had long enjoyed a certain priority and privilege. It was an apostolic seat, a fact which gave it seniority. Moreover, through the previous centuries it had proven the soundness of its doctrine, and had been intransigent and tenacious in the face of heretics. Triumphant in all trials, it had overcome the Arian crisis with the aid of Athanasius, its great mentor. While Alexandria was jealous for its own glory, and confident in its ability to neutralize Antioch, a combination of circumstances suddenly gave rise to another rival, Constantinople, which became the seat of the Roman emperor. The prestige of its bishop steadily rose, to reach its peak in 381, when Constantinople came to be called "the New Rome." From this moment, the disagreement between these two large cities became a fierce and open struggle. This happened because Constantinople chose its bishops from among the monks of Antioch, who were mostly illustrious disciples and advocates of the dualistic Christology.

Exasperated and jealous, the bishops of Alexandria attacked, and attempted directly to interfere in the religious affairs of Constantinople. We shall consider only two important events. First was the conflict, around the end of the fourth century, between Theophilus, patriarch of Alexandria, and Saint John Chrysostom, the learned Antiochian monk. In 398, John was nominated patriarch of Constantinople. We shall not elaborate here on the odious intrigues of Theophilus to oust Patriarch John and send him into exile.

The second event was the debate, which lasted through the fifth century, between Cyril, nephew of Theophilus, and Nestorius, a former Antiochian monk who became patriarch of Constantinople. The incidents of this lengthy debate deserve to be reported in more detail since, in our opinion, it was the direct cause of the building of the monastery of Saint Maron in the vicinity of Apamaea and of its attachment to the monastic order founded by the disciples of Marcian.

In 428, having learned of Nestorius's homilies as the new bishop of Constantinople, Cyril of Alexandria was indignant. He organized a coalition against Nestorius and worked relentlessly to involve the other patriarchates. Pope Celestine approved Cyril's line, and charged him with rectifying the error. Patriarch John of Antioch asked for time to allow him and his bishops to try and persuade Nestorius to renounce his views. The conflict seemed to be moving toward a peaceful solution, when suddenly Nestorius received from Cyril a letter, "The Anathemas," and the quarrel was aggravated. The Antiochians recognized in this letter the style and the controversial spirit of Apollinarius, the ex-bishop of Laodicea. Theodoret was responsible for the refutation, which turned out to be decisive. In fact, Cyril's letter itself lay open to attack. It insisted excessively on the existence of only one nature in Christ and herein lay its weakness, since such an error was no less serious than that of Nestorius, who put too much stress on the separation between the two natures. As we have seen, in 431 the First Council of Ephesus was held. The two schools of Antioch and Alexandria were represented by Theodoret, bishop of Cyr, and Cyril, bishop of Alexandria, respectively. They were the two most brilliant theologians of the period. In 433, a joint declaration, the "Union Formula," seemed to have put an end to the discord. While this famous "Union Formula" was of Antiochian inspiration, it did not fail to include expressions favorable to a better and deeper understanding of Alexandrine thought. Thus, an agreement was reached, and both sides exchanged compliments, where each acknowledged the merit and the learning of the other. This agreement clarified and developed many theological concepts, producing even some uniformity in terminology. Yet, it was only a lull.

Years passed, and many of those who had played important roles in the Nestorian tragedy passed away. Leo the Great, who was attracted by the Antiochian Christology, succeeded Pope Sixtus III. In 442, John of Antioch died. His relative and successor, Domnus, was confident of Theodoret's knowledge and abilities, and made him his counselor, submitting to him doctrinal questions for judgment. Domnus built Theodoret a house in Antioch, where he could organize meetings with his friends and associates. In 444, Cyril died, and was succeeded by his relative, Dioscorus. The most important survivor now was Theodoret, who noticed that the general opinion in monastic circles was inclined to the Alexandrine theology, perhaps due to Cyril's influence.

This can be understood if we remember that the unitarian Christology favors mystical contemplation and rapture; and that thanks to Saint Anthony, Thebaid and Alexandria were in the eyes of the monks the cradles of monastic life and therefore holy places. They were constantly inspired by them in their mystical and ascetic methods.

III. Third Section: The Role of the Monks in the Doctrinal Struggles between Antioch and Alexandria

As we have seen, during this period of calm, Theodoret seized the opportunity to give concrete expression to his ideas in a well-structured book: the *Religious History*. It was effectively more than a history of coenobitic life in northern Syria, for Theodoret's intention was to consolidate the seriously threatened unity among his monks, to make them rediscover their moral value, and regain confidence in their vocation and local traditions. This would reduce the monks' enthusiasm and leaning toward Cyril's doctrine and everything imported from Egypt. It is enough to read the title to see that it is basically a claim for the rights of Syria usurped by Egypt. The author mentions in his book only the Syrian hermits who lived in a single stated and well-defined region: Cyr, Apamaea, Antioch, and Hierapolis. It was this same region which was later to become the first cradle of those who were to be called "Maronites." On the other hand, the author does not deal with all the hermits of Syria. It is no accident that he concerns himself only with those who lived according to the Antiochian plan and principles. They are all natives of Cyr, Apamaea, and Antioch. It was they also who, after the Council of Chalcedon, were to form a solidly united group. Their seat was to be Apamaea, the town that was particularly distinguished by the purity of its patriotism. Their objective was the defense of the Chalcedonian doctrine elaborated by the work of the Antiochians, especially that of Theodoret himself.

Theodoret wrote his book around 445, that is to say, after the death of Cyril. In 448, Eutyches appeared, superior of the monks of Constantinople. Already an old man, and a friend of Saint Cyril, he had rallied to the unitarian Christology and had much influence in the capital and in particular with the emperor Theodosius II. Dioscorus of Alexandria hastened to help him. Two other bishops retaliated immediately, Flavian, bishop of Constantinople, and Domnus, bishop of Antioch. It was natural that the last two would make use of Theodoret. He, in turn, set to work and wrote a three-part book titled *Eranistes*, in which he refuted Eutyches with a rarely equaled logic and dialectic.

Theodosius II was anxious to support Eutyches and Dioscorus; he therefore decided to hold a second council in Ephesus. We have seen how carefully the council was stacked against Theodoret, its decisions, and also how Pope Leo refused to approve the council's conclusions, which he described as the "brigandage of Ephesus." He also nullified the excommunication of Theodoret, at the same time declaring his acceptance of Theodoret's opinions and doctrines. Theodosius II, however, did not yield. He issued a second order sending the bishop of Cyr into exile. Theodoret replied that he preferred to go either to Rome to be judged or to his old monastery in Nikertai. The emperor agreed to the second proposal, which was put into effect. In one of his letters, Theodoret says, "he was escorted by a great number of his friends and followers."

Those two years from 449 to 451 at Nikertai, not far from Apamaea, were to be the most fertile of his life. He wrote a considerable number of books and letters. Upon the death of Theodosius II (451), a sudden political shift occurred. The orthodox general Marcian seized power, and banished Eutyches. Then he gave orders for Theodoret and his followers to be recalled from their exile, who now demanded a new council in which the errors and aberrations of the Ephesus Council of 449 would be eradicated. Marcian agreed to this request. Thus, on 8 October 451, the Council of Chalcedon was held not far from Constantinople. We have covered this above. Concerning this council, we have to consider two important points related to our thesis:

1. Modern historical research has established that the canon of the Chalcedonian faith was formulated according to the directives and under the influence of Theodoret in agreement with Pope Leo the Great's legates, who on a number of occasions showed some reserve concerning Cyril's expressions. Further, Theodoret probably deserves credit for introducing into the Chalcedonian creed the term "hypostasis" (of Alexandrine usage), making it the equivalent of "prosopon" (person). In doing so, he paved the way for neo-Chalcedonianism, a system which would attempt to coordinate the respective expressions of both schools so as to unify the language. It is one of Theodoret's claims to fame and deserves our greatest respect. This same neo-Chalcedonianism was adopted by the monks of Apamaea and particularly by those of the monastery of Saint Maron.

2. The monastic reform desired by Emperor Marcian was decreed by the council in its sixth session, which was attended by the emperor and his wife Pulcheria. After having thanked the Lord for having established concord and peace in the empire, Marcian threatened to punish severely whoever dared to cause new doctrinal problems, be they clergy or laymen. He then proposed three projects to the bishops, of which the two main points were as follows: (1) the founding of any new monastery comes within the competence

of the emperor and the local bishop, and (2) all monks would be submitted to the authority of the bishops.

The council approved these plans and drafted the rules of the monastic reform to stamp out the centers of unrest and insecurity in the empire created by the monks who had followed Eutyches and Bar Sauma. These rules viewed the monastic reform under two aspects, one positive and one negative. Positively, they promoted monastic life, and negatively, they eliminated the subversive elements and replaced them with men dedicated to peace, meditation, and continuous prayer. The council had barely come to an end when Marcian began to issue a series of orders to hasten the execution of these decrees. *On 28 June 452, the monks of Bar Sauma and Eutyches were the object of a measure forbidding them to meet or build new monasteries, requisitioning those which they already had, together with their property, and mandating them to leave all the regions of the empire.*

Also during the year 452, the emperor gave orders to build a monastery in the vicinity of Apamaea, which he named the monastery of Saint Maron. Abū l-Fidā, governor of Ḥamah, tells us: "During the second year of his reign (452), Marcian gave orders to build the Monastery of Maron in Ḥoms."

IV. Fourth Section: The Circumstances of the Founding of the Monastery of Saint Maron

The founding of this monastery by a special order of Marcian (451–57) is therefore nothing other than a first stage of the plan elaborated by the emperor with the help of the bishops of the Council of Chalcedon to maintain peace in the empire and at the same time support the Chalcedonian doctrine. As we have seen above, the evidence converges to this conclusion. The monks of the new monastery were distinguished by the importance they attached to prayer, fasting, and control of the passions. It bore the name of Maron, their pioneer. They devoted themselves equally to studies,[2] learning, prayer, contemplation, and the practice of asceticism.

[2] In 718, the monastery of Saint Maron had one of the largest libraries in Syria. Only one manuscript remains, conserved in the British Museum. One learns from it that three monks were devoted to the care, running, and organization of this great library. Wright, *Catalogue*, 454.

Theodoret had a particular affection for it. It was he who decided that the monastery should be in the region of Apamaea and not of Cyr. Being poor, deserted, and not easily accessible, Cyr could not be a center of influence and open relationships. On the other hand, Apamaea was a meeting point for diverse civilizations, and the capital of Syria Secunda where the Aramaic culture prevailed over the Hellenic culture. It offered more opportunities for the example and efforts of the monks of the monastery of Maron to spread. Moreover, the bishops of Apamaea practiced the same well-defined religious policy as approved and defended by Theodoret. Among these bishops, special mention should be made of Polychronius, brother of the founder of the school of Antioch, Theodore of Mopsuestia. Shortly after its founding, the new monastery flourished to such an extent that all the other monasteries of Chalcedonian Syria admitted its supremacy. It was, as Arthur Vööbus, historian of Eastern monasticism, wrote, a solid and impregnable citadel of the Catholic doctrine as defined by the Council of Chalcedon.

The time has come to state the evidence and arguments taken from the early sources and scientifically established documents:

1. The monastery of Beit Maron was founded near Nikertai, in the middle of a religious confederation dear to Theodoret, in a region which offered him, more than any other center of northern Syria, opportunities for orthodoxy.

2. There is a complete and total silence in the documents concerning the activity of the disciples of Saint Maron in the region of Cyr after the Council of Chalcedon. Does this not suggest that they went elsewhere? There is plenty of information about the monks, disciples of Saint Maron, living and working during this same period in the region of Apamaea and especially in the neighboring regions of the south. As for Theodoret, none of his biographers mentions his return to Cyr, his diocese. The overwhelming majority tend rather to think that he passed the rest of his life within one of the monasteries of Apamaea.

This thesis has in its favor a letter written by Theodoret before the Council of Chalcedon and after the death of the emperor Theodosius. In it we read that he will no longer return to Cyr and that, if he had struggled so much, it was not at all to regain an exhausting post, but solely to make the truth triumph, that truth which alone deserves to be defended and to have sacrifices made for it.

3. The monks of Beit Maron were marked by an unfailing attachment to the doctrine and terminology of Chalcedon and to Theodoret even unto death. The connections between Theodoret and the monks of Beit Maron were not entirely broken off. The disputes concerning the incarnation which had so troubled his life troubled also his memory and his friends, the monks of Beit Maron and of Syria Secunda. Theodoret was the object of several posthumous anathemas. The Monophysites had him anathematized under Anastasius by a council held at Constantinople in 499 and by that of Sidon in 511. In 553, Justinian was made to believe that the Monophysites would easily be reunited with the imperial church if the leaders of the school of Antioch, and notably Theodoret, and their theology were condemned as Nestorian in tendency. Theodoret's friends could have disowned him, but in fact the anathemas revived their memories of him. This could partly explain any discreet silence on the part of these monks toward Theodoret's legacy. But, as we have already seen, the Monophysites knew very well what intimate relations and doctrine bound the monks of Beit Maron and their partisans to Theodoret of Cyr and the Council of Chalcedon. Also, in 517, following the carnage at Larissa, which followed the provocative appointment of Peter to the archbishopric of Apamaea, the monks of Beit Maron at the head of the orthodox party drew up a petition to Pope Hormisdas, the general tenor of which recalls the appeal of Theodoret to Pope Saint Leo after 449.[3]

From 529 to 545, the monks of Beit Maron were considered by the Monophysites to be the theological advisors of Ephraim of Amid, the patriarch of Antioch (529–45) and so promoters of the neo-Chalcedonian theology whose direction was traced out by Theodoret himself. In the eighth century a Maronite chronicler invoked the authority of Theodoret in exegesis.[4]

[3] Azéma, III, ep 113.

[4] Noldeke, *Fragments d'une chronique maronite*, in Z.D.M.G. (1875), t. 29, 82–89; Nau, *Opuscules Maronites*, in *Orient Chrétien*, t. IV (1889), 175–76.

In 517, only sixty-five years after its foundation, the monastery of Saint Maron was already a hive of activity with daughter houses. Thirty monasteries owed to it their origin, setting up and organizing into a beautifully structured religious order. It is worth noting that all these monasteries were to be found in Syria Secunda, and none were far from Apamaea. All of them acknowledged the leadership of the monastery of Saint Maron and conformed to its directives. In spite of being more ancient than the monastery of Saint Maron, the two monasteries founded respectively by Simon and Agapetus, disciples of the hermit Marcian, who was a contemporary of Saint Maron, aligned themselves with it.

It seems to us that another principal objective of this new religious order was the defense and the protection of the Chalcedonian doctrine. As soon as the adversary of this doctrine, Severus, was appointed to the episcopal seat of Antioch, he hastened to nominate his collaborator Peter as bishop of Apamaea. This provocative nomination aroused the anger of the monks who were under the patronage of the monastery of Saint Maron. They agreed to attend a meeting near the monastery of Saint Simon in Syria Prima in a place not under the territorial jurisdiction of Bishop Peter. But he, anticipating their initiative, set an ambush for them in which 350 of them were slaughtered, and seven monasteries were either set on fire or pillaged. The few survivors of these tragic events reported them in two letters written, one to the pope of Rome, Hormisdas, and the other to the chapter of their bishops.

However, Ephraim of Amid, who occupied the patriarchal see of Antioch from 529 to 545, supported and was himself aided by the monks of the monastery Beit Maron. The patriarch kept them close to him, and both sought and gave great weight to their advice. This is shown in a letter by a Monophysite, now held in the British Museum, stating that the monks of Beit Maron were Ephraim's teachers and masters, that this same patriarch persecuted the Monophysites, devoted all his energy to confirming the Chalcedonian doctrine, and wrote massive volumes on the subject. By 536 the Chalcedonians had regained their prestige, and brought the bishops together in a new council in Constantinople. The monasteries of Syria Secunda delegated a monk from the monastery Beit Maron to sign the decrees of the council in his capacity as representative of that monastery, being one with authority over them all.

In 610, the emperor Heraclius visited Syria. His first visit was to the monastery of Saint Maron, then at the head of the Chalcedonian party. On the same occasion, the emperor, who did not hide his pro-Chalcedonian preferences, gave orders to add to the property of the monastery of Saint Maron, a great part of the property belonging to the Monophysite monasteries. Such actions explain the rumors according to which Heraclius was thought to be a Maronite.[5]

4. The Monophysites were unremittingly hostile to the monks of Beit Maron, and to the monastic confederation of Apamaea. Around the year 517, as we have just seen, Monophysites attacked the Chalcedonians without warning, killed 350 of them, wounded a still greater number, and burned down or demolished a great number of their monasteries. This hostility did not abate. As late as the second quarter of the sixth century, Monophysites advised the emperor Justinian, who felt threatened by external dangers, and wished to secure the unity of the empire, to hold a new council. This was the council held in 533, which excommunicated the now deceased teachers of the school of Antioch. It did not, however, attack the Chalcedonian doctrine itself for fear of arousing the pope's anger. Theodoret was the first of the founders and leaders of the Antiochian school to be excommunicated. One hundred years after his death, Theodoret's opponents burnt his books. Of all his writings dating before the Council of Chalcedon, few remain. Inevitably that excommunication had unfavorable repercussions on Theodoret's followers, the monks of Beit Maron. François Nau informs us of the existence in the British Museum of an ancient Syriac manuscript which deals with this subject.

We have indeed found a certain number of letters which were exchanged in 592 (that is to say, forty years after the date of the excommunication) between the monks of Beit Maron and those of Beit Abaz. This correspondence followed a public debate between the representatives of the Catholic party, which supported the Council of Chalcedon, and the representatives of the Monophysites. In the

<hr>

[5] *P.G.*, Migne, III, col. 1089.

very beginning of their letter, the latter designated the addressees, the monks of Beit Maron, using these words: "To the plant of the Chalcedonian vine, to the offspring of the root of Leo, to the acid germ produced by the vine of Theodoret and, to say it in a few words, to the sons of the great and principal schism to have taken place in the church [Chalcedon, 451], which scatters the members of the Messiah and divides his body into many parts, to . . . those of *Beth Maron*, . . . who are in the territory of *Apamaea*." From the signatures we can deduce that the senders were Monophysites. They took pride in having been able to get rid of Eutyches and blamed the Maronite monks for not yet having liberated themselves from the yoke of the leaders of the school of Antioch and particularly from Theodoret. "The excommunication of these," they add, "will in due course reach you, as well as your mother, the Chalcedonian community." Then they propose a solution: "If you want to be safe from excommunication, it is essential for you to reject the teachings of the list of impostors and insulters, at the top of which figures the name of Theodoret. This would be just the first step. The second will consist of your regaining the camp of the true Christians (the Monophysites)."

What remains is to identify with precision the real founder of Beit Maron. Usually, a foundation would be the work of a strong and original personality, who himself assumes the role of superior. Only rarely does a founder stay outside his monastery, simply retaining a certain right to intervene in its running.

Was this founder the bishop of Cyr himself? Did Theodoret retire in fact to return to "the peaceful life which is dear to him," as he wrote to John of Germanicia? Or was it Jacob, the famous disciple of Maron called by the Monophysites Resh Dairâ of Kaphrâ Reḥimâ? We know that the collection of ruins of an ancient monastery, thought to have been the monastery of Saint Maron, lies near an ancient village called Kaphrâ Tobâ. Do we have the grounds for identifying Kaphrâ Reḥimâ with Kaphrâ Tobâ?

On the other hand, according to Theodore the Lector, Jacob after his death was laid in a tomb prepared in Cyr at the request of Theodoret.

Both hypotheses have a considerable degree of probability. Our present means, it must be admitted, do not allow the verification of either hypothesis. Will the last word on this subject come from archaeology or from the numerous manuscripts of the Syriac patristics? The question remains in suspense. Far from being sufficiently researched, these two sources need to be patiently submitted to deeper investigation.

Here, then, is the argument we have brought up in support of our hypothesis, one that may be summed up as follows. The monastery of Saint Maron, founded near Apamaea in 452, following the Council of Chalcedon, bore the weight of the cultural and theological heritage of the school of Antioch for a period that has not yet been sufficiently explored. We have ascertained that Maronitism was more than a community limited in number struggling for its existence within a confessional setting; it was an intellectual and theological heritage transmitted from generation to generation, and having a distinctive feature which takes it back to the great, ancient Antiochian civilization, and confers on it a specific local and regional character.

Appendix

DOCUMENT I
Petition of the Monks of *Syria Secunda*
to Pope Hormisdas (517)

Coll. Avellana, Pars II, Vindobonae (1898), 565–71, Ep 139, Ed. Otto Guenther

The grace of Christ, the savior of us all, has led us to find refuge with Your Beatitude as a haven of tranquility before the winter and the storm. Thus protected, we consider ourselves never cast down by the calamities which afflict us. Whatever our sufferings in this world, we rejoice in them, "knowing that they are as nothing in relation to the future glory that awaits us" [Rom. 8:18]. Since Christ our God has established for us a prince of pastors, a doctor and physician of our souls, it is right that we should expose to your holy angel the sufferings that have afflicted us and that we should show him (and denounce) the pitiless wolves that scatter the flock of Christ, that you might chase them from amongst the sheep by the authority of your staff and that by the word of doctrine you might cure our souls that have at last found peace through the effect of prayer.

But you have no doubt heard who are these cruel people and who has armed them against us, Blessed Father; they are that infamous Severius and that Peter who have never been counted among the faithful Christians, who every day attack and publicly anathematize the holy synod of Chalcedon and our most holy and blessed Father Leo, and who, despising the judgment of God, trample underfoot the canons used by the holy fathers, and who by their desire to force us to despise the above-mentioned holy synod

135

inflict on us extreme tortures. What is more, certain ones among them, not satisfied with these punishments, have gone further and massacred a considerable number of us.

While we were going to the monastery of Saint Simon, for the purposes of the church, these wicked ones prepared an ambush for us and hurling themselves upon us, they killed 350 and wounded others; they even killed those who had managed to take refuge at the altars; they burnt our monasteries and under the cover of night they sent a band of seditious persons, creatures who had been bought, to snatch from us the little that we had in our monastic poverty.

Your Beatitude will learn the details of our misfortune from the venerable brothers John and Sergius, whom we sent first of all to Constantinople in the hope of obtaining justice for all that had happened to us. But not only did he (the emperor) not deign to listen to them but he chased them shamefully away, threatening those who tried to expose their causes for complaint. Consequently we have learned, too late, that all this wickedness and shamelessness in committing such evils against our communities had been concerted in agreement with himself.

We beg you, Blessed Father, imploring you with insistence, to rise up with ardor and zeal, sharing the suffering of the sundered body (for you are the head of all), and to avenge the faith so despised, the canons trampled underfoot, the fathers blasphemed and the illustrious synod smitten with anathema. To you God has given the power and the authority to bind and to loose. "For it is not the healthy but the sick who have need of the doctor" [Matt 16:19; Matt 9:12].

Rise, holy fathers, and come to save us! Be like the Lord Christ who from heaven came down to earth to find the lost sheep, who chose Peter as prince of the apostles, whose see you so worthily occupy, and Paul, this vessel of election, to voyage across the earth, giving it light. Great wounds need great aid. The hired shepherds, when they see the wolves come, let the sheep scatter [John 10:12], but it is to you, the true shepherds and doctors, that the care of the salvation of sheep has been committed, you towards whom runs this flock that knows its shepherd, and which once freed from the most savage beasts follows his voice, for as the Lord says, "My sheep hear my voice and I, I know them, and they follow my voice" [John 10:3 et seq.]. So do not disdain us, Blessed Father, we who every day are torn apart by ferocious beasts. For the perfect information of your holy Angel we anathematize in this [official] petition the following authors already excommunicated by your Holy See, to wit: Nestorius, who was bishop of Constantinople, Eutyches, Dioscoros and Peter of Alexandria called Ballus and Peter called the Fuller of Antioch, and also Acacius their partisan, who was bishop of Constantinople, and all those who defend any one of these heretics.

The Signatories

1. I, ALEXANDER, by the mercy of God priest and Archimandrite of the Monastery of Saint Maron, I implore
2. SIMEON, by the mercy of God priest and Archimandrite "ut supra"
3. JOHANNES, by the mercy of God deacon and Administrator "ut supra"
4. PROCOPIUS, by the mercy of God priest and Archimandrite "ut supra"
5. PETRUS, by the mercy of God priest "ut supra"
6. EUGENIUS, by the mercy of God priest "ut supra"
7. GELADIUS, by the mercy of God priest "ut supra"
8. BASSUS, by the mercy of God priest "ut supra"
9. ROMULUS, by the mercy of God priest "ut supra"
10. EUSEBIUS, by the mercy of God priest "ut supra"
11. MALCHUS, by the mercy of God priest "ut supra"
12. LEONTIUS, by the mercy of God priest "ut supra"
13. STEPHANUS, by the mercy of God priest "ut supra"
14. CARUFAS, by the mercy of God priest "ut supra"
15. THOMAS, by the mercy of God priest "ut supra"
16. SAMUEL, by the mercy of God priest "ut supra"
17. THEODORUS, by the mercy of God priest "ut supra"
18. JOHANNES, by the mercy of God priest "ut supra"
19. JOHANNES, by the mercy of God priest "ut supra"
20. THOMAS, by the mercy of God priest "ut supra"

In all 209 Archimandrites, priests and some deacons.

DOCUMENT II
Hormisdas, to the Priests, Deacons and Archdeacons
of Syria Secunda (518)

Coll. Avellana, Pars II, Vindobonae (1898), 572–84, Ep 139, Ed. Otto Guenther

I have read your affectionate letter in which you denounce the madness of the enemies of God and, as you say in pain, the tenacious rage of the infidels, who in unceasingly reborn hatred of the Lord, set themselves criminally against his members; how I praised God when I heard the news of your constancy, God who preserves in adversity the faith of his soldiers. On the other hand, considering the shocks suffered by the churches and trials and sufferings of the servants of God, I cried out with the prophet: "Rise up, Lord, plead your cause; remind yourself of the madman who blasphemes you each day! Do not forget the voice of those who seek you, nor the proud ardor of your enemies which is forever increasing" [Ps 73:23].

For, just as we must have constancy in faith, so it is not right to doubt the judgments of God. This trial of the church is not new, brethren, however he who is humiliated shall be raised up, and he shall be enriched by those hurts which one would believe would weaken him. It is the practice of the faithful of God to gain life by the death of the body; they renounce perishable goods to win eternal ones and, insofar as persecution opens the way to being tested, that testing is the cause of merit. The furious madmen and blind ones are ignorant, for they are leading to the kingdom of God those whom they believe themselves to remove from the vicissitude of men. Hence, in those very perils, there are joys and the search for suffering; for he awaits the struggle of his own ones, this rewarder of great services; for who could fail to be broken by adversity unless he were consoled in his misfortune by recompense? Faith is that which does not allow falling into despair, seeing that it excludes the bitterness of the tribulations by the sweet savor of the virtues. Who would therefore attach any importance to things present while knowing how to appreciate future things? Who would refuse the loss of his life while considering the things that he will surely receive?

Persevere, my dear [ones] and, while serving the unshakable faith with firm courage, consider the glory of the perseverance in which resides salvation and the prize for good works. Great are those things to which we are called despite our unworthiness; may human weakness put no obstacle, for he who calls us faithfully rewards and is a powerful helper. Let us not mislead ourselves with hope of prosperity or with indolence or propose to ourselves easy solutions.

The Lord has promised us neither pleasures nor ease. It is not for tranquility that he has promised us recompense. Glory does not come with rest. How shall one who has no care for virtue have an opportunity for merit?

The door is indeed narrow, but the kingdom immense, accessible to only a few but they are an elite. Were these not the first words that he said to his disciples: They shall pursue you and flog you in the synagogues? It is by our patience, as it is written, that we shall gain our own souls, by fear of suffering we shall lose them by our impatience. The first master of patience, Our Lord, carried his cross, giving an example to those whom he will help. He himself holds the balance between virtues and pains, opposing himself to the flails of the furious ones, so that he himself would give the crown of the eternal kingdom according to the violence of the persecution.

Reflect on the glorious devotion of the Machabees as told in ancient history, when Judas and the famous phalange of his faithful brothers met a glorious death and when all was accomplished in the eyes of the people who stood on the mountain. And all these virtuous ones to save the Law, shadows and forms of things to come, merited so many examples; we follow the example of our fathers that we have seen, touched and tried. Who is not drawn on by events? What can we refuse to the truth? What is there not owed to the Redeemer? It is most willingly that we communicate to you this teaching. "Blessed is he," says Solomon the Wise, "who preaches the word to ears that accept." It is a joy to address ourselves to people who accept and to exhort those who do not hang back from advancing along the straight path. We hold as a guarantee for your faith the constancy with which, far from the influence of the pernicious aggressors, you turn to the doctrine and instructions of the Apostolic See. *Late have you been in taking the road of truth; but blessed be God, who remains not forgetful to the end, who reprimands and heals, and who does not allow the sheep of his flock to be continually rent by the rapacity of faithless wolves and who by moderation of rigor fails neither to reprimand nor to save his own.* But what reason is there to be astonished if, far from the one true shepherd the bloodthirsty and rapacious cheat has disturbed and scattered the sheep by his snares? Those who do not defend themselves expose themselves to the dangers that tear them apart. So for now walk with a firm tread along the road of the fathers to whom you have had recourse and hold to it. Great shall be the mercy of God who adds to your merit the correction of the others if you bring them back to righteousness. But free yourselves completely from the mire in which the heretics are constantly plunged; rejecting the filth of the dust that sticks to all, condemn with horror all those who stray from apostolic teachings. No communion between darkness and light, and may those who walk on the right road not turn their footsteps towards those who stray. One must hold fast to the bond of faith and defend it against the influence of a perfidious society, for according to the apostle just as he who unites himself to the Lord forms one spirit with him, so he who unites himself with a courtesan forms one body with her.

The virtuous love those who are like them and impiety causes those who attach themselves to her to be swallowed up with her. We have before our eyes, on our lips, even in our hands, those dogmas of our fathers that we recommend should be safeguarded; every day the venerable councils call on us to conserve them as a duty.

It would take long to recall them each in turn; we must know and preserve the Council of Chalcedon which enjoys the respect of all, but also the teaching of the venerable Leo drawn from the apostles. Behold the banner of the faith, behold the ramparts of truth, behold the cause and the hope of our redemption!

And here, according to what we read in [the writings of] the apostle is this foundation by which whoever seeks to build on straw which fire devours deceives himself.

In these councils there were destroyed the poisons of Eutyches and Nestorius, who maintained against each other contradictions contrary to the saving mystery and economy of the Lord, who equaled each other in sacrilege; one by denying that the Virgin Mary was the Mother of God separated what was united and the other, by confusing that which is distinct and that which is proper in the natures, destroyed the mystery of our redemption. One fell into the arms of the sect of Fontinus while the other by an impious affinity bordered on the folly of Manes. Against them, beloved brethren, apply with firm courage the appropriate remedies which, as you see, are feverishly combated by the impious heretics. Do not let the affirmation of truth be half-hearted! With what ardor should you not cherish salvation on seeing the mortal perdition loved by the others! One should blush to defend only half-heartedly the canons of truth when errors are upheld with such obstinacy. As for the other wicked inventions denounced above, the synodal constitutions pursue them with their just condemnations. As for ourselves, we also warn you against their partisans known by the Apostolic See to be like their leaders, and we would add Dioscoros and the sacrilegious Timotheus, Peter of Alexandria, Acacius of Constantinople with his partisans, Peter of Antioch also like the one above-mentioned of the same name and the same error, and also Severus of the same country and same poison, Xenaius of Jerusalem, Cyrus of Edessa, Peter of Apamaea, all condemned for the same reason not only to their own perdition but also for that perdition to which they have led others. When these wretches enshroud themselves in their ignominious opinions they also soil others by teaching them the doctrines that they have wrongly conceived.

I remind you of this general salutary principle; reject anything which might undermine the rules of the fathers, whatever these commentaries may be. Let nobody disturb you with inappropriate precepts or by new doctrines; if they are worldly people, they cannot concern the churches, for it would be better for them to learn than to teach. It is calamity to bring to the holy altars offerings that are foreign, for God has prescribed certain limits to the religious disciplines and, since the beginning, to his own worship. He divided the duties between the Levites and his people.

The power of men is one thing and priestly function is another. He who had the temerity to introduce fire from outside into the holy sanctuary angered the Lord more than he pleased him.

Who is he who can arrogate to himself the right to give orders in the institutions of others when there can be no doubt enjoying the honor of offering sacrifice motivated only by the enjoyment of the office will be punished?

At the court and in the administration of Ozias respect would have continued if, instructed by the example of so much rigor, he had regulated the best customs, fearing rather than assuming religious principles. But as in his headstrong audacity he did not give up the adorers forbidden in the temple, he was stricken with the abominable disease of leprosy and lost his office as he was taking on priestly functions.

Let it be known then that the measures taken by presumptuous persons about the holy orders are not acceptable to God when the punishment imposed in the rigorous and dishonoring sentence will preserve one individual and raging fire consume others.

What are these things that have taken on a superficial religious appearance, having no efficacy and no authority?

The apostle Paul has said: "Well, if we ourselves, or an angel from heaven, were to proclaim a gospel different to that which we have preached to you, let him be anathema!" [Gal. 1:8]. "We have already said, and now I repeat, if anyone proclaims to you a gospel different to the one that you have received, may he be anathema" [Gal. 1:9].

Then let him who follows the apostolic discipline use this great precept for keeping the faith. Certainly we have not been lacking in solicitude, for we have charged a double legation with what is humble in prayers, what is reasonable in the complaints and what is salutary in the orders.

But can the way of justice for that be neglected, when error is loved with such perfidious obstinacy?

There must be no attachment to the errors of the damned; may they perish without contaminating us, they who do not turn away from their errors because they are held back by their impiety.

4th of the Ides of February, P.C. Agapiti V.C.

(10th February, 518)

DOCUMENT III
Copy of the Petition Presented by the Community of the Monks of the Region (of Apamaea)

To the Most Reverend Bishops our Lords, to all the Most Reverend Holy Fathers the Bishops of *Syria Secunda*, from Alexander, John, Simon, Palladius, Procopius, Eugenius Stephanus and other archimandrites and monks of the region of Apamaea.

(See: ACO Coll. Sabbaitica, ed. Schwartz, t. III, Berolini, 1940, 106–10)

(Also: Mansi, VIII, cols. 1129–38; Hardouin, II, cols. 1387–94)

(Also the summary in Héfélé-Leclercq, Histoires, t. II, 2nd part, 11)

The divine Scriptures teach us how the very necessity of things often "serves the moment" [Eccl 3:1]. Therefore during the previous periods we have been silent, forced to be so by the power of those who were in government and by the fury of the heretics. But as God has now granted a just liberty and graciously allows some much-desired hope for our affairs, and has caused a Christian orthodox emperor to rise up for the churches and the whole world, those who were oppressed and voiceless must now make themselves heard.

You know in effect to what degree violence follows situations that are impossible or even inexorable. Since God has shown his clemency (he who in his great goodness never leaves his faithful and those who hope in him without counsel, but gives them consolation), he has restored peace to the world with a good emperor taking care of government; those who endeavored to loot the straight path of the orthodox faith being now set aside, it remains for us to speak, though with moderated voice, of the lamentable conduct of the heretic Severus, as also of the shameful and abominable manner of acting of Peter.

When in truth we were proceeding towards the locality of Kaprokerameh, not far from the venerable temple of the blessed confessor Simon, with only peace, union in love, and a just vow in our thoughts, manifesting a purely monastic attitude and intention, we did not know that we had an enemy in the impious Severus, whom Christianity ignored and never welcomed, and who in no manner or time whatsoever ever took part in the communion of truth, so much was he in the power of the enemy of the truth; most

certainly we would have all perished when the Jews or at least
lay persons and even monks hurled themselves upon us, coming
down from the folds of the steep heights. What could we do, how
could we resist the fury of those who threw themselves against us
and of the pitiless leader of impiety? For some they put to death,
others they led away into captivity; some were stripped of their
garments and others were taken in triumph clad in torn rags, as if
according to their idea they led a degrading life. For we ourselves,
in truth, we found honor in these events, supporting the trials and
holy wounds with firm hope for Christ our God.

But judging such great injustices as only benign, they sent on
[to Nikertai] an army of peasants greater in number than the first,
making a second assault on the above-mentioned monastery. They
destroyed a part of the wall and filtered in taking advantage of the
night; they cut the throats of some and rained blows on the greater
number, stealing the modest provisions of the monastery in such a
way as to put up trophies in the sight of the pious, in answer, they
said, to the vehement complaints. And these after their many acts
of violence were driven away with great difficulty.

As for Severus, who was the enemy of the whole world and to
be more precise of those who contemplate heavenly realities, he
never had enough of the stain of murder.

Severus, therefore, not being enough it seems to disfigure the
beauty of the world, Peter in his turn rose up against the city of
Apamaea and took charge of it, he said, he who should rather have
been taught the alphabet and syllables and not dreamt of oracles
and sacred rites.

This is why on several occasions he brought the unreasoning
petulance of youth into the venerable monastery of DOROTHAEA,
publicly pulling in a crowd of women inclined to enjoying themselves with no holding back. For they were women leading bad
lives and not respectable people. Raining blows on the monks of this
place, he led them into the town and put them on several occasions
in prison.

Who could count the evils already recounted and the harm
inflicted on the monastery of MATRONA? Even today the features
of the ISAURIANS who followed him and formed his escort are
recollected, features which proclaim aloud the enormity of the

drama that was enacted that day. And those who pass cannot hold back their tears on seeing the broken doors of the monastery.

And if we dare speak of acts of homicide, for which more than once he misused his own hands and, although seeing the blood staining the altars, dared make offering [the Eucharist], something about which the orthodox will not hesitate to speak—but who on the other hand would not be happy to pass all that over in silence?

But if once again we were to recall the deeds formerly perpetrated at the monastery of ORAGA, what letter could suffice to enumerate so many wrongs? They did not hesitate at all to knock down the monastery as if they were besieging it and to lead away like prisoners of war the monks who were chanting there because, after having fallen into error, they had finally loved the word of truth and had entered into total communion with us.

The combat of LARISSA is known from reliable sources, and the abominable frenzy of FAUSTUS, and the number of those he struck down with impious arrows; likewise, inhabitants of this region know what happened during the attack of NICERTA. What nature endowed with reason could without shedding tears relate how many things were perpetrated in the venerable dwelling of the victorious martyr ANTONINUS and in how many different ways? Thus, having got into the habit of massacring monks, considering what is abominable in the eyes of men as advantageous profit, he got his henchmen, whom he led on the warpath in a way not at all religious, to slit the throats of the venerable orthodox monks who had gathered there for a solemn ceremony; then he presented himself at the altar with his hands all bloodied from this deed.

You have heard in the presence of the most honorable governor of this province the most illustrious Amelius, of the most honorable NARSES and several others, what was told by the venerable priests here present, the deacons, subdeacons and clergy of the Catholic church of Apamaea; how he lived in the company of prostitutes and immoral women, what insulting words he pronounced against God, blaspheming in his drunkenness Christ crucified and leading to the sacred pool [font] of Christians women judged still unworthy to receive holy baptism. Further, if we wanted to give details of everything, the present occasion would not be enough and we would need another. Also, leaving aside the many faults of Peter and of Severus, from the tips of our fingers we now expose with timid hesitation the true accusations against them. But it would not be right to pass in silence over the reason for the sorrow of the venerable JULIAN. In point of fact, as certain stories had been spread around in the sanctuary of Saint STEPHEN, when the feast was being celebrated the aforementioned venerable man replied that our most pious emperor had right and holy faith. Peter, enemy of the truth, as if overwhelmed and pierced to the depths of his soul by this word so rightly placed, accused and condemned the Emperor, so they say; never did he say a good word, but, impetuous in everything, only opposed here also the Christian and orthodox sentiment of he who after God is the master of the whole universe.

Indeed, how well this is all confirmed; many members of the clergy of Apamaea have affirmed it in the presence of the most honorable governor of the province and of certain illustrious nobles of the metropolis. They also add what tender affection he had for STEPHANA, the former actress, whom he persuaded by his flattery to throw herself into a convent. At all times he remained continually by her side, finding himself again an indecent place of repose and a dishonest opportunity, that he himself called "teaching and exhortation," thinking to deceive all the superiors and hide the truth; there lies the wrong in which he engaged in this liaison, to speak only discreetly about such a subject.

So we beg and demand Your Beatitude to consider the word of truth that you honor and that at all times you serve with piety and the orthodox purpose worthy of praise of our pious emperor and of our highest magistrates; imitate and follow the holy footsteps of the blessed patriarch of the imperial city and of the holy synod assembled at his sides. Approve the just expulsion of the arch-heretic Severus; depose also Peter, whose name we blush to pronounce but which we say driven by necessity. We implore you to depose him and to set him apart from the sacred choir and from the priesthood to which he has been so far completely foreign; for he took on nothing but the external appearance of the priesthood, in illicit fashion.

This being admitted, God will accept your righteous will which is agreeable to him and the great emperor will praise the rectitude of your justice and efface for you the diseases which torment the members of the church.

May you (and to the pleasure of heaven it has already been thus in the past) by procuring for the churches the remedy and apostolic treatment bring the immaculate [faith] of Christians back into order and to its integrity, in order to render glory to God, Lord of the universe, and may hymns and chants unceasing be offered him by the celestial powers as by mankind.

May the just in this way be reunited in the unity of the Church Catholic according to the divine word, that there may be only one flock and one shepherd, Christ our God.

The Signatories

1. I, ALEXANDER, priest and Archimandrite of the *Monastery of the Blessed Maron*, have made public this letter above, signing it with my own hand . . .
2. SIMON, by the mercy of God priest and Archimandrite of the *Monastery of the Blessed Agapetus* . . .
3. PROCOPIUS, by the mercy of God priest and Archimandrite of the Monastery of the Blessed Theodosius . . .
4. EUGENIUS, by the mercy of God priest and Archimandrite of the Blessed Heschii, I also subscribe . . .
5. PALLADIUS, by the mercy of God priest and Archimandrite of the Monastery of the Blessed Valentinus in Capriole . . .
6. STEPHANUS, by the mercy of God priest and Archimandrite of the Monastery of the Blessed Theodorus in Vasala . . .
7. JOANNES, priest and Archimandrite of the Monastery of the Blessed Belius . . .
8. MARAS, priest and Archimandrite of the Monastery of the Blessed Basilius . . .
9. MUSILUS, priest and Archimandrite of the Monastery of the Blessed Barsaba . . .
10. SERGIUS, priest and Archimandrite of the Monastery of the Blessed Tahalasius . . .
11. TIMOTHEUS, priest and Archimandrite of the Monastery of the Blessed Gaianus . . .
12. SIMON, deacon and Archimandrite of the Monastery of the Blessed Eugraphius . . .
13. JULIANUS, by the mercy of God priest and Archimandrite of the Monastery of PAPULIS . . .

14. DOROTHEUS, priest and Archimandrite of the Monastery of the Blessed Cyrillus . . .
15. ROMULUS, priest and Archimandrite of the Monastery of the Blessed Jacobus (Joannis) . . .
16. THOMAS, priest and Archimandrite of the Monastery of the Blessed Joannis . . .
17. CAIUMAS, priest and Archimandrite of the Monastery of the Blessed Paullus . . .
18. SAMUELIS, deacon and Archimandrite of the Monastery of the Blessed Isaacius . . .

Sunt autem et in lingua Syrorum multae et infinitae monachorum subscriptiones . . .

DOCUMENT IV
Supplica dei Chierici e dei Monaci d'Antiochia al Patriarca Giovanni e al Sinodo Radunato Contro Severo

Aco Coll. Sabbaitica, Ed. E. Schwartz, T. III, Berolini (1940), 60–62

Supplica dei chierici e dei monaci del trono apostolico della grande città d'Antiochia della chiesa santa cattolica di Dio, al santissimo e beatissimo arcivescovo patriarca ecumenico Giovanni e al sinodo radunato.

Ora è il tempo, se mai ve ne fu uno, o beatissimi padri, che tutte le sante chiese di Dio nel mondo, gridino come da una sola bocca il detto profetico: "Si rallegrino i cieli ed esulti la terra, e tutto ciò che è in essa, perché Dio ha avuto pietà del suo popolo." E come i fedeli non sono giustamente convinti di proclamare questo grido, dal momento che, confidato lo scettro dei Romani agli imperatori pii e amati dal Cristo, anche la libertà e la fiducia è stata data a coloro che coltivano la religione ortodossa? Ma in una festa tanto comune del mondo, sola fra tutte, o con poche, la chiesa d'Antiochia è ripiena di mestizia e di lutto. Ricevette infatti un lupo al posto del pastore (e non sappiamo in che modo), ed è afflitta. Quale tragedia infatti non fu superata e sorpassata dai mali, attentati da Severo? In primo luogo costui sembra non abbia avuto mai comunione con alcuna chiesa (lasciamo, per non offendere le vostre orecchie, come costui sia vissuto); inoltre colpi con le saette della calunnia e dispose tutto per cacciare il giustissimo e beatissimo pastore Flaviano, rapì violentemente e contro i canoni la sede di lui, e poi, come un mercenario, non solo non condusse al pascolo il gregge di Christo e non fuggì, (cosa che era preferibile), ma egli faceva ciò che proprio delle bestie feroci, sgozzando e dispergendo le pecore. Fabbricando delle novità e delle bestemmie contro Dio, non risparmiò alcun santo padre: continua tutto il giorno, interdicendo i sinodi radunati per la religione [= per la pietà]. È chiaro che colui che osò anatematizzare e impugnare il santo sinodo calcedonense, che stabilì principalmente il simbolo dei 318 santi padri, che ricevette anche 150 santi padri, costui [= il medesimo Severo] è avverso inoltre e soprattutto ai santi padri i quali ad Efeso si raccolsero contro l'empio Nestorio ed [è avverso] ai predetti sinodi e li odia come delle sorelle di questo [sinodo].[1] Né a noi, né agli altri è nascosto quanti omicidi di santi monaci egli abbia fatto, o santissimi; e che egli abbia comandato con mani di giudeo una simile impiccagione. Furono un triste spettacolo di unomini, che avevano combattuto in combattimenti religioso fino alla vecchiaia, nudi e insepolti, oltre trecento, nati nella seconda provincia della Siria, gettati ai cani e agli uccelli per essere lacerati. Cose di questo genere e similmente misere le compì pure negli *xenodochi*, cioé negli ospizi.

Ore poi costruisce delle carceri; e così uccide molti incarcerandoli per la fede e flagellandoli nelle tenebre. O santissimi, egli osò fare tali cose anche presso le fonti di Dafne; ivi facendo uso di sortilegi, rese culto ai demoni con sacrifici turpi; e questo è cantato [= attestato] da tutta quella grande città. Non risparmi ò neppure i santi altari: non risparmiando neppure le cose sacre [1040/8], alcune le distrusse, altre invece le conservò per darle ai suoi simili. O beatissimi, costui ebbe la presunzione di fare anche questo: insieme al altre cose, si appropriò delle colombe d'oro e d'argento, appese in forma di Spirito Santo sui divini battisteri e gli altari, dicendo che

---

[1] Sinodo in latino è di genere femminile; perciò parla di "Sorelle."

non conviene designare sotto forma di colomba lo Spirito Santo. Per il denaro prese poi sia le case sia tutto ciò che era nei migliori fondi e lo spese; opprime la chiesa con gravissime usure. Ma, beatissimi padri, non è possibile ricordare tutto ciò che egli presunse di fare. Perciò ci contentiamo di queste poche e grandi cose e preghiamo il vostro santo sinodo, benché in ritardo, di sedare i mali che occupano la nostra chiesa e quasi tutto l'oriente. Vi preghiamo di liberarci da quest'uomo pessimo, esigendo de lui il castigo di ciò che fece contro le leggi divine e . . . la condotta legale. Vi preghiamo di provvedre alle cose che rimasero, se ne rimasero, convincendo il principe [= imperatore?] piissimo e valorosissimo di mandare alcuni di buoni costumi affinché, con qualcuno dei nostri rimasto fuori dell'affare, esigano che si renda ragione di ciò che è stato compiuto dell'inizio fino ad ora, e delle molte cose che essi hanno rubato; affinché pure essi custodiscano quanto troveranno, affinché non venga asportato assolutamente tutto. Il buon uomo [= ironia verso Severo] non cessa [di agire] contro ciò che appartiene alla chiesa di Dio, dissipando ciò che appartiene alla stessa chiesa. Benché giustamente abbia persa ogni speranza in Dio, ha speranza negli uomini perversi, dai quali è nutrito. Preghiamo anche di inviare degli avvocati, affinché i nostri fratelli che sono stati esiliati, siano vescovi, siano chierici, siano monaci, o laici vengano restituiti alle proprie città e ai propri uffici.

Inoltre, chiedendo perdono per il dolore che ci occupa, scongiuriamo vostra beatitudine, per la santa e consustanziale Trinità e per la pietà e la vittoria e la perseveranza dei sempre augusti Giustino ed Eufemia padroni di tutto il mondo, di muoversi a pietà e di soccorrerci opportunamente e di non disprezzare le nostre suppliche. [Vi scongiuriamo] anche di fare presenti tutte queste cose ai nostri pii e cristiani imperatori e persuadere le loro serenità [= titolo nobiliare], affinché per il loro e il vostro interessamento derivi tutto il bene alla nostra santissima chiesa.

Sottoscrizioni

1. TEODOSIO, per misericordia di Dio presbitero di Antiochia, presentai.
2. LONGINO, diacono, ugualmente presentai.
3. STEFANO, diacono, ugualmente presentai.

4. MAURIZIO, suddiacono, ugualmente presentai.
5. GIULIANO, diacono, ugualmente presentai.
6. TOMMASO, diacono, ugualmente presentai.
7. GIOVANNI, per misericordia di Dio presbitero, ugualmente presentai.
8. ANDREA, presentai.
9. GIULIANO, ugualmente presentai.
10. MARCELLO, diacono, ugualmente presentai.
11. SERGIO, per misericordia, ugualmente presentai.
12. GIOVANNI, per misericordia, ugualmente presentai.
13. MAURIZIO, per misericordia di Dio presbitero, ugualmente presentai.
14. GIOVANNI, consiliere, presentai.
15. **GIOVANNI**, monaco del convento del beato **Marone**, ugualmente presentai.
16. GIACOMO, monaco del convento del beato Bizone, ugualmente presentai.
17. COSTANTINO, monaco ed apocrisiario di Astere di santa memoria, presentai.
18. NONNO, diacono del convento del beato Paolo, presentai.
19. Salomone, monaco del convento del beato Valentino di Caproele, presentai.
20. SIMEONE, monaco del convento del beato **Agapito**, ugualemente presentai.
21. **SERGIO**, monaco del convento del beato **Simeone**, ugualmente presentai.
22. ALFIO, monaco del convento del beato Giacomo, ugualmente presentai.
23. FELICE, monaco del convento del beato Giovanni, ugualmente presentai.
24. SIMEONE, monaco del convento (. . .) del beato Paolo, presentai.
25. Paolo, monaco del convento del beato Esichio, ugualmente presentai.
26. CHIRIACO, monaco del convento del beato Doroteo, ugualmente presentai.

DOCUMENT V
The Maronites, Inquisitors of the Catholic Faith
in the Sixth and Seventh Centuries

*Bulletin De L'association De St. Louis Des Maronites, No. 97
(January 1903), 343–50; No. 98 (April 1903), 367–81*

Introduction

We have copied from a manuscript of the eighth century, conserved in the British Museum in London,[1] an unpublished Syriac text comprising a letter from the monks of Beth Maron to the Jacobites together with the answer of the latter. This emphasizes once more the orthodoxy of the monks of Saint Maron from the sixth to the seventh century, their struggles with the Jacobites and the pre-eminence then enjoyed by their monastery over the other monasteries of Syria Secunda.[2]

According to this text, the monks of Saint Maron, who represented the orthodox party, partisans of the Council of Chalcedon and of Pope Leo, held a conference at Antioch with the sectaries of Peter of Callinice, Jacobite Patriarch from 578(?)to 591. The latter had not been able to answer them, even during a supplementary postponement of five days that had been allowed them. Nor had they answered a letter that the monks of Saint Maron had sent them by a certain Mar Constantine.

The Maronites Philip and Thomas then composed the letter of which we have given the translation and charged Isaac and Simon with taking it to the Jacobites and convoking their monks, advocates, and bishops either to give an answer or to renounce

[1] Add. 12155, fol. 163.

[2] The monks of Saint Maron spoke Greek and Syriac, for their representatives signed in Greek, the works of Saint Jean Maron, as we have said when publishing them, show a deep knowledge of Greek, and in any case the monastery library, as we shall see later, certainly contained Syriac manuscripts; these monks therefore were entirely suited by their situation, their number, their regularity, and their orthodoxy to enjoy a certain preeminence over the other monasteries, both Greek and Syriac.

their errors. The role of the Maronites in this affair and the tone they adopted towards the Jacobites show clearly that they were the leaders of the orthodox party just as previously they had been recognized as leaders of the monks of Syria Secunda at the Council of Constantinople in 536.[3] It seems quite probable, although this was once contested, that their orthodox supporters had adopted their name and thenceforward called themselves "Maronites."

Theodore, of the monastery of Beth Mar Abaz, gave them a lengthy answer; he treats them as "offspring of the root of Leo" and of the "plant of the Chalcedonian vine" and accuses them of using the rod against the Jacobites. All these insults now turned to the glory of the Maronites, for it is a remarkable fact that this bitter enemy accuses them of no other dogmatic error than that of not professing his own.

In order to fix the date when this letter was written, we shall point out that here there was the question of a quarrel at Antioch involving Peter [of Callinice] and that we know of a meeting of monks called at Antioch to discuss matters of faith involving this same Peter shortly after his death, that is to say soon after 591. It seems clear that it was a question of the same event in both cases. This means that our letter would have been written soon after the year 591.

---

[3] At this council, just as Marianos, Abbot of Saint Dalmatius, was called primate of the monasteries of Constantinople, so the Monastery of Saint Maron, represented by the deacon and apocrisarius Paul, was called primate of the holy monasteries of Syria Secunda (Cf. *Perpétuelle orthodoxie des Maronites*, by Msgr. Debs, 70). "The principal" of the monasteries clearly signifies that it had some authority over the others, for the Greek text says "exarch of the monasteries." This quality of primacy had been conferred by the Council of Ephesus on the Monastery of Dalmatius; it is not known when it was conferred on the monastery of Saint Maron, a fact which used to lead to doubts about the title despite the text of the Council of Constantinople just referred to. The present letter leaves no more room for doubt that the Maronites spoke in the name of all the orthodox of Syria, that is to say, exercising the functions of primacy which must therefore have been recognized by them. We have already seen them discussing with the patriarch and bishops of the Jacobites and getting the better of them at Damascus in front of Moawiah in the year 659. Cf. *Opuscules Maronites*, second part (Paris, 1900), 6; and first part, 36 of the Syriac text.

Denis of Tellmahreh quoted by Assemani[4] relates in fact that
Probus and John Barbur, both learned and eloquent men, after
having supported the Jacobite patriarch Peter of Callinice, finally
turned against him by accepting the Council of Chalcedon and by
causing numerous defections among the Jacobites in the region
of Antioch. After the death of Peter [591] they asked Patriarch
Anastasius[5] to convoke all the monks of Antioch to discuss the
faith and to show that the doctrine of Peter, which affirmed the
difference of the natures and denied that there were two of them,
was a novelty in the church. The monks were taken to Antioch even
by force and kept there for six months. It was at this meeting that
the below cited letters were written.

It will be noticed that here *the Maronites are called "monks of Beth
Maron[6] who are in the territory of Apamaea"* and that their letter was
written to Armenaz [or Armaz].

This manuscript *add.* 17169 written by a certain Sergius in 581
was bought by the monks of the monastery of Saint Maron and
placed in their library in the year 745. Here incidentally are the two
notes in the manuscript that inform us of this capital fact:

"May the happy memory and recollection of justice be with God
the Father Almighty, with his Son Our Lord Jesus Christ, and with
his living Holy Spirit, of the priest Mar Matthew of the village of
Qolab, country of Tsofanoïeh, who dwells in the monastery of the
blessed Mar Maron and of his disciples, who bought this work of
the monk John[7] with a number of other similar books for their use."

"This book therefore entered the library of Mar Maron in the year
one thousand and fifty-six [745] during the time of the superior Mar

[4] *Bibl. Orientalis*, II, 72.

[5] Patriarch of Antioch from 559 to 599.

[6] Here the expression is not "those of the monastery of Maron," as is to be
found elsewhere, but, as in the Maronite chronicle, we simply find "those of
Beth Maron." Now in the letter that we are going to publish "those of Beth
Petra" designates the Jacobite partisans of Peter. It is therefore possible that the
locution "those of Beth Maron" designates not only the monks of the principal
monastery but also all their supporters.

[7] This manuscript contains a Syriac translation of the ascetical writings of
"John the Monk, the Seer of the Thebaïd"—no doubt John of Lycopolis.

George of Kharba`medoï[8] when the second [in charge] of the library was Athanasius of . . .[9] and Mar Sergis of Delam and Mar Cozma of Ma`rath Metsrein[10] and Mar Zacharia of Ramtha."[11]

This monastery of Saint Maron was therefore still in existence in 745. But it was no doubt destroyed during the following century, for another note in the same manuscript followed by an anathema written by somebody's hand in the ninth or tenth century, according to M. Wright, tells us that it was given [before the writing of this anathema] to the Church of the Mother of God of the Syrians in the desert of Sceteh by two brothers Matthew and Abraham, monks of Tagrit.[12]

Finally, towards 1835, this manuscript was removed from the monastery of the Syrians by a Greek named Pacho and sold to the British Museum in London, where we saw it.

To justify our title we also point out that the Maronites clearly appear here towards 592 as inquisitors, for the Jacobite Theodore will say: "You carry cudgels, chase, pursue and insult the priests and faithful of the Messiah who do not agree to associate themselves with your wickedness. You resemble the thieves and evildoers who inhabit the mountains and the devastated desert places to commit their deeds like to yours." Bar Hebraeus, whom we have already quoted,[13] tells us that towards 630 there were still "the monks of Maron, of Maboug and Emesus [Homs] [who] showed their cruelty and destroyed many churches and monasteries [of the Jacobites] and when our people complained to Heraclius he did not answer them.

"So the Lord of Vengeance sent the Arabs to deliver us from the Romans. Our churches were not returned, for each kept what he owned, but at least we were saved from the cruelty of the Greeks and their hatred towards us."

---

[8] The letter "d" of this word is not certain.

[9] This word is illegible.

[10] Village halfway between Antioch and Aleppo. Cf. *Studia sinaïtica*, t. IX (London), 1900, XXIV.

[11] Cf. Wright, *Catal. of Syr. Man.*, 454.

[12] It is known that the monastery of the Syrians was founded in Egypt in the desert of Sceteh by merchants from Tagrit (Tekrit).

[13] *Opuscules Maronites*, first part.

However, the hatred of the Maronites towards the heretics was not yet extinguished with the arrival of the Arabs. For, as Bar Hebraeus says, according to the chronicle we have published,[14] they had the upper hand over the Jacobites in front of Moawiah, who every year took twenty thousand dinars from the Jacobite patriarch in return for the protection he gave him against "the sons of the Church."

If certain of our readers feel unsympathetic towards these inquisitors, precursors of the Spanish Dominicans, we would at least remind them that the Jacobites had first acted harshly against the Maronites at the time when the Jacobites enjoyed the favor of the emperor Anastasius. They had even gone much further than their adversaries were to go, for they had not confined themselves to molesting them and taking away their material resources—the only actions with which they reproached the Maronites—but had actually killed them. In the petition to Pope Hormisdas written towards the year 517, Alexander, priest and archimandrite of Saint Maron, says:[15] "As we were going to the Monastery of Saint Simon, for reasons concerning the Church, these wicked ones [the Jacobites] prepared an ambush for us on the road; and, coming to hurl themselves upon us, they killed three hundred and fifty of our people and wounded others. They even killed those who had taken refuge near the altars.

"They burnt the monasteries, sending by night a multitude of seditious persons won over by money, who looted the little that was there. You will be informed about everything by the notifications of our venerable brothers John and Sergius. We sent them to Constantinople, hoping to be justified after all these excesses, but the emperor, without deigning to say a word to them, drove them out shamefully, which gave us to understand that he himself was the author of all these evils."

This text helps us to better understand the reprisals that followed during a century and a half, particularly when one notes that the Maronites did nothing against the lives of their enemies and therefore only pursued in them their error and its manifestations.

---

[14] This has been quoted above.
[15] Mansi, t. VIII, col. 1129, and Fleury, , XXXI, 32. Cf. , 70.

Elsewhere they behaved perfectly towards each other as a story shows that we have already published:[16] a periodeute said to a former ascetic unhappily fallen into sin: *"I advise you to go down to this Monastery of Mar Maron the Blessed, to remain there and to weep there for your sins. For there one finds a monastic life that will do complete penance for the sins committed; in a word, one finds an excellent practice of perfection."*

F. Nau

I. Letter of the Maronites

Questions[17] *of the monks of Beth Maron,* which are:

Sentence on the tonsured of the party of *Peter*,[18] who is one of the many schismatics of the party of Eutyches, and of Severus, whose names are soiled and whose habitations are like those of brigands and thieves; from the orthodox monks of Beth Maron, sons of the Catholic Holy Church.

The Divine Book has said: *Subjects of confusion cover our fathers and they do not let themselves be reprimanded.* It is above all in you that such a word is accomplished, for you have faces of brass, and what is more you are opinionated, unless *you have said to the mountains, fall on us and to the hills, cover us.*[19] Indeed, for five days we have been waiting for you to give us an answer to the five questions concerning which your faith leaves something to be desired,[20] and you have not been able to. After that, we again concerned ourselves with you in a testimonial letter in which we addressed you by the intermediary of the illustrious Mar Constantine, preserved of God, and again you have made no answer. This witness, for which we

---

[16] *Opuscules Maronites*, second part.

[17] Literally, chapters. The Syriac text will be published in Beirut by Msgr. Debs with an Arabic translation of the present work.

[18] Peter of Callinice, Monophysite patriarch of Antioch from 578(?) to 591.

[19] Cf. Luke 23:30. The Maronites reproach their adversaries for not having answered them and ask if they have disappeared from the face of the earth.

[20] Literally, into which you have fallen.

asked you at Antioch,[21] we demand it again of you by this letter, before God and before man; if you are able, and if you have a just and appropriate answer to these five questions that we have raised against you, with the whole town and with the outsiders to be found there as witnesses between ourselves and you, answer us in all piety, according to the chosen doctors and saints, concerning whom there is no division between us and you or any Christian, namely:

First, that the Messiah is not said to be twofold; second, that the Messiah has a composite nature; third, that the nature, the person and the hypostasis are all the same thing in the Messiah; fourth, that Dioscoros, your master, has anathematized Eutyches after having received him in your communion; fifth, show also that you submit to the anathema whoever confesses two natures in the Messiah before the union [of the natures], or in the union, or after the union. That is all. As for those advocates that you have, if they take it on themselves to apologize for the errors[22] into which you have fallen, let them first do so for the five above questions, and then if they have anything to say or to have heard in justice, let them do so boldly. If they do not judge that it is well to apologize for such stupidities, let them anathematize by their signatures the four above propositions, let them show that Dioscoros anathematized Eutyches, then we shall go to discuss together without equivocation in order to know whether or not there should be said to be two natures in the Messiah. Outside any one of these points we do not agree to discuss with you nor to listen to you. We adjure you, by the Holy and Consubstantial Trinity, and by your venerated habit, if indeed it is venerated by you, to show this writing to all the bishops close to you[23] in the direction of the east[24] and to give us an answer as stated above.

Now we have to make known the answer of the Jacobites. It is rich above all in insults against the Maronites, but is nonetheless

---

[21] Literally, in the town of God. This is the Greek name for Antioch translated into Syriac. We therefore think it probable that this letter was written in Greek and that here we have only a Syriac translation.

[22] Literally, the falls.

[23] Your neighbors or perhaps your coreligionists.

[24] Mesopotamia.

important, for as we have already said,[25] all these insults now turn
to the glory of the Maronites, since their bitter enemies reproach
them only with professing the faith of Saint Leo and of the Council
of Chalcedon and accuse them of no other error than that of not
professing the same faith. Our readers—the heirs and emulators
of these valiant monks who are insulted and calumniated in the
following pages—will raise their spirits to God and say with the
psalmist: "The zeal of your house devours me, and the outrages of
those who insult you fall on me."[26]

F. Nau

II. Response of the Jacobites

Response and summary solution to the five questions sent from
the village of Armaz[27] by the monks of Beth Maron, after their
leaving Antioch, to the orthodox monks in the holy monasteries
of Mesopotamia.[28]

*To the plant of the Chalcedonian vine, to the offspring of the root of Leo,
to the acid germ produced by the vine of Theodoret*[29] *and, to say it in a few
words, to the sons of the great and principal schism to have taken place
in the church, which scatters the members of the Messiah and divides his
body into many parts,*[30] *to Philip and to Thomas, those of Beth Maron,*[31]
*who have not ceased corrupting to the best of their ability the true faith
preached by the Apostles, who are monks in name [only],* who lead the
life that God knows well and is not unknown to many men, [such

---

[25] See above.

[26] *Zelus domus tuae comedit me et opprobria exprobrantium tibi ceciderit super
me* (Ps 68:10).

[27] Written as Armenaz by M. Wright.

[28] As we have already noted, the letter of the Maronites was addressed to
the whole Jacobite party.

[29] The Jacobites, unlike the Maronites, rejected the Council of Chalcedon
and condemned Pope Leo and Theodoret.

[30] It is hardly necessary to say here that the schismatics are the Jacobites and
not the partisans of the Council of Chalcedon.

[31] No doubt we have here the names of some of the two principal authors
of the letter from the Maronites.

are those addressed here by] *Theodore*,[32] his brother who is the least of all the church founded through the hands of God, whose walls are stones of election, I mean to say *Peter* and all his successors: the apostles, the prophets and doctors and [to such is addressed] the [following] discourse which resolves their infirm studies against the truth and its representatives.

We have received your insults and we have examined your outrageous words; know you well that they cause us no hurt, but if one may say it in such a way, they have filled us with great joy, for through them we have learnt the feebleness of your thoughts, and [we have seen] your lack of any work capable of defending your bad heresy other than this compilation.[33] You busy yourselves with compiling and with hiding yourselves under insults, according to the words of the Theologian,[34] who said of the sophists in his discourse on the arrival of the bishops: "They prepare darkness, that they might attack while hiding themselves and that it might be difficult to attack them."

You, likewise, having nothing to answer what the disciples of truth asked you at Antioch in writing and not in writing [orally], you hide your shame under insulting words and you try to escape any clear point by cunning. But that is not enough for you, for you say that *the Lord does not see, that he who has made the ear does not hear, that he who chastises the disputants will not reprimand*,[35] and you go all over the place, rejoicing in nothing; you put your hope in falsehood, you take refuge in lies, you deceive the simple and you recount misleading dreams. As the prophet has said of you and of those like you,[36] you lie in your words and in your writings.

"For five days we have been waiting for you to give us an answer to the five questions concerning which your faith leaves something to be desired and you have not been able to."[37]

---

[32] This is the author of the response of the Jacobites.

[33] Or, this accidental work (of small value).

[34] Gregory of Nazianzen.

[35] Ps 93:9-10.

[36] Cf. Jer 9:5, 8.

[37] Here the author is quoting the words of the Maronites themselves. Cf. above, 157.

We could not know when, what day, what hour, what moment you did that and sent us writing in the town of Antioch. Then you heap iniquity on iniquity, and you raise proud heads in alleging a writing of *Constantine;*[38] by his intermediary, you say, you have sent us letters as evidence. If he were present and swore in the name of the Holy Trinity, I do not think he would associate himself with your hypocrisy and would hide the truth on your behalf, and so your calumny would be exposed, according to the word of *Solomon*: The man whose eye is wicked hastens to enrich himself and does not know that poverty is coming upon him.[39] Your wealth, it seems, is the evil that you suspect of being ours, *for it is not before the judges that you have acquired it*, according to the words of *Jeremiah, like the partridge that calls to those to whom it has not given birth*, it is not *in the middle of the days* but on the very instant—in accord with the divine David—that you abandon *the help of Jesus Christ.*[40] For here is what you write:[41]

1. "If you are able, and if you have a just and appropriate answer to these five questions that we have raised against you, with the whole town and with the outsiders to be found there as witnesses between ourselves and you, answer us in all piety, according to the chosen doctors and saints, concerning whom there is no division between us and you or any Christian, namely that the Messiah is not said to be twofold."

I am astonished by your ignorance, and how can you, you who are the doctors of Ephrem,[42] can you fail to know that! You are like a man who would look for light at the third, sixth and ninth hour, when the sun gives light more than the stars. If however you wish for a demonstration of these things that are so well-known and evident, address yourselves to Saint Cyril, about whom alone between us there is no controversy, he being received with complete persuasion

---

[38] See above.

[39] Prov 29:22.

[40] This is an adaptation of Jer 17:11.

[41] See above.

[42] Perhaps this means that the Maronites were the advisors of Ephrem, patriarch of Antioch from 529 to 545, and amongst the harshest persecutors of the Monophysites. If so, this passage is of great importance.

of the spirit and recognized as the ax which cuts the artisans of heresies and his teachings believed by us to be Gospel.

In the great and illustrious letter that he wrote to Nestorius, enemy of God, he seems to say in his definition that the Messiah should not be twofold: "We do not separate the words of the Gospel consecrated to our Savior in two persons nor in two hypostases, for this one and only Messiah is not double even though he is recognized as [formed] from two things which were united in one indivisible unity, just as a man is formed of soul and body but is not therefore double, but one, formed from two. In confirmation of this, we shall call to witness in their time the words of Our Savior which run: *Let he who has ears to hear listen,*[43] and: *That which I say to you I say to all.*" So in this passage he decides that the Messiah is not twofold and that man cannot be said to be twofold, one [formed] from two.

If you still wish to listen, on account of one piece of evidence not being enough, we shall quote again this same doctor and we shall see what he says in his second tome against the blasphemies of Nestorius when he writes: "It is not because the Son the Word has become man when he became flesh that you will describe him as double." So he tears up one may say by the roots, deep in the very inside of your opinion, you who call him [Christ] double because he has taken on flesh and become man, and he proclaims to you *Maronites partisans of the two natures*[44] and to all the Council of Chalcedon: "It is not because the Son the Word, in taking on flesh from God [that he was], became man that he should be called double."

If you wish to combat Saint Cyril and if you still try, after this prudent decision of this wise doctor, to say that the Messiah is twofold, I would ask you also in what manner and using what formula you say it, for this doctor has decided in what he said earlier [above] that it is not for having taken on flesh that has a rational soul that he should be said to be double. If you have another formula [opinion] which agrees with the Divine Book, answer us; if not, put a lock on your lips and according to your words anathematize your

[43] Matt 11:15.

[44] This is the Catholic doctrine. As for the words of Saint Cyril, they were toned down or explained by Saint John Maron. Cf. *Opuscules Maronites*, first part, 25, etc.

reproaches to be found in the writing where you have said: "Show us something that decides the Messiah is not said to be double." Thus your first reproach is annulled and reduced to fragments *as the potter's vase and not a fragment will remain in which one might carry the fire of the hearth or draw a little water*, as Isaiah said.[45]

2. For your second word [question], you seem to be saying something for those who listen to you and who share your error; but those who stand on the solid ground of the Messiah laugh or weep at such stupidities. You show that you are without any intelligence when you say and write things professed by many, without discussion, so to say; and that not only by estimable doctors, but even by those whom your fathers charged with defending their doctrine; but you know that you are little learned in literature[46] and that you do not even look at books, or, to say what is nearer the truth, you show that you are strangers to the Holy Books[47] and especially to the fathers who interpreted them. In fact you say: "Show us that the Messiah has one composed nature." You resemble those who remember having dreamt something and then ask somebody to bring what they have dreamt about. When you hear "one incarnate nature" which the divine doctors everywhere recognize in the Messiah, I cannot understand how it is you ask about the words "one composed nature," unless because of your ignorance you do not try to understand the word *incarnate*—applied to him who is formed of both, in the simple meaning.[48] If you wish, we offer you more to drink from the same source, from Cyril who will bring you closer to the divine mysteries. *If you are thirsty, come close to the waters*, said Isaiah.[49] He writes in his thirteenth discourse: "When, then, certain things which are not like each other in nature come together to unity of composition, there will however remain something [of each of them] in the latter [composed], it is not right

[45] Isa 30:14.
[46] Literally, in the word or in discourse.
[47] Literally, to the witness of the books.
[48] The Maronites interpreted "one nature incarnate" in the sense of "two natures," "for by incarnate (the holy Fathers) announce and recognize a (second) nature." Cf. *Opuscules Maronites*, first part, 25.
[49] 55:1.

to separate them into two because the assembling that has taken place for the unity cannot be destroyed in any way, when each of the things united would be named by us separately, as soon as [the whole] is completed by the two."

By these words the doctor teaches us that by placing the composition first, one does not break up the things which are joined in one and which have completed one person and nature of the incarnate Word. So, O clever men, if you do not recognize the composition and assembly of the unity of the nature and the person, you certainly do wrong to the parts that are not assembled, as the pious doctor has said; and if you say that it is impossible to say that it is composed because unity cannot be attributed to things that are composed, approach, eat the bread of wisdom, instruct yourself in the proximity of the same doctor, who wrote in his second letter to *Successus*:

"It is not only to things simple of nature that one may apply in truth the notion of unity, but one can also do it to those which are assembled in something composed; so a man is a certain thing [composed] of body and soul. Such things are of different kinds and do not resemble each other, but when they are united they complete the unique nature of the man."[50]

You see how [this doctor] who approaches the divine mysteries says "one nature" rendered perfect by the things which were assembled in one composed thing [to arrive] at unity without confusion. The same wise doctor, when the impious Andrew[51] reproached him over the words *with* and *at the same time*—then he added much of his own against him, following his theory—because he had said: The Son is enthroned with his flesh "at the same time" "so like the Father," gave an explanation about chapter eight and wrote:

[50] Saint John Maron quotes a text of Cyril analogous to this one in favor of the Catholic doctrine of the two natures: "(Cyril) : If we seek a demonstration in the composed thing that composes us other men, we are composed of soul and of body and we see in ourselves two natures, one the soul and the other the body; and because we are composed of two natures we are far from being two men, but one composition, as I have said, formed of soul and body, and not of a destruction of the two," *Opuscules Maronites*, first part, 25.

[51] Andrew of Samosata.

"When on the subject of hypostasis and nature, that is to say of a person, the discourse studies the elements of which it is formed or composed, naturally he employs the word 'at the same time' or 'with.' I have left the latter in order that it should thereby be understood that he is one, even in the composition, and that he is not an aggregation of two separable things."

3. O dart hurled vigorously by a young man[52] against your two reproaches—I speak of the second and of the third—that were installed behind a wall of earth, and as says Isaiah, [one heard] a great noise of destruction[53] caused by his fall! O stone hewn not by [human] hands in order to break and to reduce to fragments your two reproaches, like straw blown from the threshing-floor, without leaving them the least place! Indeed just one word pronounced by the Holy Spirit will show in the Messiah the nature, the person, and the composed hypostasis are the same thing and remained "one" in composition he who is completed with the help of two in an ineffable manner and without confusion. For you ask to be shown thus about the Messiah "that the nature, person, and hypostasis are the same thing."

But I am going to interrogate you as well: Do you say that the nature, person, and hypostasis are the same thing in the Messiah or that they have different significations? If you say that this is the same thing, you will show that your inept questions and quarrels on this subject are vain. If you say that this is not the same thing, it follows that you must confess three things in the Messiah: the nature, the person, the hypostasis and still many other things, such as being the Son, the Lord, the Word of God and all the other names that are given him in the Books.

If you suffer from such hallucinations, it is not only two natures and persons[54] that you must lightly propose—according to your blasphemies and those of your doctors up till today—nor a quadrity

---

[52] Cf. Ps 126:4.

[53] Cf. Isa 29:6.

[54] We have already noted that the Monophysites, for whom nature is not distinct from person, accused the Catholics who recognized two natures of also recognizing two persons, so making Nestorians of themselves. Cf. *Les Plérophories de Jean, évêque de Maioumai* (Paris, 1889), 5, 15–16, 61.

instead of the Trinity that you must adore, but all that we have said above must still flow from the folly and ignorance that come from the bad doctrine in which you have been baptized and have erred until today. If you have not asked questions about this subject and wish to instruct yourself—or rather you do not even know how to ask questions—about these natures which constitute and complete the unity of the Messiah, that is to say the person of God the Word and a flesh animated by a rational soul and endowed with knowledge that he is united in nature and person in the unity of nature and person, know well that we do not recognize *Emmanuel* [formed] of two hypostases as we recognize it of two natures, that is to say two persons,[55] and in that we follow the holy and illustrious *Cyril* and the other pious[56] doctors of the church.

He wrote in fact in the letter to Nestorius: "This unique Jesus Christ must not be divided into two sons, for such a word is in no way appropriate to the true word of faith, although some propose the union of the hypostases, for the Book has not said that the Word united himself to the hypostasis of the man, but *that he was flesh.*"[57] In the first tome of the interpretation of the Epistle to the Hebrews, he decrees and says in the same way: "It is good to proclaim that the unity has been made by the concourse of the natures, but one must not introduce into the teaching of the church that it has been done by the concourse of particular hypostases, this is pure imagination which cannot be demonstrated." And in the third tome of the same interpretation he expresses in writing words which are sisters to the former ones: "We have said that according to the Holy Books, but those who care little for the true unity, I wish to say the unity of person, and have found only and simply unity of hypostases, they do not accept to call *Emmanuel* a true son." Saint Julius, bishop of Rome, in his letter to *Prodocius* makes an analogous decision and says: "For the perfection of the faith, one shall announce as Son of God he *who is incarnate* of Mary *and has remained among men,*[58] not

[55] For the Monophysites, the nature does not exist without a corresponding person.

[56] Literally, clothed with God.

[57] Cf. John 1:14.

[58] John 1:14.

that he has supplanted the man, for one finds in the prophets and in the apostles: *Perfect God in the flesh and perfect man in the spirit;* there are not two sons, one the true son who took on the man, and other a mortal man who was taken by God; he is not a [being formed] of two hypostases, but is alone and unique in heaven and on the earth." And a little further on: "If anybody says that Jesus son of Mary is a man who was taken by God and if he says that two perfect hypostases became one, such a one will be a stranger to the divine hopes to come [will not go to heaven.]"

Our Holy Father Patriarch Severius followed these illustrious doctors and wrote on the subject chapter XXI of his second discourse against the grammarian, preparing his subject in the following manner: "When I read this letter addressed to Maron, I was pained to see still there this difficulty which I had already answered and which I had answered in the following manner." And a little further on: "It has come to this, but our adversary has the audacity to ask us:—But you yourself, what do you say of two natures and persons? You say that *Emmanuel* is even composed of two hypostases—We reply to this that when these persons subsist in their proper substance separately, then we write for each of them the word hypostasis, but when, by the concourse of both, natural unity arrives and they form one nature and one person without any confusion, as one sees for a man [the body and the soul], then the parts of which this one [being] is constituted do not appear with their particular characters in two hypostases." He gives the same clarifications in the letter to the priest *Thomas* and his syncellus, and says: "After these clarifications, one first sees that it is foreign to those who profess the personal unity to call hypostases persons, that is to say natures, which concur in an ineffable manner to the unity and constitute *Emmanuel;* also they will avoid saying that the unity is formed of two hypostases. That is all very well for those who profess deceptive unity, for whom the man and God exist apart each in his own substance, and who draw this conclusion out of arbitrariness and a similitude of names."

4. After having shown you this on the subject of the Word, we pass to the fourth reproach, which is cold, insipid and tasteless and would not even merit being proposed to the children who

play in the public places. Leave those who busy themselves with such quarrels. These doctors give themselves praise,[59] but as the *Theologian* says: "The wise are ephemeral when they have no care for wisdom but to ask questions." Here then is the writing[60] of your broken reed: "Show us that *Dioscoros*, your master, anathematized *Eutyches* after having received him in his communion."—Know well, before all else, that all your reproaches are cold and deprived of all learning, and that the one which we now answer is more unreasonable that the most unreasonable and encloses more ignorance than the most ignorant. For first you ought to speak not to us but to your fathers, that you ask their opinion as friends and coreligionists, and that you say to them, "Tell us, admirable ones, do you know whether *Dioscoros* anathematized *Eutyches* the impious and inventor of fantasies after having received him in communion, after he had made at *Ephesus* a long *libellus* for himself and those with him?"—If they reply negatively, ask them again and say: "Why then at Chalcedon, when you spoke much about him, did you not blame Anatolios, Patriarch of Constantinople, when he said aloud before the Council: 'It is not for a reason of faith that we depose *Dioscoros* but because he opposed the letter of Pope Leo and because when called three times he did not come.'" The emperor *Justinian* again confirmed this in his edict received at the council that you call the Fifth. He wrote: "Dioscoros has not sinned against the faith." So you should have said to him: "O clever man, why do you not write the truth, that he did not wish to anathematize Eutyches, the inventor of fantasies?"

And how was it that the council, when it heard it said to *Anatolios*: "It is not for a motive of faith that we depose Dioscoros," was silent on this subject? It was that the council had nothing to say and in truth you have nothing to say either—for they said nothing, particularly when they were given a moment in which to accuse him. Show us then what the council replied to *Anatolios*, or rather interrogate the fifth council and the emperor Justinian, as we have said above, and tell us what they reply.

---

[59] Literally, make impositions of hands upon themselves.
[60] Literally, the support.

For ourselves, with the confessors of God *Dioscoros* and *Timotheus*, we anathematize *Eutyches* with *Nestorius*, the Council of *Chalcedon* and the partisans of these three schisms, for they are equally opposed to the religion; we put them with the infidels. But you, look inside yourselves, go into the fables imagined by your spirits, and reflect on what we have just said. Even if the council which illegally deposed Dioscoros [said] by the mouth of *Anatolios*, urged by truth, that it did not do so because of faith, one knows in any case that *Dioscoros* was never called on to anathematize Eutyches—which he in any case did—because the Council of *Chalcedon* liked and respected the doctrine of the impious *Eutyches*, for we have even now in our hands the letter of your *Leo*, who calls Eutyches his spiritual son, his coreligionist, his companion, and exhorts him to correct what is weak in the opinion of *Nestorius*; I judged it of no purpose to mention it here.

If I have to show that the reproach is vain in the same way as I have done for the others[61] and to throw myself into vain labors, as *Gregory* the Theologian for all the reproaches and spiteful acts of the pagan *Julian, come listen and I shall relate to you* as it is written. I shall go to find the martyr of the sufferings of the Messiah [Dioscoros] and he himself will answer that your reproach against him is vain.

I shall let him repeat before you what he cried aloud at your impious Council of *Chalcedon*, where he anathematized *Eutyches*, saying: "If *Eutyches* has thought anything outside the teachings of the church, he deserves not only to be excommunicated but also to be delivered to the fire. For myself, I care only for the Catholic faith, and not for any man, whoever he may be."

In his letter to Seqendes which he wrote from *Gangres* where he was then in exile for the Messiah, he said:[62] "I omit many things, and I arrive at what is the question now and which one must say is a stranger[63] to our body, that which he took from holy *Mary* by

---

[61] By quotations.

[62] Quoted by Michael the Syrian, except the last sentence, ed. Chabot, II-7, m, 58. According to Michael, the letter is addressed to Secundinus, the textual differences being numerous but the meaning remaining the same. One may suppose that the present text and that of Michael are two different translations of the same Greek text.

[63] Literally, *alienus et peregrinus*.

means of the Holy Spirit, Our Lord, according to a word [a means] that he knows. If things are according to the impiety of these, Paul must have lied when he wrote to us: *He took not from the angels, but he took from the race of Abraham;*[64] for *Mary* was not a stranger to *Abraham*, as can easily be shown by many books. Also he says, *he had to resemble his brethren in everything.*[65] This *in everything* lets nothing of our nature escape; this flesh of Our Savior, born of *Mary*, only without seed of man and woman, animated by a rational soul, is composed of nerves, hair, veins, bones, a belly, a heart, kidneys, a liver, lungs, in a word of all of what we are composed.

If it were not so, and according to the evil lunacy of the heretics, how could he be called a brother if he used a strange body unlike ours. How could he be truthful when he said to his Father: *I shall preach your name to my brothers?*[66] Then despise and hold in horror those who think such things. He was with us, like us, for us; he was not there in semblance or in appearance, according to the heresy of the impious Manicheans, God protect us! But he truly came out of *Mary*, Mother of God. As for his arrival among us he came to renew [repair] the broken vase, in truth he is called: *Emmanuel. He was poor*, according to the word of *Paul, in order to make us rich through his poverty.*[67] He made himself like us by his providence, that by his grace we might be like him; he was the son of man without destroying what was Son of God. That is what we confess and we think. If anybody should try to think otherwise, he will be a stranger to the traditional and apostolic faith."

* * * * * *

The authors show that the words of Dioscoros condemn Eutyches and come to the fifth question:

5. You write: "Show also that you put under the anathema whoever confesses two natures in the Messiah before the union [of the natures] or in the union or after the union." *Let us take*

---

[64] Heb 2:16.
[65] Heb 2:17.
[66] John 17:6, 26. This is not, however, the text quoted by Dioscoros.
[67] 2 Cor 8:9.

as a witness on this subject the Lord of Lords, as the divine Micah[68] somewhere said about the iniquity of *Israel.*

Let us reflect a little together. Do you, you who are looking for a quarrel with these reproaches, do you confess all these words without controversy? I hope so, otherwise you would have to divide them. Why then, since you confess two natures before the union, do you not embrace *Eutyches* who also confesses them vainly. Why also do you accept the Council of Chalcedon in drawing down on your heads the anathema [delivered] against this [proposition]. All the friends of truth will recognize that you profess these three propositions since you blame those who do not profess them and you ask the doctors, as something impossible, to show you that they condemn all three of them. Do you not know that we were able to show you immediately the condemnation of one of these propositions, that which concerns the two natures before the union, according to a comminatory decision of Chalcedon? But if you have masters and doctors, O *Philip* and *Thomas,*[69] they were bound [they also] by the decision that fits [attains] you for a time, until you make for this error the right response; but their eyes, like yours, bear only on ineptitudes and gossip, to throw calumnies against the disciples of truth; like courtesans, they seek wrongly to fix their opprobrium on persons who are pure.—As for the demonstration that you equally demand of the anathema pronounced against [the two natures] in the union and after the union, who does not know, however little intelligence he may have, that it is easier still to answer this. We shall show this without difficulty.

* * * * * *

The author then quotes Saint Cyril *"In the fourth tome of the interpretation of the Epistle to the Hebrews," then* Probus *in the letter to the Armenians, then* Julius, *bishop of Rome, in his words against those who attack the divine incarnation. Here is the translation of this latter text:*

---

[68] Mic 1:2.

[69] These are the Maronites already mentioned at the beginning of this answer.

"The Virgin, when she gave birth in the flesh, gave birth to the Word and she is the mother of God. The Jews, when they crucified the body, crucified God. One finds no distinction in the divine books between the Word and his body; but it is one nature, one person, one operation, one hypostasis, the same all God and all man."

* * * * * *

Then come quotations from Gregory of Nyssa in his Discourse on the Creation of Man, *etc., etc., in all, five pages of quotations, from folio 167 recto to folio 169 verso. Here is the translation of the end of the letter:*

As you have adjured us to place under the eyes of our fathers your ignominy, that is to say your little letter or your imperfect conceptions that you have sent us from *Armaz* [Armenaz], by *Isaac* and *Simon* after burying yourselves secretly in the face of the reprimand [given you] at Antioch, we have done [as you asked] for your salvation and on account of your adjurations. We have shown to the holy fathers who were here that your factum was not worthy of their powerful words like unto the iron which cuts stone, as it is written, but they have asked of me and of my young brother *Theodore* of the monastery of *Beth Mar Abaz*, to give you the appropriate solution, something that I have done according to my feeble forces.—I adjure you also by the holy and consubstantial Trinity which is divided while remaining one and which is one while being divided, to read what we have written, containing the solution of your reproaches before the whole assembly of *Beth Maron;* perhaps you will find some profit if you sometimes listen, if you understand it and if you let yourself be persuaded and if you abandon your machinations to turn yourselves towards God, according to the words of the prophet inspired by the [Holy] Spirit.—If you adjure by your venerated habit as you have done for us, I know that you lie because it is not venerable but despicable and vile in your eyes. [I know] that you seem stranger to it, you who carry cudgels, who strike, who pursue and who vilipend the priests and the faithful of the Messiah who do not accept to be associated with your wickedness. You resemble the thieves and the evildoers who keep to the mountains and the desert and devastated places, to do their deeds like unto yours. You will receive like retribution from God, he who renders to each according to his works in his just and righteous judgment, as it is written.

End of the solution to the senseless questions of the monks of *Beth Maron* who are in the territory of *Apamaea*.

DOCUMENT VI
The Kings of Roum*

Book of the Warning and of the Revision, French Trans. Carra De Vaux, National Press (Paris, 1897), 211–12

"The twentieth was Maurice, who reigned twenty years and four months. Under his rule there appeared *a man of the town of Hamat,* in the province of *Emessa,* called *Maroun,* to whom the Maronite Christians at our time of writing trace their origin. This sect is famous in Syria and elsewhere. Most of its members live in *Mount Lebanon and Mount Sānir at Emesus* and in the districts depending on them, like those of *Hamat,* of *Chaïzar,* of *Maarrat-al-Nōman.*

"Maroun had a great monastery, which bears his name, *to the east of Hamat and of Chaïzar,* composed of an immense building, surrounded by three hundred cells where the monks lodged. This monastery possessed in the form of gold, of silver and of jewels considerable wealth. It was devastated together with all the cells that surrounded it following the repeated incursions of the Bedouins and the violent actions of the Sultan.[70] It rose near the river Orontes, river of Emessa and Antioch.

"Maroun expressed opinions not in conformity with Christian faith, for example on the subject of the will. He had many adepts. We have already described his belief. Together with the Melkites, the Nestorians and the Jacobites, he admitted the Trinity, but he differed from them by counting two natures in the Messiah, one person and one will, an opinion intermediate between that of the Nestorians and that of the Melkites. This is what we have explained, together with other things, in our book 'Doctrines on

---

[70] Perhaps Seif-ed-Daulat, according to De Sacy, *Les Prairies d'or,* t. IX, 339.

the Foundations of the Religions.' One of the sectaries, known by the name of Kaïs the Maronite, is the author of an excellent book on chronology, the origin of the world, the prophets, books, cities, nations, the kings of Roum and others, and their histories. He ends his work with the caliphate of Mouktafi [901]; I do not know of the Maronites composing any other book on these same matters."

*AL-MASᶜŪDĪ Kitāb al-tanbīh wal ischrāf, ed. Dār at-Turāth (Beirut, 1968), 131–32.

Sources

(ABBREVIATIONS AND INITIALS)

I. MANUSCRIPTS

AL-BIRUNI
Abū l-Rayḥān Muḥammad AL-BIRUNI, *Al-Kānūn al Masʿūdī fī l'hay'a wa-l-nūjūm*, cf. *Catalogue des Manuscrits orientaux de la bibliothèque d'Oxford* d'Alexandre Nicoli, t. II, pp. 360–63, n. CCCLXX, Oxford, 1835.

BIBLIOTHEQUE NATIONALE Paris, 203 (1878), ZOTNEBERG, *Catalogue*, pp. 154–55.
Paris, 204 (1657 based on a copy from 1173), ZOTENBERG, *Catalogue*, pp. 155–56.

BRITISH MUSEUM
Add. 12.154 (VIIIe–IXe s.), WRIGHT, *Catalogue*, II, pp. 986 et ss.
Add. 12.155 (VIIIe s), WRIGHT, *Catalogue*, II, pp. 921 et ss.
Add. 17.169 (581), WRIGHT, *Catalogue*, II, pp. 450 et ss.
Add. 17.216 (664), WRIGHT, *Catalogue*, II, p. 1041.

II. PRINTED BOOKS

ABŪ L-FIDĀ, *Abrégé*
ABŪ L-FIDĀ, *Abrégé de l'histoire du genre humain*, ed. Dār al-Kitāb Allubnānī (in Arabic), Beirut, 1960.

ABŪ L-FIDĀ, *Hist. Anteislamica* ABŪ L-FIDĀ, *Historia ante-Islamica*, arabice. E duobus codicibus bibliothecae regiae parisiensis, 101 et 615, edidit Henricus. orthobius Fleischer, versione latina notis et indicibus auxit, Lipsae, 1831.

ACTS OF THE COUNCILS,

CHALCEDON:

ed. LABBÉ -COSSART, t. IV.

ed. HARDOUIN, t. II.

ed. MANSI, t. VI.

ed. SCHWARTZ, ACO, t. II. = Acta Conciliorum Œcumenicorum, tome II in six volumes, Berlin 1932–38. Vol. I, Lettres et Actes grecs; vol. II, 1 et 2, coll. Novariensis et Vaticana; vol. III, trad. lat. des Actes grecs (Rusticus); vol. IV, Lettres de St. Léon. The letters concerning the affair of Eutyches and the Council of Chalcedon were edited by C. Silva-Tarouca (*Textus et documents*, 15 and 20), Rome, 1934.

COLL. AVELLANA

Epistolae imperatorum, pontificum, aliorum A.D. 367–553, ed. Otto Günther, Vindobonae, 1895–1899.

CONSTANTINOPLE (536):

ed. LABBÉ -COSSART, t. V.

ed. HARDOUIN, t. II.

ed. MANSI, t. VIII; Suppl. I.

ed. SCHWARTZ, ACO, t. III, Coll. *Sabbaitica.*

EPHESUS (431):

ed. LABBÉ -COSSART, t. III.

ed. HARDOUIN, t. I.

ed. MANSI, t. IV–V.

ed. SCHWARTZ, ACO, t. II, Coll. *Casinensis*

EPHESUS (449):

MARTIN, *Actes du Bringandage d'Éphèse,* Amiens, 1874 (from the *Revue des sciences ecclésiastiques*).

FLEMMING

Johannes FLEMMING, *Akten der ephesinischen Synode vom 449,* in *Abhandlungen der Koniglichen Gesellschaft der Wissen-schaften zu Goettingen.* Philologisch-Historische Klasse, Neue Folge, Band XV, n. 1, Berlin, 1917.

THÉODORET DE CYR

THÉODORET DE CYR, *Correspondance,* ed. Yvan Azéma, in *Sources Chrétiennes,* t. I, n. 40 (Epist. I-LII); t. II, n. 98 (Epist. Sirm. 1-95); t. III, n. 111 (Epist. Sirm. 96–147), Paris, 1955–65.

THÉODORET DE CYR, *Hist. Eccl.*

THÉODORETI CYRENSIS, *Historia ecclesiastica*, ed. L. Parmentier (in le Corpus de Berlin), revised by F. Scheidweiler, Berlin, 1954.

THÉODORET DE CYR, *H.R.*

IDEM, *Historia Religiosa*, *P.G.* (Migne), t. LXXXII, col. 1283 ss., Trad., intro., and notes by Pierre Canivet and Alice Leroy-Molinghen, in *Sources Chrétiennes*, *Histoire des moines de Syrie*, t. I, 1977, no. 234; t. II, 1979, no. 257.

Bibliography

(ABBREVIATIONS AND INITIALS)

AAES

Publications of an American Archaelogical Expedition to Syria in 1899–1900, New York, 1903–30.

ABŪ L-FIDĀ, *Géographie*

ABŪ L-FIDĀ, *Takwin al-Buldan*, ed. J. T. Reinaud and Mac Guckin de Slane, Paris, 1840; trad. and Reinaud, Paris, 1848 and S. Guyard, Paris, 1883.

ACO

Acta Conciliorum Œcumenicorum, ed. Ed. Schwartz, Berlin, 1914–.

AL-DOUAIHI

E. AL-DOUAIHI, *Histoire de la Communauté Maronite* (en arabe) éd. Chartouny, Beirut, 1890.

AL-MASʿŪDĪ

Abū al-Ḥasan ʿAli AL-MASʿŪDĪ, *Kitab at-tanbih wal-ischraf*, éd. De Gœje, Leiden, 1894.

AL-MASʿŪDĪ

IDEM, *Les Prairies d'Or*, ed. Barbier de Meynard and Pavet de Courtelle, rev. and corrected by Charles Pellat, *Publications de l'Université libanaise, Section des études historiques*, XI, Beirut, 1966.

AZÉMA, I, II, III

Yvan AZÉMA, *Correspondance de Théodoret*, Intro., trad., and notes in *Sources Chrétiennes*, t. I, n. 40 (Epist. I-LII); t. II, n. 98 (Epist. 1-95); t. III, n. 111 (Epist. 96-147), Paris, 1955–65.

AZÉMA, *inédit*

IDEM, *Théodoret de Cyr d'après sa correspondance. Étude sur la personnalité morale, religieuse et intellectuelle de l'évêque de Cyr*, Paris, 1952.

BACHT, *Das Konzil* — H. BACHT, *Die Rolle des orientalischen Moenchtums in den Kirchenpolitischen Auseinandersetzungen um Chalkedon* (431–519) dans *Das Konzil von Chalkedon*, t. II, PP. 193ss.

BALUSE — BALUSE, *Concilium appendix*, Paris, 1683.

BARDENHEWER — O. BARDENHEWER, *Geschichte der altkirchlichen Literatur*, Fribourg-en-Brisgau, Herder, 1913–32, 5 vols.

BARDY, *D.T.C.* — G. BARDY, *Théodoret de Cyr* dans *D.T.C.*, t. XV, I, c. 299–326.

BAUMSTARK — A. BAUMSTARK, *Geschichte der syrischen Literatur mit Ausschluss der christlich-palästinensischen Texte*, Bonn, Marcus-Weber, 1922.

BESSE — J. M. BESSE, *Les moines d'Orient antérieurs au concile de Chalcédoine*, Paris, 1900.

BIDEZ — J. BIDEZ, *Le philosophe jamblique et son école*, in *Revue des études grecques*, XXXII, 1919.

BIHLMEYER-TUCHLE — C. BIHLMEYER et H. TUCHLE, *Histoire de l'Église*, t. I, Paris, 1962.

CAMELOT, *Éphèse et Chalcédoine* — P. TH. CAMELOT, *Éphèse et Chalcédoine, Histoire des conciles œcuméniques*, n. 2, éd. de l'Orante, Paris, 1961.

CANIVET, *Entreprise* — P. CANIVET, *Histoire d'une entreprise apologétique au Ve siècle*, in *Bibliothèque de l'Histoire de l'Église*, Paris, 1957.

CANIVET, *Messalianisme* — IDEM, *Théodoret et le Messalianisme*, in *Revue Mabillon* LI (1961).

CANIVET, *Mission en Syrie* — IDEM, *Mission en Syrie du Nord* (Août-Septembre, 1955).

CANIVET, *Théologie* — IDEM, *Théodoret et le monachisme syrien avant le concile de Chalcédoine*, in *Théologie de la vie monastique*, Aubier, 1961.

CANIVET, *Thérapeutique* IDEM, *Thérapeutique des maladies hellé-niques*, Intro., trad., and notes in *Sources Chrétiennes*, n. 57, in two volumes, Paris, 1958.

CAVALLERA F. CAVALLERA, *Le schisme d'Antioche*, Paris, 1905.

CHAPOT M. CHAPOT, *Frontière de l'Euphrate*, Paris, 1907.

CUMONT F. CUMONT, *Études Syriennes*, Paris, 1917.

CUQ CUQ, *Manuel des institutions juridiques des Romains*, Paris, 1928.

C.S.C.O. *Corpus Scriptorum Christianorum Orientalium*, Louvain, 1955.

D'ALES A. D'ALES, *La lettre de Théodoret aux moines d'Orient*, in *Ephemerides théologicœ lovanienses*, 1931.

DAOU Père Antoine DAOU, *Histoire des Maronites* (in Arabic), ed. Dar an-Nahar, Beirut, 1970.

DE BAUER DE BAUER, *Der Heilige Chrysostomus und seine Zeit*, Munich, 1929.

DELEHAYE H. DELEHAYE, *Les saints stylites, Subsidia hagiographica*, t. XIV, Brussels, 1933.

DE MEESTER P. DE MEESTER, *De manachico statu iuxta disciplinam Byzantinam statuta selectis fontibus et commentariis instructa*, Vatican, 1942.

DEVRESSE, *Le Patriarcat d'Antioche* R. DEVRESSE, *Le Patriarcat d'Antioche*, dans *Études Palestiniennes et Orientales*, Paris, 1945.

DIB, *Histoire* Mgr. P. DIB, *Histoire de l'Église Maronite*, Beirut, 1962.

DRAGUET R. DRAGUET, *Les Pères du désert, Textes choisis*, Paris, 1949.

D.T.C. *Dictionnaire de Théologie Catholique*, A. VACANT, E. MANGENOT and E. AMANN.

DUCHESNE, *Histoire*

L. DUCHESNE, *Histoire ancienne de l'église*, 3 vols., Paris, 1906–10.

DUSSAUD, *Topographie*

R. DUSSAUD, *Topographie historique de la Syrie antique et médiévale*, Paris, 1927.

FESTUGIÈRE, *Antioche*

A. J. FESTUGIÈRE, *Antioche païenne et chrétienne, Libanius, Chrysostome et les moines de Syrie dans Bibliothèque des écoles françaises d'Athènes et de Rome*, Fasc. 194, Paris, 1959.

FLICHE-MARTIN

A. FLICHE and V. MARTIN, *Histoire de l'Église depuis les origines jusqu'à nos jours*, Paris, Bloud et Gay, 1936 ss.

GLUBOKOVSKIJ, *Blazennyi Feodorit*

N. N. GLUBOKOVSKIJ, *Blazennyi Feodorit episkop Kirrskie, Ego jizn i literaturnaia diéiatehrost. Tserkoivno istoriceskoe izlidovanïe* (Blessed Theodoret, bishop of Cyr, his life and literary activity. Studies in Church History), Moscow, 1890.

GRANIC'

B. GRANIC', *L'acte de fondation d'un monastère dans les provinces grecques du Bas-Empire au Ve et VIe siècles*, in *Mélanges Ch. Diehl*, 1, Paris, 1930.

GRILLMEIER-BACHT, *Das Konzil*

A. GRILLMEIER, H. BACHT, *Das Konzil von Chalkedon, Geschichte und Gegenwart*, Echter-Verlag Wurzburg, 1953.

HARDOUIN, *Acta conciliorum*

J. HARDUINUS, *Acta conciliorum et epistolae decretales ac constitutiones summorum pontificorum*, 12 vols. (up to 1714), Paris, 1715.

HARTMANN

Martin HARTMANN, *Das Liwa Haleb, Zeitschrift der Gesellschaft für Erdkunde*, Berlin, 1894.

HÉFÉLÉ-LECLERCQ, *Histoires*

C. J. Von HÉFÉLÉ and H. LECLERCQ, *Histoires des Conciles*, Lib. Letouzey, Paris, 1907 ss.

HENDRIKS, O. S.

O. HENDRIKS, *La vie quotidienne du moine Syrien* in *Orient Syrien*, 5 (1960).

HENDRIKS, P.O.C. — IDEM, *L'activité apostolique des premiers moines syriens*, in *Proche-Orient Chrétien*, t. VIII. 1959.

HITTI — P.K. HITTI, *History of Syria*, London, 1951.

HONIGMANN, *Évêques* — Ernest HONIGMANN, *Évêques et évêchés monophysites d'Asie antérieure au VIe siècle*, C.S.C.O., subsidi a 2, Louvain, 1936.

HONIGMANN — IDEM, *The Monks Symeon, Jacobus and Baradatus, Patristic Studies*, in *Studi et testi*, n. 173, Vatican, 1953.

HONIGMANN, *Topographie* — IDEM, *Historische Topographie von Nord Syrien im Altertum*, dans *ZDPV*, 1923.

IBN AL-ATIR — IBN AL-ATIR, *Al-Kāmil fi l tāriḥ*, en 12 vols., Brill, 1867.

KIRCHMEYER — J. KIRCHMEYER, *Le moine Marcien* (de Bethléem), *Conférence d'Oxford*, 1959, vol. V, Part. III, Berlin, 1962.

KUHN — M. E. KUHN, *Über das Verzeichnis der rœmischen Provinzen aufgesetzt um 297*, in *Jahrbücher für classische Philologie*, t. CXV, 1877.

LABBE, *Concilia* — PH. LABBE and G. GOSSART, *Sacrosancta concilia*, 17 vols., Paris, 1671–74.

LAMMENS, *Le Liban* — H. LAMMENS, *Le Liban*, Beirut, 1906 (taken from *Al-Machriq*).

LASSUS — J. LASSUS, *Inventaire archéologique de la région au Nord-Est de Ḥama, Documents d'études orientales de l'Institut français de Damas, IV*, 2 vols., Damascus, no date (1935).

LEBON — J. LEBON, *Ephrem d'Amid*, dans *Mélanges d'Histoires offerts à Charles Moeller*, t. I, Louvain-Paris, 1914.

LEBON — IDEM, *Le moine Marcien*, dans *Miscellanea historica in honorem Alberti De Meyer*, t. I, Louvain-Bruxelles.

LEBON — IDEM, *Le moine Marcien*, Louvain, 1968.

LEBON, *R.H.E.* — IDEM, *Restitutions à Théodoret de Cyr*, in *R.H.E.*, 26 (1930).

LE QUIEN	M. LE QUIEN, *Oriens christianus quo exhibentur ecclesiae, patriarchae, etc. totius Orientis*, Paris, 1740.
MANSI, *Sacrorum conciliorum*	J. D. MANSI, *Sacrorum conciliorum omnium nova et amplissima collectio*, 31 vols. (jusque 1439), Florence and Venice, 1759–98; anastatic reproduction by J. B. MARTIN and L. PETIT (up to 1902), 53 vols., Paris, 1901–27.
MARIN	MARIN, *Les moines de Constantinople*, Paris, 1897.
MARQUARDT	J. MARQUARDT, *Organisation de l'empire Romain*, Paris, 1892.
MARROU, *Nouvelle Histoire*	J. DANIÉLOU and H. MARROU, *Nouvelle histoire de L'église*, t. I, *Des origines à Grégoire le Grand*, éd. du Seuil, Paris, 1963.
MATTERN	J. MATTERN, *Villes mortes, dans Mélanges de l'Université Saint-Joseph*, Beirut, 1933, V. XVII.
MICHEL LE SYRIEN	*Chronique de Michel le Syrien, patriarche Jacobite d'Antioche* (1166–99), ed. and trans. by J.-B. Chabot, 4 vols., Paris, 1899–1924.
MOELLER	*Das Konzil*, Ch. MOELLER, *Le chalcédonisme et le néo-chalcédonisme en Orient de 451 à la fin du VIe siècle*, in *Das Konzil von Chalkedon*, I, p. 659 ss.
MOELLER, *R.H.E.*	Ch. MOELLER, *Nephalius d'Alexandrie*, in *R.H.E.*, t. XL (1944–45).
MONDÉSERT	R. MONDÉSERT, *Inscriptions grecques de la Syrie*, in *Studia Patristica, Conférence d'Oxford*, 1955, Berlin, 1957.
MOULARD	A. MOULARD, *Saint Jean Chrysostome, sa vie, son œuvre*, Paris, 1941.
MOUTERDE-POIDEBARD	R. MOUTERDE and A. POIDEBARD, *Les limes de Chalcis*, Paris, 1945.

M.S.R.	*Mélanges de Science Religieuse*, Lille, Facultés Catholiques, 1944 ss.
MUYLDERMANS	J. MUYLDERMANS, *Evagriana Syriaca*, Louvain, 1952.
NAU	F. NAU, *Les Maronites inquisiteurs*, dans *Bulletin de l'Association de Saint Louis des Maronites*, n. 97 (Jan., 1903).
NAU, *O.C.*	F. NAU, *Opuscules Maronites*, dans *Revue de l'Orient Chrétien*, t. IV, 1899.
NEWMAN	J. H. NEWMAN, *Historical Sketches*, vol. II, London, 1876.
NOLDEKE, *ZDMG*	Th. NOLDEKE, *Zur Topographie und Geschichte des damaszenischen Gebiets und der Haurangegend*, in ZDMG, 29, p. 419 ss.
PAES	*Publications of the Princeton University Archaeological Expeditions to Syria in 1904–1905 and 1909*, Leiden, 1907–49.
PALANQUE	J. R. PALANQUE, *Histoire Universelle*, dans *Encyclopédie de la Pléiade*, Paris, 1957.
PAULY-WISSOWA, *realenc.*	PAULY et G. WISSOWA, *Realencyklopadie des Klassischen Altertumswissenschaft*, Stuttgart, 2e éd., en cours depuis 1894.
PEETERS, *Hypatius et Vitalien*	P. PEETERS, *Hypatius et Vitalien*. Taken from *L'Annuaire de l'Institut de Philologie et d'Histoire Orientales et Slaves*, t. X (1950), Mélanges H. Grégoire, II, Brussels, 1950.
PEETERS, *Tréfonds*	P. PEETERS, *Le tréfonds oriental de l'hagiographie byzantine*, Brussels, 1950.
P.G.	J.-P. MIGNE, *Patrologia cursus completus*. Series graeca, Paris, 1851–79, 161 vols.
P.L.	J.-P. MIGNE, *Patrologia cursus completus*. Series Latina, Paris, 1844–55, 221 vols.
POIDEBARD	A. POIDEBARD, *La trace de Rome dans le désert de Syrie*, Paris, 1934.

PUECH

H. CH. PUECH, *Numérius d'Apamée et les théologies orientales au second siècle*, in *Mélanges Bidez*, Brussels, 1934.

P.U.G.

Textus et Documenta, PONTIFICIA UNIVERSITAS GREGORIANA, *Textus et Documenta, Series Theologica*, 20, Pars Secunda, *Epistolæ post Chalcedonense concilium missae*, ad codicum fidem recensuit C. Silva-Tarouca, Rome, 1935.

RICHARD, R. Biblique

Marcel RICHARD, *Les citations de Théodoret conservées dans la chaîne de Nicétas sur saint Luc*, in *Revue Biblique*, 1934, pp. 88–96.

RICHARD, *R.S.P.T.*

IDEM, *L'activité littéraire de Théodoret avant le concile d'Éphèse*, in *Revue de sciences philosophiques et théologiques*, XXIV (1935), pp. 83–106.

RICHARD, *R.S.P.T.*

IDEM, *La lettre de Théodoret à Jean d'Égées*, in *R.S.P.T.*, n. 30 (1941–42), pp. 415–33.

RICHARD, *R.S.P.T.*

IDEM, *Notes sur l'évolution doctrinale de Théodoret*, dans *R.S.P.T.*, t. XXV (1936), pp. 459 ss.

RICHARD, *M.S.R.*

IDEM, *Théodoret, Jean d'Antioche et les moines d'Orient*, in *Mélanges de sciences religieuses*, II, 1946, pp. 137 ss.

RICHARD, *R.S.R.*

IDEM, *Un écrit de Théodoret sur l'unité du Christ après l'Incarnation*, in *Revue des sciences religieuses*, 14 (1934), pp. 34–61.

ROSTOVTZEFF

M. ROSTOVTZEFF, *Social and Economic History of the Roman Empire*, Oxford, 1926.

R.S.P.T.

Revue des sciences philosophiques et théologiques, Paris, 1907.

R.S.R.

Revue des sciences religieuses, of the Faculté de théologie catholique de Strasbourg, Paris, 1921 ss.

RUCKER

J. RUCKER, *Florilegium Edessenum Anonymum*, in *Sitzungsberichte der Bayer Akademie der Wissenschaften phil.-hist. Abt.*, Munich, 1933.

SALTET, *R.H.E.*   L. SALTET, *Les sources de l'Eraniste*, in *Revue d'histoire ecclésiastique*, t. VI (1905), pp. 289–303.

SAUVAGET   B. SAUVAGET, *La poste aux chevaux dans l'empire des mamlouks*, Paris, 1941.

SCHIWIETZ, *Das morgenlandische Moenchtum*   S. SCHIWIETZ, *Das morgenländische Moenchtum*, III, *Das Moenchtum in Syrien und Mesopotamien*, Moedling bei Wien, 1938.

SOURDEL   D. SOURDEL, *Ruhin, lieu de pélerinage musulman de la Syrie du Nord au XIIIe siècle*, in *Syria*, t. XXX, 1953.

SOZOMENE, *Hist. eccl.*   SOZOMENE, *Histoire ecclésiastique*, P.G. (MIGNE), t. LXVII.

STEIN   E. STEIN, *Histoire du Bas-empire*, Paris, 1959.

STEIN   A. STEIN, *Surveys on the Roman Frontier in Iraq and Trans-Jordan*, in *Geographical Journal*, 1940, p. 430 ss.

TCHALENKO, *Villages*   G. TCHALENKO, *Villages antiques de la Syrie du Nord*, in *Bibliothèque archéologique et historique de l'Institut Français d'archéologie de Beyrouth*, t. L, Paris, 1958.

THÉODORET, *P.G.*   THÉODORET DE CYR, *Discours sur la charité*, in *P.G.* (MIGNE), 82, 1508 ss.

THÉODORET, *Thérapeutique*   IDEM, *Thérapeutique des maladies helléniques*, ed. Pierre Canivet, in *Sources Chrétiennes*, n. 57, 2 vols., Paris, 1958.

THÉODORET, *H.R.*   IDEM, *Histoire des moines de Syrie*, ed. Pierre Canivet and Alice Leroy-Molinghen, in *Sources Chrétiennes*, 2 vols.: vol. I, no. 234, Paris, 1977; vol. II, no. 257, Paris, 1979.

TILLEMONT, *Histoire*   Le Nain De TILLEMONT, *Histoire des empereurs*, Paris, 1700–1738.

TILLEMONT, *Mémoires* IDEM, *Mémoires pour servir à l'histoire ecclésiastique des six premiers siècles*, Paris, 1693–1712.

UEDING, LEO Von, *Das Konzil* UEDING, LEO Von, *Die Kanones von Chalkedon in ihrer Bedeutung für Mönchtum und Klerus*, in *Das Konzil von Chalkedon*, t. II, 569–676.

VOGUÉ M. de VOGUÉ, *Syrie centrale, Architecture civile et religieuse, du Ier au VIIe siècle*, 2 vols., Paris, 1865–77.

VÖÖBUS, *History of Asceticism* A. VÖÖBUS, *History of Asceticism in the Syrian Orient*, t. II, *Early Monasticism in Mesopotamia and Syria*, C.S.C.O., CXCVII, subs., t. XVII, Louvain, 1960.

WRIGHT, *Catalogue* W. WRIGHT, *Catalogue of Syriac Manuscripts in the British Museum*, London, 1870–72.

ZDMG *Zeitschrift der Deutschen Morgenlandischen Gesellschaft*.

ZDPV *Zeitschrift des Deutschen Palästin-Vereines*, 1923 ss.

ZOTENBERG, *Catalogue* H. ZOTENBERG, *Catalogue des manuscrits syriaques de la bibliothèque nationale*, Paris, 1874.

Geographical and Historical Index

Index of Names and Persons

Peter of Callinices: 45, 152, 153, 154, 157, 160
Peter of Chalcis: 68
Peter the Fuller: 30, 137
Peter of Alexandria: 137, 141
Peter of Antioch: 141
Philoxenus: 31
Photius: 86
Polychronius (bish. of Apamaea): 34, 64, 119, 129
Pompey: 14, 24
Posidonius: 32
Proclus: 84, 85
Pulcheria: 10, 11, 12, 13, 88, 127

R
Rabbula of Edessa: 103
Romulus: 7, 87, 137

S
Sabellius: 49
Salamanes: 53
Seleucids: 24, 32
Senator (Patrices): 10, 77
Sergius (I) (bish. of Cyr): 30, 31
Sergius (II) (bish. of Cyr): 31
Sergius (m. of St. Symeon): 44, 136, 147, 154, 156
Severus of Antioch: 14, 17, 20, 21, 31, 34, 35, 43, 44, 131, 141, 143, 144, 146, 157
Shnoudi (m. of Egypt): 97
Simon the Elder: 41, 68
Simon the Stylite (= Simon Stylites): 41, 55, 72, 76, 77, 78, 82, 98, 99, 104, 106, 118, 121, 131, 136, 143, 147

Simon the zealot: 30
Simon (m. of Apamaea): 41, 44, 46, 48, 64, 65, 66, 114, 118, 119
Siricius: 30
Sixtus III (pope): 84, 125
Sozomenes: 11
Stephen: 109
Sulpicus Quirinus: 32

T
Takī al-Dīn ʿUmar: 3
Thalassius: 55
Theodore (m. of Beit Abaz): 45
Theodore of Mopsuestia: 31, 34
Theodore the Lector: 46
Theodore the Studite: 47
Theodosius (m.): 10, 70, 79
Theodosius 1: 67, 86, 87, 88
Theodosius II (emp.): 13, 90, 92, 97, 98, 100, 126, 127, 129
Theodotus: 39
Theophilus of Alexandria: 124
Tiberius (emp.): 28
Timothy Elures: 77, 121
Titus (count): 99

V
Valens (emp.): 52, 58
Vespasian: 28
Vincomale: 89, 90, 107

Z
Zebinas (m. of Cyr): 52, 59
Zenobiana: 39
Zenon (m. of Cyr): 63, 68

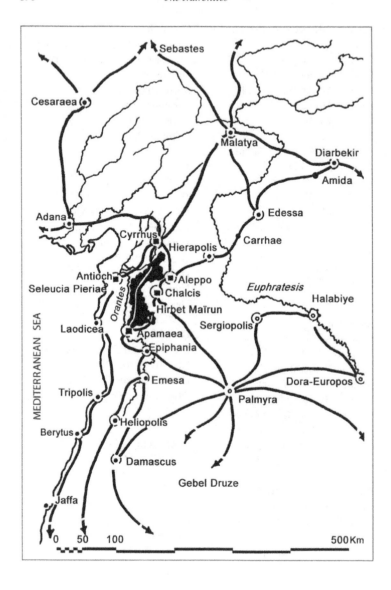

Map I: Old Communication Roads in Syria

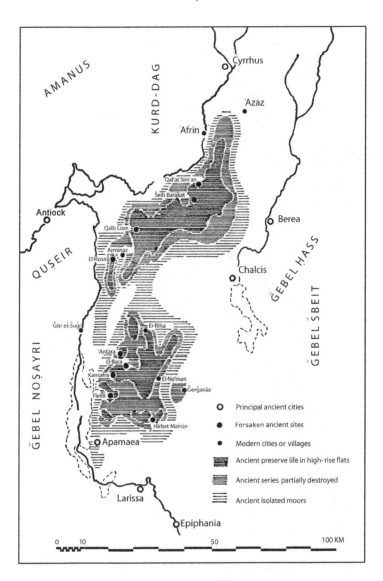

Map II: Archaeological Regions of Limestone Massif

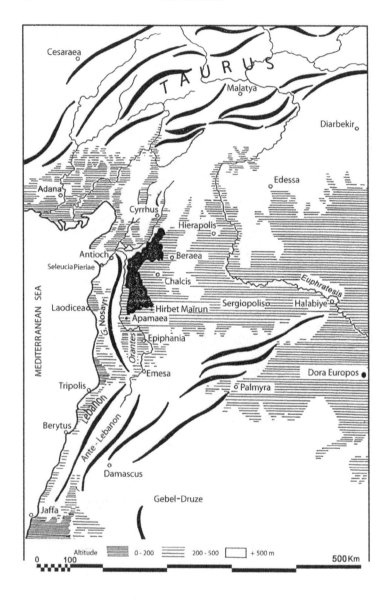

Map III: Position of Limestone Mountains

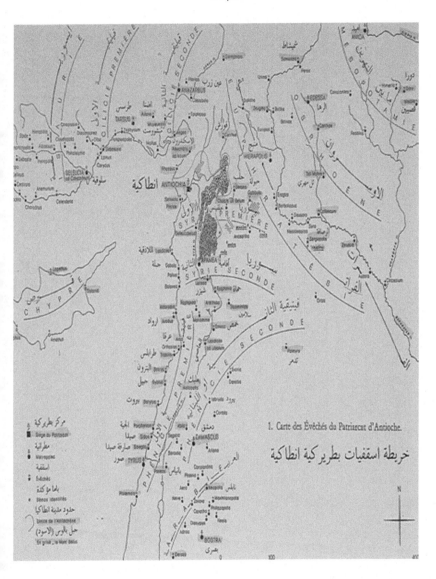

Map IV: Antiochian Patriarchate and Dioceses

Made in United States
Orlando, FL
26 October 2023

38269043R00124